Crowdfunding and Alternative Financing Models for Women Entrepreneurs

Naveeda Katper
University of Sindh, Pakistan

IGI Global
Scientific Publishing
Publishing Tomorrow's Research Today

Vice President of Editorial	Melissa Wagner
Director of Acquisitions	Mikaela Felty
Director of Book Development	Jocelynn Hessler
Production Manager	Mike Brehm
Cover Design	Phillip Shickler

Published in the United States of America by
IGI Global Scientific Publishing
701 East Chocolate Avenue
Hershey, PA, 17033, USA
Tel: 717-533-8845
Fax: 717-533-7115
Website: https://www.igi-global.com E-mail: cust@igi-global.com

Library of Congress Cataloging-in-Publication Data

Names: Katper, Naveeda, 1984- editor.
Title: Crowdfunding and alternative financing models for women entrepreneurs / Naveeda Katper.
Description: Hershey, PA : IGI Global Scientific Publishing, [2025] | Includes bibliographical references and index. | Summary: "By investigating these areas, this topic aims to provide a comprehensive understanding of how crowdfunding and alternative financing can empower women entrepreneurs in developing regions, offering them new opportunities to overcome traditional financial barriers and achieve business success"-- Provided by publisher.
Identifiers: LCCN 2024055595 (print) | LCCN 2024055596 (ebook) | ISBN 9798369391938 (hardcover) | ISBN 9798369391945 (paperback) | ISBN 9798369391952 (ebook)
Subjects: LCSH: Businesswomen--Developing countries. | Crowd funding--Developing countries.
Classification: LCC HD6053 .C87 2025 (print) | LCC HD6053 (ebook) | DDC 331.409172/4--dc23/eng/20250312
LC record available at https://lccn.loc.gov/2024055595
LC ebook record available at https://lccn.loc.gov/2024055596

British Cataloguing in Publication Data
A Cataloguing in Publication record for this book is available from the British Library.

This book is dedicated to all the women entrepreneurs who dare to dream, innovate, and challenge the status quo. Your resilience, creativity, and determination continue to inspire and shape the future of entrepreneurship worldwide.

To the trailblazers who have paved the way, the aspiring entrepreneurs who are just beginning their journey, and the mentors who guide and support them. This work is a tribute to your unwavering spirit and commitment to breaking barriers.

May this book serve as a beacon of hope, empowerment, and transformation for generations to come.

Naveeda Katper
University of Sindh, Jamshoro, Pakistan

Editorial Advisory Board

Table of Contents

Foreword xii

Preface xiv

Acknowledgment xx

Chapter 1
Empowering Women Entrepreneurs: Innovative Crowdfunding and Alternative Financing Models for Sustainable Business Growth 1
Muhammad Usman Tariq, Abu Dhabi University, UAE & University College Cork, Ireland

Chapter 2
Analyze the Factors that Contributed to Their Success and Lessons Learned ... 35
Shiney Chib, Datta Meghe Institute of Management Studies, India
M. Karthigeyan, Karpaga Vinayaga College of Engineering and Technology, India
Falguni Sanjay Pawar, Datta Meghe Institute of Management Studies, India
P. Selvakumar, Motilal Nehru National Institute of Technology, India
T. C. Manjunath, Rajarajeswari College of Engineering, India
P. C. Neena, Jain University, India
Mohit Sharma, Maharshi Dayanand University, Rohtak, India

Chapter 3
Scaling Up Women-Led Businesses: A Critical Analysis of Crowdfunding and Alternative Financing Models 65
K. Balaji, Christ University, India

Chapter 4
A Systematic and Bibliometric Analysis of Venture Capital Exit Strategies ... 101
Poonam Singh, Manav Rachna International Institute of Research and Studies, India
Nupur Mishra, Galgotias University, India
Mohd Shamshad, Galgotias University, India

Chapter 5
Women Technopreneurship in a Developing Economy: Understanding the Growth Prospects and Barriers 133
Zelda Arku, University of Mines and Technology, Ghana
Sheena Lovia Boateng, University of Ghana, Ghana
Stephen Boateng, University of Mines and Technology, Ghana
Desmond Kwadjo Kumi, University of Ghana, Ghana

Chapter 6
Impact of Crowdfunding on Women-Led Business Sustainability by Mediation of Alternative Financing in the Horn of Africa 171
Shashi Kant, Bule Hora University, Ethiopia
Tafese Niguse, Bule Hora University, Ethiopia
Metasebia Adula, Bule Hora University, Ethiopia

Chapter 7
The Interplay of Climate Change and Inflation in Sindh 205
Ghazala Shaukat, University of Sindh, Pakistan
Farhat Jokhiyo, University of Sindh, Pakistan
Saima Shaikh, University of Sindh, Pakistan

Compilation of References 219

Related References 253

About the Contributors 293

Index 301

Detailed Table of Contents

Foreword xii

Preface xiv

Acknowledgment xx

Chapter 1
Empowering Women Entrepreneurs: Innovative Crowdfunding and Alternative Financing Models for Sustainable Business Growth 1
Muhammad Usman Tariq, Abu Dhabi University, UAE & University College Cork, Ireland

To empower women entrepreneurs and promote sustainable business growth this chapter examines the role that creative crowdfunding and alternative financing models play. It offers a thorough examination of several funding choices highlighting their applicability to women in overcoming conventional financial obstacles. These options include impact investing peer-to-peer lending microfinance and crowdfunding platforms. The chapter looks at these models' efficacy accessibility and regional adoption while emphasizing the difficulties faced by female entrepreneurs including platform fees marketing requirements and project failure risks. The chapter highlights women entrepreneurs who have used these financing options to grow their companies and attain long-term sustainability through case studies and success stories. The impact of social and cultural factors on the adoption of these models is also explored as is the function of government regulations and non-governmental organization assistance in promoting financial accessibility.

Chapter 2
Analyze the Factors that Contributed to Their Success and Lessons Learned ... 35
Shiney Chib, Datta Meghe Institute of Management Studies, India
M. Karthigeyan, Karpaga Vinayaga College of Engineering and Technology, India
Falguni Sanjay Pawar, Datta Meghe Institute of Management Studies, India
P. Selvakumar, Motilal Nehru National Institute of Technology, India
T. C. Manjunath, Rajarajeswari College of Engineering, India
P. C. Neena, Jain University, India
Mohit Sharma, Maharshi Dayanand University, Rohtak, India

Success analysis is a comprehensive approach that delves into the multifaceted factors driving achievement across various domains, including personal development, education, career, and entrepreneurship. Understanding success is not merely about defining it; It requires examining the intricate web of influences that contribute to an individual's or organization's ability to reach their goals. in the face of setbacks. This resilience is often correlated with higher levels of achievement, as those with a growth mindset are inclined to embrace effort, seek feedback, and cultivate their skills continuously. Conversely, those with a fixed mindset may avoid challenges, fearing failure and consequently limiting their potential for growth. Another critical component is goal setting. Clear, achievable goals provide a roadmap for success. Research shows that individuals who set specific goals are more likely to achieve them compared to those with vague aspirations. This process involves not only identifying what one wants to achieve but also breaking down the steps necessary.

Chapter 3
Scaling Up Women-Led Businesses: A Critical Analysis of Crowdfunding and Alternative Financing Models 65
K. Balaji, Christ University, India

Women-led businesses have gained significant traction globally, yet many still face barriers to accessing traditional forms of financing. Crowdfunding and alternative financing models present new opportunities for these entrepreneurs to scale up and grow their ventures. This study critically examines how these models impact the growth, profitability, and long-term sustainability of women-led businesses. It identifies both the advantages and limitations of using crowdfunding and alternative financing mechanisms, such as peer-to-peer lending and microfinance, in fostering entrepreneurial success. The research further explores the challenges women entrepreneurs encounter in adopting these models, including the gender bias present in many crowdfunding platforms. This paper presents actionable solutions for improving the effectiveness of alternative financing in supporting women-led businesses. The study's findings contribute to both academic research and practical business strategies, offering a roadmap for empowering women entrepreneurs in the evolving financial landscape.

Chapter 4
A Systematic and Bibliometric Analysis of Venture Capital Exit Strategies ... 101
Poonam Singh, Manav Rachna International Institute of Research and Studies, India
Nupur Mishra, Galgotias University, India
Mohd Shamshad, Galgotias University, India

the study aimed to explore and synthesize the current knowledge clusters in the venture capital exit strategies or routes. The paper adopted a robust and scientific protocol to retrieve the 436 journal articles published in the Scopus-indexed journals from 2002-2022. Then, bibliometric analysis is carried out using the VOS viewer, Science of Science (Sci2), and Gephi. Keyword co-occurrence, prestige analysis, bibliographic coupling, and citation analysis are performed to merge knowledge clusters. The results of keyword co-occurrence and co-citation analysis suggest that there exist mainly two prominent exit strategies in venture capital which are Initial public offering (IPO) and M&A. These clusters have significant relation with other parameters but limited research observed on them. The findings also indicate that, of all the tactics employed, secondary sales and strategic sale are the technique that has received the least research. Also, at the same time IPO and Merges and acquisitions are the most prevailed exit tactics of venture capitalists to retain investment.

Chapter 5
Women Technopreneurship in a Developing Economy: Understanding the Growth Prospects and Barriers 133
Zelda Arku, University of Mines and Technology, Ghana
Sheena Lovia Boateng, University of Ghana, Ghana
Stephen Boateng, University of Mines and Technology, Ghana
Desmond Kwadjo Kumi, University of Ghana, Ghana

This study examines the growth prospects and barriers for women technopreneurs in Ghana, focusing on their landscape, challenges, and key growth drivers. Using data from 60 women technopreneurs in Ghana and Nigeria, it explores four critical factors—Entrepreneurial Culture, Technopreneurship Capabilities, Staged Financing, and Business Support Mechanisms—and evaluates the moderating role of the regulatory environment. Partial Least Squares Structural Equation Modeling (PLS-SEM) was used to analyze causal relationships. Findings show women-led technopreneurs are profit-driven, leveraging technologies like social media and cloud computing but face barriers such as taxation, limited financing, and cultural biases. The regulatory environment moderated Technopreneurship Capabilities, Entrepreneurial Culture, and Staged Financing but did not significantly moderate

Business Support Mechanisms. These results are thoroughly discussed, and relevant recommendations made.

Chapter 6
Impact of Crowdfunding on Women-Led Business Sustainability by Mediation of Alternative Financing in the Horn of Africa 171
Shashi Kant, Bule Hora University, Ethiopia
Tafese Niguse, Bule Hora University, Ethiopia
Metasebia Adula, Bule Hora University, Ethiopia

This investigation looks at the influence of crowdsourcing on the viability of female owned firms in the East Africa, with a special emphasis on the mediating function of alternative means of finance. A quantitative research technique was used to collect information from 385 female venture innovators using structured questionnaires. AMOS software was used to conduct the investigation, which assimilated Kaiser-Meyer-Olkin (KMO) measurements, Exploratory Factor investigation (EFA), and Structural Equation Modeling (SEM). The findings show that crowdsourcing augments access to alternative means of finance, which helps to the long-term viability of female owned firms. The investigation reveals a large direct influence of crowdsourcing on venture viability while emphasizing the considerable intermediary effect of alternative means of finance. Specifically, the findings show that effective crowdsourcing campaigns not only give immediate cash resources but also promote other financing options, hence increasing long-term viability.

Chapter 7
The Interplay of Climate Change and Inflation in Sindh 205
Ghazala Shaukat, University of Sindh, Pakistan
Farhat Jokhiyo, University of Sindh, Pakistan
Saima Shaikh, University of Sindh, Pakistan

Sindh, located in southeastern Pakistan, faces significant socio-economic challenges that have been exacerbated by climate change and rising inflation. The 2022 floods, the most devastating in Pakistan's recent history, exposed the province's vulnerability to climate-induced disasters and deepened existing economic and social inequalities. This chapter examines how climate change, particularly floods, has contributed to inflationary pressures in Sindh and analyzes how inflation has, in turn, worsened the province's ability to respond to natural disasters. By focusing on the floods of

2022, we explore the direct and indirect impacts on various sectors, such as health, education, employment, food security, and infrastructure.

Compilation of References 219

Related References 253

About the Contributors 293

Index 301

Foreword

Entrepreneurship has long been recognized as a powerful engine of economic growth, job creation, and social transformation. Yet, despite their immense potential, women entrepreneurs continue to face significant barriers to accessing finance. Traditional financial systems often impose constraints that limit their ability to secure funding, thereby hindering their business growth and economic contribution. In response to these challenges, crowdfunding and alternative financing models have emerged as revolutionary mechanisms, enabling women to overcome financial hurdles and turn their entrepreneurial aspirations into reality.

This book, Crowdfunding and Alternative Financing Models for Women Entrepreneurs, is a timely and much-needed contribution to the discourse on women's economic empowerment. By examining innovative financial tools such as reward-based crowdfunding, equity crowdfunding, peer-to-peer lending, and microfinance, this book sheds light on new pathways that enable women to access capital beyond conventional banking systems. It presents a compelling blend of theoretical insights, empirical studies, and real-world case studies that highlight the transformative potential of alternative financing models.

Beyond providing access to capital, crowdfunding and alternative finance models foster a sense of community, collaboration, and financial inclusion. These platforms empower women to leverage digital tools, expand their networks, and connect directly with supporters who believe in their entrepreneurial vision. Moreover, these models facilitate financial literacy and resilience, equipping women with the skills necessary to sustain and scale their businesses in competitive markets.

This book serves as an essential resource for policymakers, academics, investors, and aspiring women entrepreneurs seeking to navigate the evolving landscape of alternative finance. It offers valuable insights into the opportunities and challenges associated with these models, while also advocating for supportive policies and ecosystems that can further amplify their impact.

I commend the editor and contributors for their dedication to this important subject. Their collective efforts in compiling this volume will undoubtedly inspire further research, dialogue, and action to enhance financial inclusivity for women entrepreneurs worldwide. I hope this book will serve as both a source of knowledge and a catalyst for change, fostering a more equitable and dynamic entrepreneurial landscape for future generations.

Muhammad Nawaz Tunio

University of Sufism and Modern Sciences, Bhitshah, Pakistan.

Preface

Access to finance remains one of the most significant barriers for women entrepreneurs worldwide. Despite their growing presence in the entrepreneurial landscape, women continue to face systemic challenges in securing traditional financing due to gender biases, lack of collateral, and limited access to networks of investors. In response, crowdfunding and alternative financing models have emerged as innovative solutions to bridge this funding gap, offering women entrepreneurs new avenues to turn their business ideas into reality.

This book, Crowdfunding and Alternative Financing Models for Women Entrepreneurs, explores the evolving landscape of non-traditional funding mechanisms and their impact on empowering women in business. It brings together contributions from scholars, practitioners, and industry experts to provide an in-depth analysis of how these financial tools are reshaping entrepreneurial opportunities for women across different economic and cultural contexts.

The chapters in this volume examine various aspects of crowdfunding, including reward-based, donation-based, equity-based, and peer-to-peer lending models. Additionally, the book delves into alternative financing options such as microfinance, impact investing, and digital lending platforms, highlighting successful case studies and best practices. Through a multidisciplinary approach, this work aims to equip researchers, policymakers, and aspiring women entrepreneurs with insights into leveraging these financing models effectively.

Beyond financial access, this book also addresses the broader ecosystem necessary for women's entrepreneurial success, including mentorship, social capital, and digital literacy. It underscores the importance of policy interventions, regulatory frameworks, and support networks that can enhance the effectiveness of alternative financing mechanisms.

As an editor, I hope this book serves as both a scholarly resource and a practical guide, inspiring further research and real-world applications of crowdfunding and alternative financing strategies. By illuminating these financing pathways, we aspire to contribute to the economic empowerment of women entrepreneurs and foster a more inclusive and equitable entrepreneurial environment globally.

I extend my heartfelt gratitude to all the contributors, reviewers, and colleagues who have supported this endeavor. Their insights and expertise have been invaluable in shaping the content of this book. I also appreciate the women entrepreneurs whose resilience and innovation continue to redefine the boundaries of business and finance.

ORGANIZATION OF THE BOOK

Chapter 1: Empowering Women Entrepreneurs: Innovative Crowdfunding and Alternative Financing Models for Sustainable Business Growth

To empower women entrepreneurs and promote sustainable business growth, this chapter examines the role that creative crowdfunding and alternative financing models play. It offers a thorough examination of several funding choices highlighting their applicability to women in overcoming conventional financial obstacles. These options include impact investing peer-to-peer lending microfinance and crowdfunding platforms. The chapter looks at these models' efficacy accessibility and regional adoption while emphasizing the difficulties faced by female entrepreneurs including platform fees marketing requirements and project failure risks. The chapter highlights women entrepreneurs who have used these financing options to grow their companies and attain long-term sustainability through case studies and success stories. The impact of social and cultural factors on the adoption of these models is also explored as is the function of government regulations and non-governmental organization assistance in promoting financial accessibility.

Chapter 2: Analyze the Factors that Contributed to their Success and Lessons Learned

Success analysis is a comprehensive approach that delves into the multifaceted factors driving achievement across various domains, including personal development, education, career, and entrepreneurship. Understanding success is not merely about defining it; It requires examining the intricate web of influences that contribute to an individual's or organization's ability to reach their goals. in the face of setbacks. This resilience is often correlated with higher levels of achievement, as those with a growth mindset are inclined to embrace effort, seek feedback, and cultivate their skills continuously. Conversely, those with a fixed mindset may avoid challenges, fearing failure and consequently limiting their potential for growth. Another critical component is goal setting. Clear, achievable goals provide a roadmap for success. Research shows that individuals who set specific goals are more likely to achieve them compared to those with vague aspirations. This process involves not only identifying what one wants to achieve but also breaking down the steps necessary.

Chapter 3: Scaling Up Women-Led Businesses: A Critical Analysis of Crowdfunding and Alternative Financing Models

Women-led businesses have gained significant traction globally, yet many still face barriers to accessing traditional forms of financing. Crowdfunding and alternative financing models present new opportunities for these entrepreneurs to scale up and grow their ventures. This study critically examines how these models impact the growth, profitability, and long-term sustainability of women-led businesses. It identifies both the advantages and limitations of using crowdfunding and alternative financing mechanisms, such as peer-to-peer lending and microfinance, in fostering entrepreneurial success. The research further explores the challenges women entrepreneurs encounter in adopting these models, including the gender bias present in many crowdfunding platforms. This paper presents actionable solutions for improving the effectiveness of alternative financing in supporting women-led businesses. The study's findings contribute to both academic research and practical business strategies, offering a roadmap for empowering women entrepreneurs in the evolving financial landscape.

Chapter 4: A Systematic and Bibliometric Analysis of Venture Capital Exit Strategies

This chapter aims to explore and synthesize the current knowledge clusters in the venture capital exit strategies or routes. The paper adopted a robust and scientific protocol to retrieve the 436 journal articles published in the Scopus-indexed journals from 2002-2022. Then, bibliometric analysis is carried out using the VOS viewer, Science of Science (Sci2), and Gephi. Keyword co-occurrence, prestige analysis, bibliographic coupling, and citation analysis are performed to merge knowledge clusters. The results of keyword co-occurrence and co-citation analysis suggest that there exist mainly two prominent exit strategies in venture capital which are Initial public offering (IPO) and M&A. These clusters have significant relation with other parameters but limited research observed on them. The findings also indicate that, of all the tactics employed, secondary sales and strategic sale are the technique that has received the least research. Also, at the same time IPO and Merges and acquisitions are the most prevailed exit tactics of venture capitalists to retain investment.

Chapter 5: Women Technopreneurship in a Developing Economy: Understanding the Growth Prospects and Barriers

This chapter examines the growth prospects and barriers for women technopreneurs in Ghana, focusing on their landscape, challenges, and key growth drivers. Using data from 60 women technopreneurs in Ghana and Nigeria, it explores four critical factors—Entrepreneurial Culture, Technopreneurship Capabilities, Staged Financing, and Business Support Mechanisms—and evaluates the moderating role of the regulatory environment. Partial Least Squares Structural Equation Modeling (PLS-SEM) was used to analyze causal relationships. Findings show women-led technopreneurs are profit-driven, leveraging technologies like social media and cloud computing but face barriers such as taxation, limited financing, and cultural biases. The regulatory environment moderated Technopreneurship Capabilities, Entrepreneurial Culture, and Staged Financing but did not significantly moderate Business Support Mechanisms. These results are thoroughly discussed, and relevant recommendations made.

Chapter 6: Impact of Crowdfunding on Women-Led Businesses Sustainability by Mediation of Alternative Financing in Horn of Africa

This chapter investigates the influence of crowdsourcing on the viability of female owned firms in the East Africa, with a special emphasis on the mediating function of alternative means of finance. A quantitative research technique was used to collect information from 385 female venture innovators using structured questionnaires. AMOS software was used to conduct the investigation, which assimilated Kaiser-Meyer-Olkin (KMO) measurements, Exploratory Factor investigation (EFA), and Structural Equation Modeling (SEM). The findings show that crowdsourcing augments access to alternative means of finance, which helps to the long-term viability of female owned firms. The investigation reveals a large direct influence of crowdsourcing on venture viability while emphasizing the considerable intermediary effect of alternative means of finance. Specifically, the findings show that effective crowdsourcing campaigns not only give immediate cash resources but also promote other financing options, hence increasing long-term viability.

Chapter 7: The Interplay of Climate Change and Inflation in Sindh

Sindh, located in southeastern Pakistan, faces significant socio-economic challenges that have been exacerbated by climate change and rising inflation. The 2022 floods, the most devastating in Pakistan's recent history, exposed the province's vulnerability to climate-induced disasters and deepened existing economic and social inequalities. This chapter examines how climate change, particularly floods, has contributed to inflationary pressures in Sindh and analyzes how inflation has, in turn, worsened the province's ability to respond to natural disasters. By focusing on the floods of 2022, we explore the direct and indirect impacts on various sectors, such as health, education, employment, food security, and infrastructure.

Naveeda Katper

University of Sindh, Jamshoro, Pakistan

Acknowledgment

The journey of bringing this book, Crowdfunding and Alternative Financing Models for Women Entrepreneurs, to fruition has been both inspiring and rewarding. This work would not have been possible without the support, insights, and dedication of numerous individuals and institutions who contributed their time, expertise, and encouragement.

First and foremost, I express my sincere gratitude to the esteemed contributors whose research, case studies, and perspectives have enriched this volume. Their commitment to exploring the evolving landscape of alternative financing for women entrepreneurs has been instrumental in shaping the depth and quality of this book.

I extend my heartfelt appreciation to the reviewers and editorial team for their meticulous attention to detail and constructive feedback, which have significantly enhanced the rigor and coherence of this work. Their valuable suggestions and keen insights have helped refine the content and ensure its scholarly and practical relevance.

A special thanks to the publishing team for their unwavering support and professionalism in bringing this book to life. Their dedication and expertise have been invaluable in transforming this manuscript into a comprehensive resource for researchers, policymakers, and aspiring entrepreneurs.

I am also deeply grateful to the women entrepreneurs whose resilience, innovation, and determination continue to inspire this field of study. Their experiences and success stories serve as powerful testaments to the potential of crowdfunding and alternative financing models in breaking down barriers and fostering economic empowerment.

Finally, I would like to acknowledge the unwavering support of my family, friends, and colleagues. Their encouragement, patience, and belief in this project have been a constant source of motivation throughout this journey.

It is my hope that this book will serve as a valuable contribution to the ongoing efforts toward financial inclusion, gender equality, and entrepreneurial success. Thank you to everyone who has played a role in making this endeavor possible.

Naveeda Katper

University of Sindh, Jamshoro, Pakistan.

Chapter 1
Empowering Women Entrepreneurs:
Innovative Crowdfunding and Alternative Financing Models for Sustainable Business Growth

Muhammad Usman Tariq
https://orcid.org/0000-0002-7605-3040
Abu Dhabi University, UAE & University College Cork, Ireland

ABSTRACT

To empower women entrepreneurs and promote sustainable business growth this chapter examines the role that creative crowdfunding and alternative financing models play. It offers a thorough examination of several funding choices highlighting their applicability to women in overcoming conventional financial obstacles. These options include impact investing peer-to-peer lending microfinance and crowdfunding platforms. The chapter looks at these models' efficacy accessibility and regional adoption while emphasizing the difficulties faced by female entrepreneurs including platform fees marketing requirements and project failure risks. The chapter highlights women entrepreneurs who have used these financing options to grow their companies and attain long-term sustainability through case studies and success stories. The impact of social and cultural factors on the

DOI: 10.4018/979-8-3693-9193-8.ch001

adoption of these models is also explored as is the function of government regulations and non-governmental organization assistance in promoting financial accessibility.

INTRODUCTION

Today, the context of entrepreneurial activity experiences radical changes and women who embark on entrepreneurship are gaining more importance in the worldwide economy. Nonetheless, women remain challenged in accessing capital that is required to finance growth and sustenance of their outfits. Online SBMs provide fewer requirements since they are founded on innovative technologies and are not restrained by conventional services' conformity to conventional financial institutions' standards and expectations, which limits women's opportunities due to high collateral, credit history, and formal finances documents' necessity. It is within this context in which crowdfunding and other forms of alternative financing have begun to take form as effective instruments for women entrepreneurs and promising routes to finance that go beyond the constrains of banking systems. This chapter focusing on the role of crowdfunding platforms and other related innovative financing techniques including micro financing, P2P lending, and impact investment, which are crucial for future empowered women entrepreneurship across the world (Soemitra et al., 2022). Introducing small amounts of money from numerous people who contribute via the internet is a relatively popular method of fundraising that has recently emerged. They are normally conducted on the internet whereby the businessmen can get a platform to exhibit their business plans or proposals to the investors. From the experiences of the female entrepreneurs, crowdfunding is perhaps the only available solution to issues of systemic exclusion by formal sources of finance. Compared to elaborate financing models in which investors and providers may have preconceived notions on gender or certain business sectors, crowdfunding provides a diverse and inclusive supporter an equal chance in choosing which projects to support by operating on the likes of Kickstarter, GoFundMe, and Indiegogo which created a worldwide repute for supporting creative projects and business. Such platforms allow women to present their concepts to a large public, get funding from those who find the idea valuable, regardless of their sex, status, or previous credit history (Adedeji, 2021). Whereas the impact of crowdfunding as related to women access pages can be expressed in concrete numbers, the role of crowdfunding as offering agency to women entrepreneurs seems to hinge largely on one crucial capacity: crowdfunding enables or helps women to avoid the gatekeepers. Across many countries of the globe, women are locked out of accessing structured financial systems to cater for their needs. For that matter, gender biases may entail discrimination, which comes in the form of either credit denial to woman borrowers, or in the granting of smaller loans at lower interest rates to male borrowers.

The restrictions are eliminated in crowdfunders since women must get funding directly from the public without the humbling and oppressive rules that complicate traditional fundraising. It does so in a manner that alters the balance of power to a more business-friendly position for women entrepreneurs while offering the capital they require to grow. But again, as noted above, while crowdfunding has huge potential, it is not without lots of difficulties. It is arduous for the entrepreneurs to dedicate long hours in the marketing of the campaigns and for developing a resourceful network, which is absolutely a grueling task for those with restricted funds and inadequate technical skills (Soemitra et al., 2022). Apart from crowdfunding, other emerging forms of financing, including micro financing, peer-to-peer financing, and impact financing have also become key financial tools in funding women's entrepreneurship. Micro credit, also known as micro banking, aims to offer small credit facilities to people especially in the developing world who cannot access any formal credit has for long been identified as an important weapon in the fight against poverty. Grameen Bank and Kiva are examples of organisations that have undertaken micro financing for woman empowering them with capital needed to setup and manage petty businesses. Micro finance institutions base their operations under the fact that women are more reputable and probable to use their profit to fund their families and community hence, enhanced cycle effect.

For instance, in Bangladesh, the provision of microfinances granted by the Grameen Bank to women has brought the poverty rate, education for children and health care services. This model has been particularly helpful in supporting the female entrepreneurship by providing a tool and enabling them to enhance financial security and fight stereotyping of women (Adedeji, 2021). Peer-to-business financing, another type of FL, means that one person can invest directly in another individual without using the services of an intermediary, such as a bank or financial services company. As a source of finance P2P lending can be an important resource for women entrepreneurs especially in the regions where commercial banks are reluctant or unable to fund female-led businesses. P2P lending enabling borrowers and lenders to meet online helps women get funds from people willing to invest in their business and take high risk, often at comparatively lower interest rates to those charged by conventional banks. Lending club and prosper for example have done much to popularize, peer to peer lending as a viable form of financing away from traditional methods, which empowers women entrepreneurs to independently access funding to grow their businesses. Like crowdfunding though, there are risks involved in P2P lending as well. Borrowers experience higher default risks and lower legal requirements than they would when dealing with the conventional bank loans, making it even more difficult for women, given the existing challenges (Ajiva et al., 2024).

Another form of fundraising is an impact investment that has recently started to pick up steam as more and more women propel their businesses driven by the desire to make social change. Social investors are those people or institutions who intend to invest their money and expect positive social outcome together with the financial gains. It appears that impact investing provides female entrepreneurs with essential funding for optimization of their business and social development objectives: sustainability, health, and education are vital determinants of a country's quality of life. The given financing model matters most in the developing nations since such women can be an essential resource when it comes to accessing clean energy or quality education within the society. Women entrepreneurs can mobilize the funds that allow them to develop businesses from the impact investors who have passion to change their world and the society at large (Soemitra et al., 2022). The relevance of these other funding systems is vested on the fact that they open other sustainable funding methods which women faced fundamental hurdles in accessing formal Institutions. A common trend that is evident in most developing countries is credit crunch or discredited rationing that hits women entrepreneurs causing them to be locked out of economic activities with resource bequests such as credit and capital. For instance, in some countries, women are legally cannot access loans without a male guarantor signing for them or they cannot own property, and property is mostly demanded as security for the traditional loans. We will see that through the various forms of alternative financing, of which crowdfunding, microfinance, peer to peer lending, and impact investing, the women can bypass these barriers and gain access to the necessary capital needed for the growth of their businesses. Besides, such models focus on providing credit to the unserved population segments and that is done much more leeward as compared to conventional banks (Ajiva et al., 2024).

As we have seen more and more women SMB owners embracing crowdfunding and new, more flexible methods of financing, it is crucial to look at the potential problems and drawbacks of such an opportunity. For instance, crowdfunding involves preaching about projects through the internet and this can be a major problem to women, especially those with little knowledge about technology and the internet. Likewise, microfinance institutions might have difficulties increasing the outreach of their services or achieving sustainable results of lending activities primarily in weak economic environments. Debt exchange markets such as P2P lending reap lower rates than banking institutions at the cost of cautionary risks since they are not regulated. As much as the concept of impact investing is vibrant, very often it put the pressure on an entrepreneur to link his/her business model with the need to hit some social or environmental outcomes, which is not always the best for all women entrepreneurs (Suseno & Abbott, 2021). I concur with the hypothesis at the onset of this chapter since crowdfunding and other alternatives to conventional financing have the possibility to greatly enhance the position of women entrepreneurs by offering them new routes to access money by sidestepping existing constraints. These models are especially important in the so-called developing nations, where women struggle to get credit and capital in the first place. However, these models should be taken with this awareness or best and worst-case scenarios, knowing that the potential of these models exists with their flaws as well. Covid 19 pandemic response measures, by increasing women employment rates and providing opportunities for receiving funding and finances for delivering working capital, these non-traditional methods fundamentally enable continued productivity recovery and positively influence the situation with female workforce in the global economy level (Ajiva et al., 2024).

BACKGROUND

Crowd funding and other innovations in financing have emerged as core issues to do with women's rights and economic enfranchisement. Crowdfunding, and all other forms of alternative finance solutions including microfinance, P2P funding and impact financing provides a different twist method compared to the conventional financial systems. But they also have specific difficulties, such as the overall accessibility, rates of success, and geographical distribution of their usage. Comparing these models outline how women are empowered to engage in business and, the ways that are still negative towards them. Despite the global growth trends in crowd-funding and other alternative financing models, they are generally like traditional models of security-based funding in that their rationale is the dem countertops and women selling groceries from Islington High Street as well as the text. For example, crowdfunding can attract wide public participation through internet-based models through which the business personality can present his/her idea or project to prospective financiers and many people can chip in small amount of money towards financing the project. This model offers women the chance to perform their work and sell their products to an international market without having to meet the stringent regulations of mainstream financial institutions. Here, women entrepreneurs can rely on the passion that people can have for a certain project rather than the creditworthiness and the presence of collateral – creativity, innovation and focus on social mission (Shaikh et al., 2021).

While a model like microfinance banks can rather have a more rigid and regional hierarchy. Micro funding involves a download of a small amount of money to individuals or groups, often in the developing world for the purpose of performing an economic activity. These institutions prefer female-headed household thinking that women will be more sensitive when using the funds provided to feed their families and friends.

Although, crowdfunding is mostly an online, worldwide activity, microfinances are closely linked to local economies, and probably institutions support borrowers in spending the funds correctly. Another type of financial model is peer-to-peer lending — a form of crowdfunding that resembles traditional lending and unites individual borrowers and lenders, more often digitally. Integrated investing focuses on making money and social or environmental change and espouses companies that promote change that both positive impact and value The two models have their strengths and weakness and are distinguished by the level of openness and performance rates of women entrepreneurs. For instance, crowdfunding such as involves requirements of the personal web presence and proper campaign promotion (Suseno & Abbott, 2021). This can be a big challenge especially to women entrepreneurs who might not have the necessary gadgets or even knowledge on how to go about matters technology especially if they operate from developing economies. Furthermore, establishing a successful crowdfunding campaign not only requires an entrepreneur to connect to many supporters, but it also poses a problem to women who lack social contacts or live in rural areas. It has however revealed that though women perform well in crowdfunding they are not capable of raising as much funding as the men. For example, studies have established that female-headed projects perform better in some industries, for example fashion and art and crafts, but do dismally in industries that are considered male preserves such as computing and video games. This disparity indicates that even though, crowd fining provides level playing ground, it is still saturated with gender biases that women encounter when seeking finances in other markets (Zhao et al., 2023).

It is found that lower interest and better gender sensitive, nontraditional sources of finance, for example micro-financing exhibits higher success rates among women entrepreneurs in developing regions. With a society visionary approach, micro finance institutions like Grameen bank in Bangladesh has concentrated more on giving loan to women and it has apparently brought about various economic as well as social transformation. For instance, micro financing operation has enhanced women business in Bangladesh and subsequently improved their families' standard of living and equally promoting education of their children. The special focus of microfinance is to provide a financial enabler along with the practical mention of support and advice that such women entrepreneurs require in setting up their businesses. But also, micro- financing has its problem. Faultfinders have claimed that high and Transformational interest rates compounded by the encourage to repay loan balances may sometimes increase tension amongst borrowers, predominantly where the economy is unstable. Finally, there is the issue of high possibility of default as a reason for microfinance institution's instability, especially where outside economic conditions influence borrowers' capacity to repay (Shaikh et al., 2021). Another source through which females can still secure funds required to finance their businesses is through peer-to-peer lending, but its effectiveness and availability depends on other issues such as the type of platform used and the legal situation back in the region of the entrepreneur. P2P lending has been beneficial to women since it affords them an opportunity to go round traditional banking institutions to access loans but through P2P lending platforms they get better offers. However, like the popular use of crowdfunding, P2P lending Marketplace platforms seemed to be more appealing to the digital savvy business owners willing and able to promote their project. Such places could be rural areas or any area that is not well connected with Information technology facilities, or the social networks that the borrowers need to mobilize to deserve such funds. Secondly, it is noteworthy that such peer-to-commerce credit platforms are often less standardized than more conventional banking organizations, which could mean higher risks of non-ere Payments and rather unstable terms and conditions for borrowers, as a rule. This makes P2P lending a high-risk venture especially for the women entrepreneurs given that the women are likely to be financially insecure (Testa et al., 2022).

With the promising opportunity for women business owners and employees in industries such as sustainability and social entrepreneurship, impact investing can be restrictive because it requires a business to meet certain social or environmental goals. For instance, issues of interest to impact investors may include climate change, health or education but not necessarily all issues affecting women businesspeople. Furthermore, impact investing usually targets large-scale investments while violence grass-root businesses are hard to get such capital funding. It could be challenging for the woman entrepreneurs in the rural setting or developing countries to measure up to the qualifiers in impact investment due to a lack of adequate social or environmental data collection and monitoring (Zhao et al., 2023).

Nevertheless, the availability of these financing models is also quite different from one geographical location to another. It forecasts that in developed countries women business owners have easier access to technology and internet which makes crowdfunding and P2P more feasible. But even in these places it is still not all easy for women due to various reasons like gender sensitive prejudice when it comes to investment, or poor employment of women in technology related fields. For instance, women startups in the United States and Europe attract considerably less venture capital funding than their male counterparts do, a gap seen on crowdfunding platforms where, on average, man founders will raise more money more often for technology or finance-based projects (Serwaah & Shneor, 2021). On the other hand, in the developing world where formal banking services are very limited, non-conventional financing opportunities such as micro-finance and social financing such as peer-to-peer lending have greatly empowered women entrepreneurship. For instance, in Africa mobile banking has accelerated development of the Peer-to-Peer lending giving women an opportunity to borrow through their mobile phones despite not have to visit a certain bank. In the same way, micro financing has been central to the economic enfranchisement of women in the south Asian/ Latin American region through provision of loans that were otherwise unattainable by such individuals for bearing small businesses. For this reason, variations in the legal systems of different regions, economic condition, and availability of technology explain the impact of these models. This means that in regions where the internet connection is restricted or only available in some selected areas, the use of crowdfunding or peer-to-Peer lending may be limited whereas in countries with unstable economies; high inflation, or volatile currency values, affect the ability of women to pay back microloan (Testa et al., 2022).

Even still and across these regional differences, crowdfunding and other realisation of financing models have irrefutably opened more possibilities and opportunities for women entrepreneurs. But they are not without any deficiencies. A crowd funding strategy can be simply attributed to aspects of visibility, marketing and technology whereas the models such as micro financing may bring financial pressure to bear on borrowers whereby loans attract high interest rates or have fixed repayment periods. Although peer-to-peer lending has been seen as a way around the traditional banking system, it is related to higher risks owing to minimal institutional control. While the case of impact investment is significant more blacks or women interested in social or environmental change, not all women will have an opportunity to access the capital (Serwaah & Shneor, 2021). Crowdfunding and other nontraditional types of financing expand the opportunities for female entrepreneurs, but their efficiency and availability depend on many factors including the level of the entrepreneur's digital literacy, a density of her social networks, regional conditions and certain requirements for each type of financing. Crowdfunding is an attractive concept in terms of rallying capital sourcing to support business ventures that do not have high visibility and the capacity to attract supporters. More formally organized models include microfinance, peer-to-peer lending and impact investing, all of which come with their very own problems. For the women entrepreneurs especially those in the developing world, these models provide essential means of unlocking traditional sources of funding, however, there is still much more that must be done to ensure that these challenges of accessibility and success are fully contained in various regions of the world and across various fields of business (Zhao et al., 2023).

Impact on Business Growth and Sustainability

This chapter has highlighted that crowdfunding and other forms of financing have gradually emerged as crucial in supporting women's entrepreneurship and more so, where more conventional funding modalities have not met the needs of the female entrepreneurs. These financing methods have a complex role in business growth and sustainability, including short term, the capacity to obtain capital, and long-term goals, including business profitability, stability, and capacity to expand. Further analysis of the case studies of women entrepreneurs reveals innovative approaches to emerging money sources such as crowdfunding, micro financing, peer-to-peer financing, and impact financing for massive growth and long-term business development (Rajagopal & Rajagopal, 2021). In the same light, one can bring an insight into the biography of Sarah Kauss who started S'well, a company focusing on the production of reusable water bottles to tackle plastic problem. When S'well was initially starting, the company used crowdfunding services such as Kickstarter to finance its products. Through self-promotion, Kauss successfully captured the attention of her target market which was employees and customers with a conscience on the environment. They managed to build a brand and tell the right story, Kauss was able to raise sufficient capital to expand production, enter new markets, and transform into a multimillion business. S'well bottles are available today, and it has grown into an international company with revenue in the hundreds of millions range. Not only did crowdfunding give Kauss the seed money to expand but also created a base of people who believed in the product and forwarded this onto the mass public (Saluja, 2024).

In the same way, the experience of Tanzanian Nasra Abubakar, who was able to bring her business to the next level due to microfinance. Abubakar, a woman from Nigeria, began by a small bakery in their village; she never received a loan from standard commercial banks with traditional credit infrastructure because she had no collateral nor credit history. But she got a small loan from the local microfinance institution and was able to expand her bakery. The money has been used by Abubakar to buy new machinery and recruit more people as a way of enhancing capacity for production and output. Years later, her bakery became one of the local success stories of small-scale businesses with several women from her local area employed. This success story is as an attestation to the fact that micro-financing does enhance business expansion in the developing area where women in particular struggle hard to get traditional credit (Ojo et al., 2022). Although these examples clearly show the potential to expand, success and profitability of businesses raised through crowdfunding and other forms of financing depends on many factors. For example, crowdfunding is a way to attract large amounts of money within a relatively short time, but it cannot guarantee constant profitability. After the first couple of rounds, may it be for marketing, expansion, or development, businesses now solely depend on their profitability or the availability of subsequent rounds of funding (Saluja, 2024).This is especially when such women filmmakers do not possess a background in either finances or entrepreneurship to undertake to do this transition from crowdfunded capital to sustainable independent operations. Studies indicate that although female entrepreneurs have been able to generate the needed funds for their businesses, few of these women-owned businesses are profitable in the long run. This gap indicates the importance of forecasting and managing funds toward crowdfunding as a platform for transition to the next phase of growth instead of a mere a workaround the absence of capital (Serwaah, 2022).

Microfinance, however, can be much more formalized, as since most microfinance institutions offer not only credit but also consultation and coaching for business persons. It has been especially helpful for women in the Third World because such opportunities for financial education are scarce. When it comes to microfinance funded businesses the ability to grow is also a critical success factor because sustainability at some point requires the business to scale up while avoiding over leveraging itself. Though proved to be with low cost of entry more than traditional banks, micro loans may be highly priced depending on the business environment volatility or the state of development of the microfinance market it operates in. If it [business] does not grow at a rate that ensures repayment of the credit, business can easily find itself struggling to repay the credits, which puts the prospects of the business in jeopardy. Consequently, microfinance funded businesses' sustainability relies largely on the ability of the business owner to manage growth with capital discipline (Ojo et al., 2022). Two other strategies for scaling up WIB are: Peer to Peer (P2P) lending While, impact investing has social impact bearing connotations that affect sustainability. Peer to peer or P2P lending, in which people lend money to borrowers inside common online marketplaces, comes with more freedom than the conventional bank loans. However, as with microfinance, there can be higher interest rates and significantly less regulation of P2P lending, which can become dangerous for borrowing individuals. Without the strict conditions of traditional loans, P2P lending can give female entrepreneurs the money they need to grow their businesses if they can effectively manage these risks. As an illustration, consider the achievements of Indian businesswoman Aditi Gupta, who obtained a peer-to-peer loan to grow Menstrupedia, an online resource that informs females about menstruation health. With the money, Gupta greatly increased the scope of her influence by spreading her educational message throughout India (Nurhayati, 2024).

Although impact investing is less popular than P2P lending or crowdfunding, it has a lot of promise for female entrepreneurs in fields like education, health, and sustainability. Impact investors are an excellent fit for companies with a mission-driven emphasis since they look for quantifiable social or environmental results in addition to financial gains. For instance, impact investment is frequently drawn to female-led social companies that offer educational services or sustainable energy solutions in developing areas. Since their profitability is frequently correlated with their capacity to bring about constructive social change, these companies typically have long-term sustainability ingrained in their business strategies. Aligning company plans with impact investors' specialized requirements, which frequently include for thorough reporting on both financial success and social impact measures, is a difficulty for many female entrepreneurs. This need may take a lot of resources, especially for small enterprises with little administrative expertise (Ajiva et al., 2024). To effectively utilize crowdfunding and alternative financing methods, female entrepreneurs must implement certain tactics that improve their prospects of sustained success. Telling an engaging tale and interacting with a community of supporters are essential for crowdfunding campaigns. Clear message, regular connection with backers, and a good web presence are frequently essential components of successful campaigns. Social media and email marketing were employed by business owners such as Sarah Kauss of S'well to increase campaign momentum and convert early backers into devoted clients. Similarly, by concentrating on money management and growth planning, women looking for microfinance or peer-to-peer loans might improve their chances of success. Borrowers that have a clear plan for growing their business and efficiently managing cash flow are frequently given preference by MFIs and P2P platforms (Al-Mamary & Abubakar, 2023).

Aligning operations with quantifiable social or environmental objectives is crucial for companies looking for impact investment. Whether it is via lowering carbon emissions, enhancing health outcomes, or generating educational opportunities, entrepreneurs should concentrate on providing precise measurements that show how their company causes good impact. For instance, women-led companies in the renewable energy space may monitor how many houses are powered by their goods or how much less greenhouse gas is released because of their work. These companies can draw in investors who are interested in both monetary gains and social change by offering thorough impact studies (Nurhayati, 2024). Women entrepreneurs also need to be aware of the competitive landscape and market circumstances to be profitable in the long run. Early business development can be greatly aided by crowdfunding and other alternative financing models, but ongoing innovation, market flexibility, and operational efficiency are necessary for long-term profitability. Regardless of the finance type used to begin, businesses may find it difficult to sustain their initial momentum if they do not change or adapt to changing market needs. For instance, as rivals appeared or market circumstances changed, some technology-based firms that had previously received significant sums of money through crowdfunding have found it difficult to stay profitable. Women entrepreneurs need to be ready to encounter more difficulties when trying to obtain follow-up finance or expand their businesses in fiercely competitive markets, especially in industries where gender prejudices still exist (Al-Mamary & Abubakar, 2023).

Thus, the expansion and viability of women-led enterprises have been significantly impacted by alternative financing models including crowdsourcing. Case studies such as those of Nasra Abubakar and Sarah Kauss show how these approaches may supply vital funding for expanding operations, breaking into new markets, and succeeding as a corporation. However, meticulous planning, sound financial management, and flexibility in response to market conditions are necessary for long-term viability. Although crowdfunding allows for community involvement and flexibility, it also necessitates a high level of digital knowledge and marketing expertise. P2P lending and microfinance offer more structured assistance, but they also include dangers to interest rates and payback plans. Although impact investment is beneficial for companies with a defined objective, it requires a clear link with environmental or social results. In the end, women entrepreneurs who successfully use these platforms can see substantial company development; nevertheless, they also must deal with the issues of sustainability and profitability in a global market that is becoming more and more competitive (Moleka, 2024).

CHALLENGES AND LIMITATIONS

Despite crowdsourcing and alternative financing's promise, women entrepreneurs may find it difficult to fully utilize these platforms due to several obstacles and restrictions. In addition to providing alternatives to conventional financing methods, crowdsourcing and models such as microfinance, peer-to-peer lending, and impact investment also present challenges that must be properly addressed. For women looking to expand their enterprises, these funding options provide both potential and hazards, ranging from platform fees and marketing difficulties to the possibility of project failure (Mahajan & Bandyopadhyay, 2021). Lack of access to the networks and resources required for the effective launch and promotion of crowdfunding campaigns is one of the most frequent challenges experienced by female entrepreneurs. Reaching and interacting with a large audience—often via social media and digital marketing platforms—is crucial to crowdfunding. Women entrepreneurs might not have as much access to these networks as their male colleagues, especially if they come from marginalized groups or poor nations. Their campaigns' exposure may be limited by this disconnect between their professional and social networks, which might lower their chances of meeting financing goals. According to research conducted on Kickstarter, for instance, women-led initiatives are less likely to succeed than male-led projects. This is mainly because women-led projects do not have the same access to networks and resources that are necessary for creating campaign momentum (Maiolini et al., 2024). Another major obstacle for female crowdfunding companies is marketing. More than simply a solid concept is needed for a crowdfunding campaign to be successful; strategic preparation, gripping narrative, and constant interaction with possible supporters are all necessary. It's possible that many female business owners lack the marketing know-how or resources necessary to develop eye-catching campaign sites, compelling tales, and focused digital marketing campaigns. For example, without access to expert marketing services or training, a rural women entrepreneur attempting to collect money for an agricultural project could find it difficult to reach a worldwide audience. On the other hand, her male counterpart in an urban environment could have easier access to a marketing team or the expertise to use social media efficiently (Mahajan & Bandyopadhyay,

2021). The financial environment for female entrepreneurs is further complicated by the fees that crowdfunding sites frequently impose, which can reduce the amount of money generated. Most well-known crowdfunding websites, such as Kickstarter and Indiegogo, impose a service fee that normally ranges from 5% to 10% of the money received. These fees can be a substantial expense for business owners with narrow profit margins or limited funds, lowering the overall amount of money available for their venture. Furthermore, even if a project does not receive the full amount of money, these costs are often non-refundable. This increases the financial risk, especially for women in underdeveloped nations who could already be working in conditions with little resources (Al-Mamary & Abubakar, 2023).

Platform fees might not be as big as a problem with peer-to-peer lending and microfinance, but there are still additional obstacles to using these alternative funding options. For example, microfinance has been a useful tool for women entrepreneurs in many poor countries, but it frequently has high interest rates that can put borrowers under a lot of financial strain. If their enterprises don't grow as planned or if their revenue sources are impacted by outside economic variables like inflation or market swings, women may find it difficult to repay their debt. Women may be compelled to take out more loans to fulfil their repayment commitments, which might result in a debt cycle that eventually jeopardizes the viability of their companies (Maehle et al., 2020). Another significant worry for female entrepreneurs who use alternative finance or crowdsourcing is the possibility of project failure. There is no assurance that the business will be successful even if a crowdfunding campaign raises the required amount of money. Unexpected obstacles that many projects face, such production hold-ups, shipment problems, or cost overruns, might cause the project to fail and, in some situations, damage the initiative's reputation among backers. For instance, there have been some well-publicized crowdfunding disasters when business owners failed to fulfil their commitments, leading to legal issues and harm to their brand. Women entrepreneurs may be more susceptible to these hazards because they might not have the knowledge necessary to handle difficult operational or logistical issues, especially if they lack mentors or substantial business experience (Mahajan & Bandyopadhyay, 2021).

When looking for alternative finance, women entrepreneurs are disproportionately impacted by systemic hurdles in addition to these difficulties. For example, gender prejudice in financial institutions is still a major problem, with many women claiming that they have a harder time getting loans or investing capital than males. Potential supporters' perceptions of campaigns can be influenced by gender prejudices, even in the comparatively equal realm of crowdfunding. According to studies, males are more likely to be seen as capable leaders, which may affect the willingness of supporters and investors to fund their campaigns. Whether overt or covert, this bias adds to the obstacles faced by women who already must navigate a financial environment that is biased against them (Maehle et al., 2020). Despite these obstacles, female entrepreneurs may use several best practices to lower the risks and improve their chances of success when utilizing alternative financing methods like crowdsourcing. First, it's critical to establish a robust network. To boost their exposure and get access to possible investors or backers, female entrepreneurs should concentrate on growing their offline and online professional and social networks. Women may reach a wider audience by taking part in women's entrepreneur clubs, going to industry conferences, and using resources like iFundWomen that assist female entrepreneurs (Zhao et al., 2023).

Women entrepreneurs might look for free or inexpensive tools to hone their digital marketing abilities to overcome marketing obstacles. Numerous websites, such as Kickstarter, provide guides and materials on how to design effective campaigns. Furthermore, several organizations and incubators offer training or mentorship tailored to the needs of female entrepreneurs. The Female Founders Alliance, for instance, provides initiatives to assist women in honing their marketing plans and increasing the likelihood that their crowdsourcing efforts would be successful (Maehle et al., 2020). Setting reasonable objectives and being ready for any setbacks are crucial components of any successful strategy. Campaigns or loan applications should be properly planned by female entrepreneurs, accounting for the obstacles that may come up. The risk of failure may be reduced by creating financial buffers to cover unforeseen costs, researching the industry to determine demand, and consulting with seasoned business owners. For instance, S'well founder Sarah Kauss carefully prepared her crowdsourcing campaign by establishing realistic objectives and anticipating any manufacturing delays (Kumar & Agrawal, 2024). In addition to helping her achieve her financial target, her meticulous planning made sure her company could continue to develop after the campaign. Women entrepreneurs can examine various crowdfunding or loan platforms to see which provide the best conditions when it comes to platform costs. For some kinds of campaigns, some platforms—like GoFundMe—are a more affordable choice since they don't impose platform fees. Women should also make sure they comprehend the price structure and how it will affect their overall funding by carefully reading the tiny print of any platform they select.

Lastly, by developing campaigns or loan applications that highlight their experience, leadership, and company potential, female entrepreneurs may endeavor to solve the problem of gender prejudice. Gender-based presumptions regarding ability can be challenged by emphasizing prior accomplishments, credentials, and endorsements from pleased clients or customers. Women entrepreneurs might also look for sponsors or investors who support women-led firms. Platforms like as SheEO, for instance, offer financing and assistance only to female entrepreneurs, lowering the possibility of prejudice in the investing process (Kumar & Agrawal, 2024). Thus, women entrepreneurs face a distinct set of difficulties even if crowdfunding and alternative financing models provide substantial opportunity. Platform costs, marketing challenges, project failure risk, and systemic gender prejudices are just a few of the barriers that might prevent women from taking full use of these models for company expansion. Nonetheless, women entrepreneurs may overcome these obstacles and raise their chances of success by establishing solid networks, honing their marketing abilities, establishing reasonable objectives, and looking for venues that assist women-led enterprises. Crowdfunding and alternative finance, when used properly, may be effective instruments for enabling women to create profitable and long-lasting enterprises.

CASE STUDIES AND SUCCESS STORIES

Crowdfunding and alternative finance have been used by several prosperous female entrepreneurs to develop their companies and get beyond conventional financial obstacles. Sarah Kauss, the creator of S'well, a business that manufactures environmentally friendly water bottles, is one such example. Because investors were dubious about the demand for her idea, Kauss first had trouble obtaining traditional finance. But she resorted to Kickstarter crowdfunding, where she not only reached but beyond her financing target. Kauss was able to draw supporters who shared her goal by emphasizing environmental sustainability and skilfully promoting her goods. She received the first funding from this campaign to start manufacturing and grow her company (Al-Mulla et al., 2022). Kauss's success was influenced by several important elements. She started by crafting an engaging story around a social cause—cutting down on plastic waste—that appealed to customers who care about the environment. Second, her polished and eye-catching marketing contributed to credibility and trust. Lastly, she made sure that funders had faith in her capacity to deliver by setting reasonable objectives and deadlines. These observations emphasize the significance of coordinating economic objectives with a more comprehensive social or environmental mission and developing a campaign that appeals to the ideals of possible supporters for female entrepreneurs (Kromidha et al., 2023).

Leah Busque, the creator of the online task-outsourcing marketplace TaskRabbit, is another example. Due of her history as a woman joining a tech-driven industry, Busque encountered difficulties getting venture financing when she founded TaskRabbit. She raised the money she needed to build her platform by using peer-to-peer lending websites like Prosper rather than traditional investors. Without giving up stock or control of her company, Busque was able to realize her vision by avoiding conventional gatekeepers. Her success was also largely attributed to her perseverance and dedication to improving her company plan (Kromidha et al., 2023). Women entrepreneurs, especially those in the technology industry, may learn a lot from Busque's story. Attracting users and investors alike was made possible by her ability to spot a glaring market gap and her dedication to making the platform better every day. She also showed the need of looking into non-traditional funding sources when access to venture capital is limited by her usage of peer-to-peer lending. Busque's flexibility and her will to get over early financial obstacles are lessons for female entrepreneurs.

In a different setting, Industree's creator, Neelam Chhiber, used microfinance to help her social company, which helps Indian rural women craftsmen. By obtaining modest loans through microfinance that would not have been accessible through traditional banking, Chhiber was able to expand her company and give thousands of women stable means of subsistence. The need of investigating alternative finance models is highlighted by Chhiber's tale, especially for women in poor nations where access to conventional banking institutions is frequently restricted (Al-Mulla et al., 2022). These case studies show that a combination of elements, including a compelling and relevant story, a skilfully organized campaign, and perseverance in the face of difficulties, are necessary for crowdfunding and alternative finance initiatives to be successful. The implications are evident for female entrepreneurs: these models need creativity, tenacity, and the capacity to engage audiences on a more profound, frequently values-based level. These illustrations demonstrate how alternative finance may be a powerful instrument for getting beyond financial obstacles and establishing sustained company expansion.

POLICY AND SUPPORT STRUCTURES

Policies and support from government and non-government organisation are also important in providing the women with access to non-conventional finance as used in many developing countries where conventional financial structures lock out the women. These support structures have increasingly concerned themselves with issues of collateral, the lack of networks, and biased credit tracking process all of which have been deemed to affect women some of which are as follows (Jamaluddin et al., 2022b). Through promoting policies that support women entrepreneurship and developing the right partnership with NGOs and Government, new funding structures such as crowdfunding, micro-financing, and P2P lending can be considered by women entrepreneurs (Jamaluddin et al., 2022a). In several countries government polices to support women entrepreneurs remained critical of any initiatives to increase access to structured and sustainable forms of funding. For example, India's government has brought measures to support women entrepreneurs, where provisions from the Pradhan Mantri Mudra Yojana (PMMY) Scheme provides collateral free access to fund micro businesses. Since this policy focuses on women-owned businesses, the gap of the gender in accessing funds has been closed well. Likewise in Kenya, the government has launched Women Enterprise Funds to finance women businesspeople who do not have the security needed by most commercial banks. That means that such policies not only enhance availability of capital but also allow women engage in the economy in a better way (Groza et al., 2020).

As applied to the use of microcredit in overall financing, NGOs are also involved in the offering of women entrepreneurs' needed support in trying out various forms of financing. Crowdfunding very as seen via the instance of Kiva, allows thousands of women across the world to order small micro loans that they might not otherwise be able to acquire from traditional institutions. Kiva can offer micro-finance and business training to women in the rural areas through its links with other local NGOs. By doing so, it is possible to create comfort that females are obtaining capital but at the same time are acquiring the appropriate competencies to sustain success in the long run (Alva et al., 2023). These NGDOs have played a big role of offering training especially in areas such as Sub-Saharan Africa where traditional cultures and values combine to deny women the opportunities to start up their own businesses by offering them role models as well as associations with other women entrepreneurs. Although such attempts have been helpful, especially in many settings, there is so much more that must be done. To increase the feasibility and effectiveness of non-traditional funding instruments the following policy interventions can be boosted further: A suggestion is that governments should encourage the use of the tax credit regime to back investors/and or crowdfunding and P2P online lending to growth-oriented women-owned businesses (Jamaluddin et al., 2022a). Using incentives such as these can elicit more action from the private actors increasing the number of resources available to women entrepreneurs. Also, more efforts should be made by the governments, to provide frameworks that facilitate partly. AP access to the digital space for crowdfunding and other alternate models of financing. This could mean extending the availability of internet connection, increasing awareness of computer illiteracy, and making mobile money cost effective (Groza et al., 2020).

Partnerships with companies and institutions somewhat also come out as an influential method of promoting the access to other sources of funds by women. An example of this kind of partnership in Turkey is the "Finance and Advice for Women in Business" an EBRD and other local banks launched program. This program in addition to offering loans also supplies customized business support services to females in business. The model of funding and technical assistance has been effective proving that with appropriate support women entrepreneurs can grow their businesses and operate successfully in quite challenging environments. Such models point out that it is necessary to complement the material support provided by the state with non-material assistance to overcome the specific obstacles that members of this category face. Other examples of successful PPP implementation are the BOI and the Aliko Dangote Foundation in Nigeria that provide low-interest credits for female entrepreneurs living in the rural areas (Alva et al., 2023). This initiative aims to eliminate poverty, encourage access to credit and financial services for women who operate small enterprises. This program has been used to help many women who do not have access to the formal financial market through assembling public and private sector funds and knowledge. These partnerships show that is possible to ensure that both the public and the private sectors work together with common aim to deliver a solution that seeks to support women entrepreneurs.

However, for these support structures to be effective it is imperative to also look at the structural vices that keep depriving women of funding (Jamaluddin et al., 2022b). This is embracing initiatives such as challenging gender stereotype in financing sector where the lending institutions categorize the women-led firms as high risk. Government should encourage policies that will increase lending to women to increase their chance of accessing loans. Similarly, the NGOs and members of the private sector should carry on campaigning for more democratization of the other forms of financing by demanding for protection of women from being charged high-interest rates or thrown into debt traps (Figueroa-Armijos & Berns,

2022). Therefore, more reassurance from the governments and non- Governmental organization is crucial to improve on the access of women to the non-conventional sources of funds. Even though much has been done to extend these models by, for example, micro-finance and crowdfunding a lot could still be done on the efficiency frontier. To increase a favourable environment for women, the governments and NGOs need to develop partnership with private sector, support tax motivations, and contribute to development of digital accessibility. Besides the financial requirements, these interventions also bring in other crucial components in the form of accompaniment in the form of coaching, development and enterprise consultancy. With more women eligible to access these financing opportunities they will be able to improve on their businesses and support the sustainable economic development.

Cultural and Social Factors

Media plays an important role as far as cultural and social perspectives toward crowdfunding and other ways of financing women entrepreneurship are concerned. Culturally and traditionally men and women have different roles to play, and it is largely through these roles that women are allowed to access money other resources for business among other things. These societal structures portray both risks and potentials for women that hope to access other forms of financing such as crowdfunding, P2P, and microcredit. For women entrepreneurs, it is therefore important to try and understand these cultural dynamics so that to ascertain the full benefits associated with these models (Figueroa-Armijos & Berns, 2022).

Because most extended cultures are traditional restrictive male chauvinistic societies, most women are locked out of accessing financial innovative institutions or networks. For example, woman entrepreneurship is still a taboo in many surrounding nations of Middle eastern countries and south Asian countries women are still barred from operating business establishments or running business establishments that encompass all sectors of business for they are expected to remain at home and be homemakers. It can restrain them from getting loans, and have contact with investors, who do not consider women's businesses serious. In less stringent environments, cultural prejudice confines women to the same perception level as in the stricter environment, making them less acceptable, less creditworthy, or simply higher risk than men in funding opportunities. Such cultivation values act as cultural barriers because they can deny women the opportunity to attract investors or to engage fully in entrepreneurship ecosystems (Arora, 2024). But crowdfunding and other nontraditional forms of financing can help women overcome traditional top-down methods of receiving funds and start raising money on more equal terms. Services like Kickstarter and Indiegogo enable an entrepreneur to gather funds directly from people, outsourcing to communities eager to invest in gender equality and social entrepreneurship. For instance, great appeal is found in advocacy campaigns such as women's rights, social justice, or improved representation for women entrepreneurs to attract funding to their initiatives.

Also, these platforms create the possibility for women to present their concepts and abilities while not coming under the scrutiny of conventional prudential financiers. Thus, this democratization of finance can be leveraged especially in societies that women have been limited in extending networks of formal Enterprise. Still, the models can be affected by societal pressure regarding how the women use or succeed with those models. In some societies, women will find it very hard to market their business online or even through the social media, which is very vital in creating awareness for a crowdfunding campaign. For instance, in certain areas of the Middle East if a woman ventures out of her home to engage in business or endorse a particular product online those in the society feel offended. This therefore brings a gap where culturally appropriate methods that will enable women entrepreneurs to advertise their businesses without violating the culture of the country are needed (Fanea-Ivanovici & Baber, 2024). And while there are these social barriers that greatly affect the overall success of the diabetes treatment and management, one can make use of the above by seeking community support and partnership. In societies that require women to be supportive of their families as well as the community, then using these relationships works in their favor. Different platforms allow women to include family members, local influencers or local leaders in the campaigns to gain public trust. Also, increasing the selling of products that are associated with cultural or religious beliefs also benefits in tackling with the resistance. For instance, where Islamic finance is well developed, providing Sharia compliant business propositions via crowdfunding can build-up the attraction to home-grown backers. It does not only make the business culturally sensitive but also resolves the conflict of the contemporary motives of financing and the cultural principles (Arora, 2024).

Knowledge of culture can also make the overall effectiveness of the other forms of financing even higher by targeting different culture-sensitive campaigns (Cruz Rambaud et al., 2022). Thirdly, it is significant that micro finance institutions, which have proved particularly effective in, for instance, South Asia or Africa, may include culturally appropriate approaches into their lending paradigms. Organizations such as the Grameen Bank have since realized the issue of lack of women's financial involvement due to but social barriers, and besides offering loans to women in batches, they ensure they support the women, thus ensuring high rates of loan repayment and enhanced togetherness. Such are realistic because women who have been empowered by microfinance do not only progress in their business ventures but are also instrumental in raising the social and economic standard of their societies.

This issue, however, is not just an example of culture as barriers, but also includes culture as an opportunity. Thus, knowledge of the social norm's values and expectations of the targeted groups and public by the women entrepreneurs means better financing to them. Crowd funding campaigns that focus on delivering social value or promoting economic growth in the predefined markets are more effective because family and community involvement is highly valued in such markets. The target backers can be sourced and recruited where the entrepreneurs are able to paint picture of the business where it is recognized as a business for purpose of generating income but also one that is proudly supporting the larger society (Cruz Rambaud et al., 2022). Finally, the study establishes that cultural and societal factors significantly influence women entrepreneurs' crowdfunding and ALF. However, at the same time these activities can prove to be effective challenges, the factors mentioned also signify opportunities where women can establish culturally relevant, profitable and popular local ventures as well as internationally. In this regard, the purpose of this chapter is to make a proposal of how the local norms and values can be adopted to ensure that the women entrepreneurs get appropriate social networks and cultural knowledge to enhance their success in the new emerging landscape of the sustainable financing. From experience it is vital to consider cultural factors when seeking to adopt such models to enhance the achievement of women's rights across the world (Arora, 2024).

FUTURE TRENDS AND INNOVATIONS

As with crowdfunding and other forms of innovative financing, this field is still developing and important trends in this area indicate that women entrepreneurs should expect even greater opportunity to access such financing in the future. They include the following: Technological innovation Changing customer preference more and efforts towards closing the gender gap in funding. With new models in place, they seek to revolutionize the traditional entrepreneurial funding by providing adequate and efficient means through which women can finance their business, expand their enterprises and integrate to the global market.

Perhaps one of the most noticeable trends for and in crowdfunding to be observed soon is the notion of equity-based crowdfunding, where backers could fund a business and receive shares in return. This model is vitally important for women entrepreneurs, as it allows them to get larger amounts of funding which might be used for the business development. Sites like Seedrs and crowed cubs have become prevalent especially in Europe and with increasing tendency in other parts of the globe, as a better substitute for traditional VCs, which form is traditionally headed by male investors and founded businesses as well. Equity-based crowdfunding fosters the concept of equal opportunities for everyone and gives women entrepreneurs an opportunity to access the large pool of people willing to invest in women-owned enterprises. And as this continues, more women businesspersons will likely have access to the capital and limelight that equity crowdfunding offers (Aziz et al., 2022). Another phenomenon that is in vogue is the application of blockchain and decentralized finance (DeFi) in non-mainstream funding. Some emerging possibilities in using of blockchain relate to the creation of an increased number of P2P, crowdfunding and micro credit in stock that is more transparent, secure and often intermediaries-free. For instance, Ethereum and Stellar; although not solely restricted to raising funds for women entrepreneurship, crowdfunded platforms have been deployed whereby female businesspersons can receive funds directly from contributors in different parts of the world without the interference of established authorities/banks. This means not only the availability of capital pathways, but also the expenses of attracting capital are reduced because transactions in blockchains are less costly and time-consuming than common payment systems. Since blockchain technology is expected to gain increased adoption going forward, business owning women especially in the developing world stand to gain from increased access to finance and new market for funding from a global network (Cruz Rambaud et al., 2022).

Alternative financing is also sponsored by AI in places like risk assessment and credit scoring as well. The conventional financial institutions have always locked women out for credit due to their inability to prove their credit worth or potential risks. Traditional credit scoring models on the other hand, lack the ability to look at other data sets such as social media activity, transaction history, and business performance to determine credit worthiness of the women entrepreneurs. These models are less prejudiced and assist more women to obtain loans and financing facilities that they would otherwise be locked out of by conventional credit rating measures. For instance, Tala and Branch, two fintech organizations, when deploying artificial intelligence for the extension of microloans to women entrepreneurs within areas that established banks avoid. This was arguably expected to progress, given the rolling advancement of artificial intelligence technologies in financial organizations (Aziz et al., 2022). Besides these technological trends, there is emerging adoption of impact investment and gender lens investment, which focuses on investment in business that creates positive social return, for women and deprived societies respectively. Female entrepreneurs seeking funding are finding access to impact investors who want to support women changemakers who address key social and environmental issues, making the goals of women-led businesses and impact investors' missions well aligned. This includes dedicated funding platforms, such as SheEO and Women You Should Fund, exclusively built on crowdfunding impact-based campaigns. With the increasing sensitisation of investors to the issue of gender imbalances in business ownership, the development of gender conscious investment strategies means that there are bound to be better prospects for women seeking funding.

In the future, more financing models for women entrepreneurs are expected to develop based on the above trends with more innovation on independence, technical support and social responsibility. The use of decentralized financing solutions, artificial intelligence in credit scoring and emphasis on the impact investment strategy will help women gain access to capital in flexible, transparent and relevant manner. These are trends inherent to the development of crowdfunding and AF models and, as such, these models will only become more attainable and affordable for women and, especially for women from the developing countries where financial systems have been traditionally getting elusive. However, with these innovations we also get some issues. New technologies and platforms continue to appear, and women entrepreneurs will have to learn the pros and cons of new solutions. For instance, with popularity such as blockchain technology and decentralised finance, there are concerns such as regulatory risks, innovations' security drawbacks and digital currency's price fluctuations. Likewise, while broader AI-based credit scoring can enhance financial inclusion the use of algorithms is not without inherent risk of bias where the models are developed and controlled. Female entrepreneurs will have to actively seek knowledge about these risks and constantly try to minimize adverse effects of unprofitable new financing models for themselves while trying to benefit in case of more favourable ones (Aziz et al., 2022). Lastly, the future of crowdfunding and other forms of funding for women entrepreneurs is bright as you will find several innovations in technology and culture striving to make funding accessible and diverse. Equity crowdfunding, blockchain financing, credit scoring by Artificial Intelligence, and gender-lens investment is some of the patterns which may redefine how women entrepreneurs seek and access capital to finance their businesses with sustainable future models. Nonetheless, as these trends evolve, it will be appropriate to respond to emerging issues related to new technologies and maintain the coherence of these models to support women entrepreneurs (Coronel-Pangol et al., 2023).

Women entrepreneurs should ensure that they are continuing learning on new changes that is happening in the financial as well as in the advancement in technology. That is why it is essential for women to have knowledge of the newest financing models like blockchain, artificial intelligence, equity crowdfunding to name a few to locate a new way to obtain the capital for their businesses and increase its size. Being active at professional conferences, being a member of the entrepreneur community, and tracking the fintech and gender lens investing in market movements are the key actions to remain relevant. It is also important for organizations to foster their digital literacies and enhance their technological competencies as well to harness new tool which use technological solutions to ease their fundraising methods. There are trends which show that by the end of the year or the next few years, any person who is using the social network, online advertising and other forms of ''new age'' marketing will have a better chance of finding backers for his or her project. Said reinforcements, women may thus wish to cultivate good relations with other women in similar businesses and influential women who have faced the said challenges (Coronel-Pangol et al., 2023). Finally, it's critical that women entrepreneurs actively pursue the right funding opportunities that are going to be right for them whilst being in line with their business principles. Microfinance, impact investing and crowdfunding provides women with funds that are intended for women venture, especially that which contributes to positive social change. Remaining relevant and in touch with new markets and economies women entrepreneurs will be ready and able to exploit new opportunities in the market as the market evolves.

CONCLUSION

In conclusion, crowdfunding and furthermore other models of financing structures hold a lot of promises for women entrepreneurs who now have a further option on how they can finance their businesses. All these models have gone a long way in minimizing key exclusions from finance that most women experience more so in areas where formal sector financial institutions are scarce or have biases towards women. Thus, crowdfunding allows women founding start-ups to attract a rather broad audience of investors, whereas other financing models, such as microfinancing, P2B lending, and impact investments are much more suitable for female entrepreneurs.

The future of these models is bright with advancement like the Blockchain, Artificial Intelligence, and Gender-lens investing that creates more opportunities inclusive for all genders. These innovations will transform accessibility, transparency and efficiency of financing for women entrepreneurs to improve their business scale and sustainability. However, the potential is still large, but there are constraints. As self-made women entrepreneurs, they must follow various cultural and social restrictions, control the platform fees, and be ready to address project failures, and to contribute their efforts to the constant improvement of technology knowledge at the same time.

While these models are slowly evolving and expanding, they should be maintained as fair and conducive for female entrepreneurship. If successfully scaled, these platforms potentially give women the opportunity to achieve their goals both socially and culturally and at the same time profit both socially and economically. First of all, crowdfunding and other forms of the non-traditional financing are not only the methods of the financial support but the instruments of the changed women's position in business and society, which in its turn allows creating efficient, generating profit companies and contributing to people's further evolution.

REFERENCES

Adedeji, A. S. (2021). Islamic financing and entrepreneurship development: Providing an alternative model for new venture growth. *Finance, Management and Entrepreneurship*, 91.

Ajiva, O. A., Ejike, O. G., & Abhulimen, A. O. (2024). Empowering female entrepreneurs in the creative sector: Overcoming barriers and strategies for long-term success. *International Journal of Advanced Economics*, *6*(08), 424–436. DOI: 10.51594/ijae.v6i8.1485

Al-Mamary, Y. H., & Abubakar, A. A. (2023). Breaking barriers: The path to empowering women entrepreneurs in Saudi Arabia. *Journal of Industrial Integration and Management*, *1*, 46. DOI: 10.1142/S2424862223500240

Al-Mulla, A., Ari, I., & Koç, M. (2022). Sustainable financing for entrepreneurs: Case study in designing a crowdfunding platform tailored for Qatar. *Digital Business*, *2*(2), 100032. DOI: 10.1016/j.digbus.2022.100032

Alva, E., Vivas, V., & Urcia, M. (2023). Entrepreneurial bricolage: Crowdfunding for female entrepreneurs during the COVID-19 pandemic. *Journal of Entrepreneurship in Emerging Economies*, *15*(4), 677–697. DOI: 10.1108/JEEE-12-2020-0464

Arora, M. (2024). Empowering the underprivileged women: Exploring entrepreneurial opportunities with microfinance. In *Women Entrepreneurship Policy: Context, Theory, and Practice* (pp. 265–285). Springer Nature Singapore. DOI: 10.1007/978-981-97-3607-2_14

Aziz, A., Iqbal, J., Murtza, M. H., Gill, S. A., & Cheema, I. Y. (2022). Effect of COVID-19 pandemic on women entrepreneurial sustainability: The role of Islamic microfinance institutions. *Journal of Economic and Administrative Sciences*.

Coronel-Pangol, K., Heras-Tigre, D., Jiménez Yumbla, J., Aguirre Quezada, J., & Mora, P. (2023). Microfinance, an alternative for financing entrepreneurship: Implications and trends—Bibliometric analysis. *International Journal of Financial Studies*, *11*(3), 83. DOI: 10.3390/ijfs11030083

Cruz Rambaud, S., López Pascual, J., Moro-Visconti, R., & Santandreu, E. M. (2022). Should gender be a determinant factor for granting crowdfunded microloans? *Humanities & Social Sciences Communications*, *9*(1), 1–13. DOI: 10.1057/s41599-022-01475-z

Fanea-Ivanovici, M., & Baber, H. (Eds.). (2024). *Alternative finance: A framework for innovative and sustainable business models*. Taylor & Francis. DOI: 10.4324/9781032713533

Figueroa-Armijos, M., & Berns, J. P. (2022). Vulnerable populations and individual social responsibility in prosocial crowdfunding: Does the framing matter for female and rural entrepreneurs? *Journal of Business Ethics*, *177*(2), 1–18. DOI: 10.1007/s10551-020-04712-0

Groza, M. P., Groza, M. D., & Barral, L. M. (2020). Women backing women: The role of crowdfunding in empowering female consumer-investors and entrepreneurs. *Journal of Business Research*, *117*, 432–442. DOI: 10.1016/j.jbusres.2020.06.013

Jamaluddin, F. A. A., Nasir, N. S. M., & Ishak, M. S. I. (2022). Cash waqf-based crowdfunding model for empowering single mother entrepreneurs in Malaysia. [JMTP]. *The Journal of Management Theory and Practice*, *3*(2), 98–104.

Jamaluddin, F. A. A., Nasir, N. S. M., & Ishak, M. S. I. (2022). Mudarabah-based crowdfunding model as an alternative fund for empowering single mother entrepreneurs. *al-Qanatir. International Journal of Islamic Studies*, *25*(2), 102–112.

Kromidha, E., Yadav, N., & Ilavarasan, P. V. (2023). Digital microfinance crowdfunding for disconnected women entrepreneurs in India. *International Journal of Entrepreneurship and Small Business*, *50*(4), 459–481. DOI: 10.1504/IJESB.2023.134687

Kumar, A., & Agrawal, G. (2024). A review of research on entrepreneurship and crowdfunding: Insights from bibliometric analysis. *Kybernetes*, *53*(9), 2824–2853. DOI: 10.1108/K-10-2022-1363

Maehle, N., Otte, P. P., & Drozdova, N. (2020). Crowdfunding sustainability. In *Advances in crowdfunding: Research and practice* (pp. 393-422). DOI: 10.1007/978-3-030-46309-0_17

Mahajan, R., & Bandyopadhyay, K. R. (2021). Women entrepreneurship and sustainable development: Select case studies from the sustainable energy sector. *Journal of Enterprising Communities: People and Places in the Global Economy*, *15*(1), 42–75. DOI: 10.1108/JEC-11-2020-0184

Maiolini, R., Cappa, F., Franco, S., & Quaratino, G. R. (2024). The impact of sustainable development goals in lending-based prosocial crowdfunding: A topic modeling analysis on the Kiva platform. *International Review of Financial Analysis*, *95*, 103441. DOI: 10.1016/j.irfa.2024.103441

Moleka, P. (2024). Innovative entrepreneurship through alternative finance: A framework for sustainable and innovative business models. In *Alternative finance* (pp. 13–28). Routledge. DOI: 10.4324/9781032713533-3

Nurhayati, N. (2024). The role of entrepreneurial finance in fueling growth and innovation. *Advances in Economics & Financial Studies*, *2*(3), 141–152. DOI: 10.60079/aefs.v2i3.271

Ojo, N. M. E., Mafimisebi, O. P., & Arndt, F. (2022). Female entrepreneurs' innovativeness in digital business ecosystems. In *Handbook on digital business ecosystems* (pp. 143–159). Edward Elgar Publishing.

Rajagopal, & Rajagopal. (2021). Crowdfunding. In *Crowd-based business models: Using collective intelligence for market competitiveness* (pp. 35-65).

Saluja, O. B. (2024). Crowdfunding to promote women entrepreneurship: A systematic literature review of the empirical studies conducted in the last decade (2012–2023). *International Journal of Gender and Entrepreneurship*, *16*(4), 500–535. DOI: 10.1108/IJGE-09-2023-0225

Serwaah, P. (2022). Crowdfunding, gender, and the promise of financial democracy: A systematic review. *International Journal of Gender and Entrepreneurship*, *14*(2), 263–283. DOI: 10.1108/IJGE-07-2021-0115

Serwaah, P., & Shneor, R. (2021). Women and entrepreneurial finance: A systematic review. *Venture Capital*, *23*(4), 291–319. DOI: 10.1080/13691066.2021.2010507

Shaikh, E., Tunio, M. N., & Qureshi, F. (2021). Finance and women's entrepreneurship in DETEs: A literature review. In *Entrepreneurial finance, innovation and development* (pp. 191-209).

Soemitra, A., Kusmilawaty, , & Rahma, T. I. F. (2022). The role of micro waqf bank in women's micro-business empowerment through Islamic social finance: Mixed-method evidence from Mawaridussalam Indonesia. *Economies, 10*(7), 157. DOI: 10.3390/economies10070157

Suseno, Y., & Abbott, L. (2021). Women entrepreneurs' digital social innovation: Linking gender, entrepreneurship, social innovation, and information systems. *Information Systems Journal, 31*(5), 717–744. DOI: 10.1111/isj.12327

Testa, S., Atawna, T., Baldi, G., & Cincotti, S. (2022). The innovation potential of Islamic crowdfunding platforms in contributing to sustainable development. *European Journal of Innovation Management, 25*(6), 1008–1035. DOI: 10.1108/EJIM-11-2021-0547

KEY TERMS AND DEFINITIONS

Crowdfunding: A financing method where small contributions from a large number of people are pooled, typically through online platforms.

Alternative Financing: Non-traditional financial methods that bypass conventional banking systems, including microfinance, peer-to-peer lending, and impact investing.

Impact Investing: Investments made with the intention to generate positive social or environmental impacts, along with financial returns.

Peer-to-Peer Lending: A form of financing that connects borrowers directly with individual lenders, often facilitated by online platforms.

Microfinance: Financial services such as small loans or insurance offered to low-income individuals or small businesses that lack access to traditional banking.

Chapter 2
Analyze the Factors that Contributed to Their Success and Lessons Learned

Shiney Chib
https://orcid.org/0000-0001-7648-9963
Datta Meghe Institute of Management Studies, India

M. Karthigeyan
https://orcid.org/0009-0006-8601-1318
Karpaga Vinayaga College of Engineering and Technology, India

Falguni Sanjay Pawar
Datta Meghe Institute of Management Studies, India

P. Selvakumar
https://orcid.org/0000-0002-3650-4548
Motilal Nehru National Institute of Technology, India

T. C. Manjunath
https://orcid.org/0000-0003-2545-9160
Rajarajeswari College of Engineering, India

P. C. Neena
https://orcid.org/0000-0002-8112-5555
Jain University, India

Mohit Sharma
https://orcid.org/0009-0007-2280-8077
Maharshi Dayanand University, Rohtak, India

DOI: 10.4018/979-8-3693-9193-8.ch002

ABSTRACT

Success analysis is a comprehensive approach that delves into the multifaceted factors driving achievement across various domains, including personal development, education, career, and entrepreneurship. Understanding success is not merely about defining it; It requires examining the intricate web of influences that contribute to an individual's or organization's ability to reach their goals. in the face of setbacks. This resilience is often correlated with higher levels of achievement, as those with a growth mindset are inclined to embrace effort, seek feedback, and cultivate their skills continuously. Conversely, those with a fixed mindset may avoid challenges, fearing failure and consequently limiting their potential for growth. Another critical component is goal setting. Clear, achievable goals provide a roadmap for success. Research shows that individuals who set specific goals are more likely to achieve them compared to those with vague aspirations. This process involves not only identifying what one wants to achieve but also breaking down the steps necessary.

INTRODUCTION TO SUCCESS ANALYSIS: UNDERSTANDING THE FACTORS THAT DRIVE ACHIEVEMENT

Success analysis is a comprehensive approach that delves into the multifaceted factors driving achievement across various domains, including personal development, education, career, and entrepreneurship. Understanding success is not merely about defining it; It requires examining the intricate web of influences that contribute to an individual's or organization's ability to reach their goals. in the face of setbacks. This resilience is often correlated with higher levels of achievement, as those with a growth mindset are inclined to embrace effort, seek feedback, and cultivate their skills continuously. Conversely, those with a fixed mindset may avoid challenges, fearing failure and consequently limiting their potential for growth. Another critical component is goal setting. Clear, achievable goals provide a roadmap for success. Research shows that individuals who set specific goals are more likely to achieve them compared to those with vague aspirations. This process involves not only identifying what one wants to achieve but also breaking down the steps necessary to reach those goals, thereby fostering a sense of purpose and direction. In addition to mindset, goal setting, and environmental influences, personal attributes such as discipline, motivation, and emotional intelligence are paramount. Discipline enables individuals to maintain focus and adhere to their plans despite distractions and obstacles. Motivation, both intrinsic and extrinsic, drives individuals to pursue their goals. Moreover, success is often non-linear. This perspective encourages individuals to reassess their strategies and approaches, paving the way for innovative solutions and ultimately contributing to long-term success. In the context of organizations, success analysis becomes even more intricate. Leaders who cultivate a culture of continuous improvement and learning empower their teams to take initiative, experiment, and drive change. In organizations, success can be quantified through key performance indicators (KPIs), customer satisfaction scores, and financial performance. These metrics help individuals and organizations gauge progress, identify areas for improvement, and adjust strategies accordingly. In conclusion, success analysis is a multifaceted exploration of the diverse factors influencing achievement. By understanding the interplay between mindset, goal setting, environmental influences, personal attributes, and organizational dynamics, individuals and organizations can develop more effective strategies for reaching their goals. Emphasizing resilience and adaptability in the face of challenges further enriches the understanding of success, highlighting the importance of continuous growth and learning. As we navigate the complexities of achievement, a comprehensive approach to success analysis not only illuminates pathways to individual and organizational success but also fosters a deeper appreciation of the rich tapestry of human potential and achievement.

SETTING THE CONTEXT: INDUSTRY TRENDS, MARKET CONDITIONS, AND GLOBAL EVENTS

Current inflationary pressures in various regions, exacerbated by supply chain disruptions and geopolitical tensions, have prompted central banks to reevaluate monetary policies. Interest rate fluctuations, currency volatility, and commodity price changes significantly impact business operations and consumer spending patterns. Companies must remain agile to navigate these challenges while seizing opportunities presented by emerging markets and innovative business models. Moreover, geopolitical events, such as trade tensions and conflicts, have created an unpredictable business environment. Companies must assess risks related to supply chains, market access, and compliance with international regulations. The recent emphasis on localization and nearshoring reflects a strategic pivot aimed at mitigating risks associated with global supply chains while addressing consumer expectations for faster delivery and greater transparency (Aburas et al., 2020). As industries adapt to these complex realities, they are also witnessing the rise of new competitors, particularly from tech-driven startups that challenge traditional business models. Collaboration across departments is crucial for achieving efficient operations. Silos within organizations can lead to miscommunication and inefficiencies, hindering overall performance. By fostering cross-functional teams and encouraging collaboration, companies can create a more cohesive and efficient operational framework. For instance, aligning sales and production teams ensures that demand forecasts are accurately communicated, leading to better inventory management and production planning. Predictive analytics can help organizations anticipate demand fluctuations, enabling them to adjust production schedules and resource allocations accordingly. This data-driven approach allows for proactive decision-making, reducing the likelihood of overproduction or stockouts. The gig economy is reshaping labor markets, providing both opportunities and challenges for employers and employees alike. Companies are increasingly adopting flexible work arrangements to attract talent and foster innovation, leading to a shift in organizational culture and employee expectations.

RESEARCH METHODOLOGY: CASE STUDIES, INTERVIEWS, AND DATA ANALYSIS

Research methodology serves as the backbone of any study, guiding the systematic investigation of complex phenomena. When exploring multi-faceted issues, especially in fields like business, social sciences, or health, employing a combination of case studies, interviews, and data analysis often yields rich insights and a more comprehensive understanding of the subject matter. Each method offers unique strengths and can complement one another, resulting in a robust approach to data collection and analysis (Adhikari et al., 2020).Case studies are particularly effective for examining specific instances in-depth, allowing researchers to explore the intricacies of particular situations, organizations, or events. This qualitative method enables a detailed exploration of the context, processes, and outcomes associated with a case. By focusing on real-world examples, case studies provide a narrative that highlights complexities and nuances that broader quantitative studies may overlook. They allow for a holistic understanding of phenomena by integrating various data sources, including archival records, reports, and direct observations. This method is invaluable for generating hypotheses and theories that can later be tested through quantitative research. Data analysis serves as a critical phase in the research process, transforming raw data into meaningful information. In qualitative research, thematic analysis is often employed to identify patterns and themes within the data collected from interviews and case studies (Ahmed et al., 2021). Quantitative data analysis, on the other hand, relies on statistical methods to draw conclusions from numerical data, enabling researchers to identify correlations, trends, and causal relationships. Combining qualitative and quantitative approaches—known as mixed methods research—can enhance the validity of findings, providing a more nuanced view of the research question. This multi-faceted approach is particularly important in complex environments where no single method can capture the entirety of the context. obtain informed consent from participants, maintain confidentiality, and uphold integrity throughout the research process (Aschemann-Witzel et al., 2017). Ultimately, a thoughtful and ethical approach to research methodology not only enhances the quality of findings but also promotes behaviour and organizational dynamics.

VISIONARY LEADERSHIP: THE ROLE OF STRATEGIC DECISION-MAKING

At its core, visionary leadership involves a clear articulation of a compelling vision that resonates with stakeholders and aligns with the organization's values and objectives. This type of leadership transcends traditional management by not only focusing on immediate operational efficiency but also emphasizing the broader implications of decisions on future growth and sustainability. Leaders who embody visionary traits actively engage in strategic thinking, allowing them to anticipate market trends, navigate challenges, and seize opportunities that may arise in a rapidly changing environment. This involves gathering and analyzing relevant data, understanding the competitive landscape, and assessing internal capabilities. A visionary leader does not shy away from making bold decisions; rather, they embrace calculated risks that have the potential to propel the organization forward. For example, companies that invested in digital transformation early on, such as Amazon and Netflix, not only adapted to changing consumer behaviors but also set new industry standards, illustrating the profound impact of strategic decision-making driven by a visionary outlook, valued, leaders can harness the collective intelligence of their teams, leading to breakthrough ideas and solutions. For instance, tech giants like Google and Apple exemplify how visionary leadership can foster a culture of innovation that continuously pushes the boundaries of what is possible, ensuring sustained competitive advantage (Bai et al., 2013). Collaboration across departments is crucial for achieving efficient operations. Silos within organizations can lead to miscommunication and inefficiencies, hindering overall performance. By fostering cross-functional teams and encouraging collaboration, companies can create a more cohesive and efficient operational framework. For instance, aligning sales and production teams ensures that demand forecasts are accurately communicated, leading to better inventory management and production planning. Predictive analytics can help organizations anticipate demand fluctuations, enabling them to adjust production schedules and resource allocations accordingly. This data-driven approach allows for proactive decision-making, reducing the likelihood of overproduction or stockouts. Effective communication is another hallmark of visionary leadership. Leaders must convey their vision in a manner that inspires and motivates employees at all levels. This involves not only articulating the vision clearly but also connecting it to the individual roles and contributions of team members. When employees understand how their work aligns with the organization's strategic goals, they are more likely to be engaged and committed. This alignment is crucial in facilitating collaboration and ensuring that everyone is working toward a common purpose, ultimately enhancing overall organizational effectiveness. Leaders must be willing to pivot their strategies in response to these changes, reassessing their goals and adjusting their approaches as necessary. This adaptability not only positions organizations to respond effectively to challenges but also to capitalize on new opportunities that align with their vision. Furthermore, visionary leadership encompasses a commitment to ethical decision-making and the importance of diversity and inclusion also cannot be overstated in the context of visionary leadership (Banik et al., 2020). Visionary leaders prioritize building inclusive environments where all voices are heard, thereby leveraging the full potential of their teams. This commitment to diversity not only enriches the decision-making process but also reflects a broader understanding of the complexities of the global marketplace. In conclusion, visionary leadership, driven by strategic decision-making, is crucial for navigating the complexities of modern organizations. By articulating a compelling vision, fostering a culture of innovation, communicating effectively, and demonstrating adaptability, visionary leaders can steer their organizations toward long-term success. Additionally, by prioritizing ethical considerations and embracing diversity, these leaders create a more resilient and sustainable organizational framework. Collaboration across departments is crucial for achieving efficient operations. Silos within organizations can lead to miscommunication and inefficiencies, hindering overall performance. By fostering cross-functional teams and encouraging collaboration, companies can create a more cohesive and efficient operational framework. For instance, aligning sales and production teams ensures that demand forecasts are accurately communicated, leading to better inventory management and production planning. Predictive analytics can help organizations anticipate demand fluctuations, enabling them to adjust production schedules and resource allocations accordingly. This data-driven approach allows for proactive decision-making, reducing the likelihood of overproduction or stockouts.

TALENT ACQUISITION AND DEVELOPMENT: BUILDING HIGH-PERFORMING TEAMS

Talent acquisition and development are critical components in building high-performing teams that drive organizational success. In today's competitive landscape, companies must not only attract top talent but also ensure that these individuals are effectively organizational skills needed for ongoing success. The process begins with a well-defined talent acquisition strategy that goes beyond traditional recruitment methods. Organizations need to employ a proactive approach that includes employer branding, a strong online presence, and engaging candidate experiences. By clearly articulating their values, culture, and mission, companies can attract ethos (Behl et al., 2019). A strategic talent acquisition plan should leverage data analytics to inform decisions. By analyzing workforce trends, skills gaps, and market conditions, organizations can better understand the talent landscape and make informed hiring decisions. Utilizing applicant tracking systems (ATS) and other technologies can streamline the recruitment process, candidate pipelines efficiently and effectively. Moreover, the use can be within the organization, reducing turnover and enhancing overall team performance. Once top talent is acquired, the focus shifts to development. Effective onboarding hires the company culture. A structured onboarding program that includes mentorship opportunities, training sessions, and regular check-ins can significantly improve new employees' experiences and accelerate their productivity. This initial investment in employee development pays dividends, as well-trained employees are more feel roles (Celik et al., 2016). Continuous development is equally important in fostering high-performing teams. Organizations should prioritize ongoing training and skill pace evolving job requirements. Offering a variety of workshops, online cross-training programs—can help employees expand their skill sets and stay competitive. Encouraging fosters adaptability and innovation, ensuring that teams can respond effectively to new challenges and opportunities. Leadership development is a key aspect of talent development that often gets overlooked. Preparing future leaders is essential for maintaining a high-performing team and ensuring organizational sustainability. In addition to collaboration, fostering diversity and inclusion within teams enhances creativity and innovation. Diverse teams bring a wealth of perspectives and experiences, enabling them to tackle problems from different angles and generate more innovative solutions. Organizations should implement inclusive hiring practices and create a culture where diverse voices are valued and heard (Chan, 2020). This commitment to diversity not only strengthens team dynamics but also improves overall organizational performance, as diverse teams have been shown to outperform their homogeneous counterparts. Finally, a focus on employee well-being is critical for sustaining high-performing teams. Organizations should prioritize mental health and work-life balance, creating an environment where employees feel supported and valued. This can include flexible work arrangements, wellness programs, and resources for stress management. When employees feel cared for and supported, their engagement and productivity levels increase, contributing to overall team performance (Craft et al., 2002). In conclusion, talent acquisition and development are integral to building high-performing teams that drive organizational success. By employing strategic recruitment methods, investing in comprehensive onboarding and continuous development, prioritizing leadership training, fostering collaboration and diversity, recognizing achievements, and focusing on employee well-being, organizations can create an environment where talent thrives. The interplay between these elements ensures that employees not only have the skills necessary to excel in their roles but also feel valued and engaged in their work. In a rapidly changing business landscape, organizations that prioritize talent acquisition and development will be better positioned to adapt, innovate, and succeed in achieving their long-term objectives.

PARTNERSHIPS AND COLLABORATIONS: LEVERAGING NETWORKS AND ECOSYSTEMS

Partnerships and collaborations are increasingly vital for organizations seeking to leverage networks and ecosystems in today's interconnected business landscape. As companies face complex challenges that require innovative solutions, the ability to form strategic alliances becomes essential. Collaborations can enhance competitive advantages, accelerate innovation, and provide access to resources and expertise that individual organizations may lack. By working together, organizations can create synergies that drive mutual benefits, enabling them to adapt to market changes and capitalize on new opportunities (Dalalah et al., 2011). One of the primary advantages of partnerships is the ability to pool resources and capabilities. This can take various forms, such as sharing technology, knowledge, and financial investments. For instance, in the technology sector, companies often engage in partnerships to develop new products or services. Collaborations between established firms and startups can lead to the rapid commercialization of innovative ideas. For example, the partnership between Microsoft and OpenAI has allowed both organizations to push the boundaries of artificial intelligence, combining Microsoft's cloud computing capabilities with OpenAI's advanced research to create powerful AI tools. Such alliances not only enhance product offerings but also accelerate the pace of innovation, enabling organizations to remain competitive in fast-moving markets. Local partners bring valuable insights into cultural nuances, regulatory landscapes, and consumer preferences, which can facilitate smoother market entry. For instance, global brands like Starbucks have successfully partnered with local companies when entering new countries, allowing them to tailor their offerings to meet local tastes and preferences while navigating complex market dynamics (Davis, 2014). Cross-industry collaborations, in particular, can yield groundbreaking innovations by combining different sectors' strengths. An example is the collaboration between automotive companies and technology firms to develop autonomous vehicles. By integrating expertise in engineering, software development, and user experience design, these partnerships are advancing the future of transportation. Such collaborations underscore the value of interdisciplinary approaches to problem-solving and innovation.

For example, distilleries shifted their production to create hand sanitizer, while automotive companies repurposed factories to produce ventilators. These collaborations demonstrated how organizations could adapt quickly through partnerships, showcasing resilience and a commitment to social responsibility recognizing the need to collaborate to achieve sustainability goals. Partnerships between companies, non-profits, and government entities can facilitate the sharing of best practices and resources, enabling collective efforts to address global challenges such as climate change and resource depletion. regardless of geographical barriers (Ding et al., 2018). This technological advancement has made it easier for organizations to establish and maintain partnerships, facilitating real-time communication and project coordination. Moreover, data-sharing agreements can enhance collaboration by allowing organizations to leverage insights from shared data, further enriching their decision-making processes. pose obstacles, particularly in cross-border collaborations. Building a shared understanding and fostering a collaborative culture are essential for overcoming these challenges. Companies should invest time and resources in relationship-building and conflict resolution to ensure that partnerships are productive and sustainable.

ADAPTING TO CHANGE: EMBRACING DISRUPTION AND INNOVATION

Adapting to change is a critical competency for organizations in an era defined by rapid disruption and relentless innovation. As technological advancements, shifting consumer preferences, and global challenges reshape industries, businesses must cultivate a proactive approach to change management. Embracing disruption is not merely about reacting to challenges but actively anticipating and leveraging opportunities that arise from evolving market dynamics. Organizations that adopt this mindset can not only survive but thrive, positioning themselves as leaders in their respective fields (Dinter, 2013). At the heart of successfully adapting to change is a culture that values agility and resilience. A resilient organization is one that embraces flexibility, allowing it to pivot quickly in response to unforeseen circumstances. This agility can be fostered through empowering employees to embrace change at all levels, encouraging a mindset that views challenges as opportunities for growth and innovation. Companies like Netflix exemplify this approach, having transformed their business model multiple times—from DVD rentals to streaming services to producing original content. By fostering a culture that welcomes change, these organizations enable their teams to explore new ideas and respond effectively to shifting market conditions (Fotopoulos et al., 2011). Innovation plays a vital role in this adaptive process. Organizations must prioritize continuous improvement and experimentation, encouraging teams to explore novel solutions and challenge the status quo. Such initiatives not only generate new ideas but also enhance employee engagement, as individuals feel empowered to contribute to the organization's vision. Furthermore, collaboration is essential in navigating disruption. In an increasingly interconnected world, organizations must break down silos and encourage cross-functional teamwork. By fostering collaboration, companies can leverage diverse perspectives and expertise, leading to more comprehensive solutions and innovative outcomes. For example, during the COVID-19 pandemic, many companies formed alliances to adapt to new challenges, sharing resources and knowledge to develop effective responses. Such collaborative efforts demonstrate the power of collective intelligence in overcoming adversity and driving change (Fuli et al., 2020). Additionally, organizations must invest in their talent to equip employees with the skills needed to navigate change. Continuous learning and professional development are essential for fostering a workforce that is adaptable and innovative. Companies should provide training programs that enhance employees' capabilities, focusing on emerging technologies and new methodologies relevant to their industries. By prioritizing employee development, organizations can ensure that their teams are well-prepared to meet the challenges of an ever-evolving landscape (Gersons et al., 2020). Cultural sensitivity is also vital in adapting to change, especially for organizations operating in global markets. Understanding and respecting cultural differences can facilitate smoother transitions and enhance collaboration among diverse teams. Organizations must be attuned to local customs, values, and consumer preferences, tailoring their strategies to resonate with various markets. Companies like McDonald's exemplify this approach by adapting their menu offerings to cater to regional tastes, demonstrating how cultural awareness can enhance market acceptance and drive success.

EFFICIENT OPERATIONS: STREAMLINING PROCESSES AND OPTIMIZING RESOURCES

Efficient operations are the backbone of any successful organization, enabling companies to streamline processes and optimize resources effectively. In an increasingly competitive marketplace, the ability to maximize productivity while minimizing waste is paramount. Efficient operations not only enhance profitability but also improve customer satisfaction by ensuring that products and services are delivered in a timely and cost-effective manner. To achieve operational efficiency, organizations must adopt a systematic approach that encompasses process analysis, technology integration, resource management, and continuous improvement (Zhou et al., 2017). At the core of streamlining operations is the need for a thorough analysis of existing processes. This involves mapping out workflows to identify bottlenecks, redundancies, and inefficiencies that may hinder performance. For example, a manufacturing firm might discover that excessive handling during the production process leads to delays. By redesigning workflows and eliminating unnecessary steps, the company can reduce lead times and increase output (Gunessee et al., 2018). Collaboration across departments is crucial for achieving efficient operations. Silos within organizations can lead to miscommunication and inefficiencies, hindering overall performance. By fostering cross-functional teams and encouraging collaboration, companies can create a more cohesive and efficient operational framework. For instance, aligning sales and production teams ensures that demand forecasts are accurately communicated, leading to better inventory management and production planning. Predictive analytics can help organizations anticipate demand fluctuations, enabling them to adjust production schedules and resource allocations accordingly. This data-driven approach allows for proactive decision-making, reducing the likelihood of overproduction or stockouts. Companies responding swiftly to changing market (Han et al., 2018a). In conclusion, efficient operations are essential for organizations striving to streamline processes and optimize resources in a competitive environment. By conducting thorough process analysis, leveraging technology, managing resources effectively, and fostering a culture of continuous improvement, companies can enhance their operational efficiency. Collaboration across departments and the use of data analytics further contribute to informed decision-making and agile responses to market changes.

TECHNOLOGY AND DIGITAL TRANSFORMATION: ENHANCING CAPABILITIES AND COMPETITIVENESS

As businesses increasingly rely on digital tools and technologies, the need to enhance capabilities and competitiveness has never been more apparent (Han et al., 2018b). These empower organizations to gather and analyze vast amounts of data, gaining insights that drive strategic decision-making. By leveraging data analytics, organizations can not only improve customer satisfaction but also optimize operations and drive profitability (Ishiwatari et al., 2020). This shift not only improves productivity but also enhances employee engagement by allowing staff to engage in more meaningful work. Companies that embrace automation can respond more rapidly to changing market conditions, gaining a competitive edge. Customer experience is also profoundly impacted by digital transformation. As consumers increasingly demand personalized and seamless interactions, organizations must leverage technology to meet these expectations. Companies like Amazon have mastered this approach furthermore, digital transformation fosters a culture of innovation within organizations. By embracing new technologies, businesses encourage experimentation and the exploration of novel ideas. This culture is crucial for staying ahead of competitors in an ever-evolving marketplace. Organizations that invest in innovation are better equipped to identify emerging trends and adapt their strategies accordingly. For instance, tech giants like Google and Apple continuously invest in research and development, ensuring they remain at the forefront of technological advancements. By cultivating an innovative mindset, organizations can drive growth and create new revenue streams (Ivanov, 2020). This involves not only investing technology usage are essential for ensuring that the workforce remains competitive and capable.

Organizations that invest in their employees' professional development not only enhance individual capabilities but also foster a culture of continuous learning and adaptation. In conclusion, technology and digital transformation are essential for enhancing organizational capabilities and competitiveness in a rapidly changing business environment. By embracing advanced technologies, streamlining operations, and prioritizing customer experience, organizations can position themselves for success. A culture of innovation, strong leadership, and a commitment to employee development further enhance the effectiveness of digital initiatives. As businesses navigate the complexities of digital transformation, those that prioritize adaptability and innovation will emerge as leaders in their industries, ready to seize the opportunities that the digital age presents. Ultimately, technology is not just a tool but a catalyst for transformation, driving growth and enabling organizations to thrive in an increasingly competitive landscape.

DATA-DRIVEN DECISION-MAKING: ANALYTICS, INSIGHTS, AND INTELLIGENCE

This approach emphasizes the use of data analytics to inform decisions, drive insights, and enhance operational effectiveness (Kaur et al., 2019). At the heart of data-driven decision-making is the process of data collection and analysis. Organizations gather data from multiple channels, including customer interactions, market research, operational metrics, and social media. This data can be structured, such as sales figures and customer demographics, or unstructured, like customer feedback and online reviews. Advanced analytics techniques, including descriptive, predictive, and prescriptive analytics, allow businesses to interpret this data effectively. Companies like Amazon utilize these techniques to enhance inventory management and personalize customer experiences, demonstrating the power of data in shaping strategic initiatives., a retail company might analyze purchasing patterns to determine which products are trending among specific customer segments. This insight can drive inventory decisions and targeted marketing campaigns, ultimately leading to increased sales. Additionally, data analytics enables organizations to segment their audiences more effectively, tailoring messages and offerings to meet the diverse needs of their customers. Such targeted strategies enhance customer satisfaction and loyalty, driving long-term business success (Lin et al., 2018). However, for organizations to fully realize the benefits of data-driven decision-making, they must address several challenges. Additionally, organizations must prioritize data security and privacy, particularly in light of increasing regulations surrounding data protection. Building trust with customers regarding data usage is essential for fostering a positive relationship and encouraging data sharing. This cultural shift may require training and development programs to enhance employees' data literacy, equipping them with the skills needed to analyze and interpret data effectively. By cultivating a data-centric culture, organizations can empower their teams to embrace standard practice, leading to more informed choices and better outcomes. Tools like Tableau and Power BI enable teams to create interactive dashboards that visualize key performance indicators, facilitating real-time decision-making. By leveraging these technologies, organizations can enhance their analytical capabilities and ensure that insights are readily accessible to stakeholders. The integration of AI and ML further amplifies the potential of data-driven insights, enabling organizations to make informed decisions with greater accuracy and speed. However, organizations must prioritize data quality, governance, and cultural alignment to fully realize the benefits of this approach. By investing in the right technologies and fostering a data-centric culture, organizations can position themselves for success, navigating the challenges of today's marketplace with confidence and agility. Ultimately, data-driven decision-making is not just a strategy; it is a transformative approach that can redefine how organizations operate and succeed in an increasingly data-rich world.

FINANCIAL MANAGEMENT: BUDGETING, FUNDING, AND INVESTMENT

Financial management is a critical discipline that encompasses budgeting, funding, and investment strategies essential for the sustainability and growth of organizations. In today's complex and dynamic economic environment, effective financial management ensures that organizations can allocate resources efficiently, manage risks, and capitalize on opportunities. This comprehensive approach integrates various aspects of financial operations, providing a solid foundation for strategic planning and performance evaluation of outcomes. Organizations must consider historical data, market trends, and economic conditions when developing their budgets. However, it may dilute ownership and control. Conversely, debt financing—such as loans or bonds—allows organizations to retain ownership but requires regular interest payments, posing a risk if cash flow becomes constrained. Investment decisions play a critical role in financial management, as organizations must strategically allocate their resources to maximize returns while managing risk. Investment strategies can vary widely, ranging from capital expenditures on new equipment and technology to research and development initiatives aimed at fostering innovation. Effective investment decision-making requires a thorough analysis of potential opportunities, including a comprehensive assessment of risks and rewards. Financial management also involves effective cash flow management, which is crucial for maintaining liquidity and ensuring that organizations can meet their short-term obligations. Cash flow forecasting enables businesses to anticipate cash inflows and outflows, allowing for proactive financial planning. This forecasting process considers factors such as sales projections, payment cycles, and operating expenses, providing insights into potential cash shortages or surpluses. By implementing effective cash management strategies, organizations can optimize working capital, ensuring that sufficient funds are available to support ongoing operations and growth initiatives. The role of technology in financial management cannot be overstated. Advanced financial management software and tools enable organizations to automate budgeting, forecasting, and reporting processes, enhancing accuracy and efficiency (Mahadev et al., 2023). In conclusion, effective financial management encompassing budgeting, funding, and investment is crucial for organizations striving for sustainable growth and competitiveness. However, for organizations to fully realize the benefits of data-driven decision-making, they must address several challenges. Additionally, organizations must prioritize data security and privacy, particularly in light of increasing regulations surrounding data protection. Building trust with customers regarding data usage is essential for fostering a positive relationship and encouraging data sharing. This cultural shift may require training and development programs to enhance employees' data literacy, equipping them with the skills needed to analyze and interpret data effectively. By cultivating a data-centric culture, organizations can empower their teams to embrace standard practice, leading to more informed choices and better outcomes. Tools like Tableau and Power BI enable teams to create interactive dashboards that visualize key performance indicators, facilitating real-time decision-making. By leveraging these technologies, organizations can enhance their analytical capabilities and ensure that insights are readily accessible to stakeholders. The integration of AI and ML further amplifies the potential of data-driven insights, enabling organizations to make informed decisions with greater accuracy and speed. However, organizations must prioritize data quality, governance, and cultural alignment to fully realize the benefits of this approach. By implementing robust budgeting processes, carefully evaluating funding options, and making informed investment decisions, businesses can optimize their financial performance and mitigate risks. Moreover, embracing technology and incorporating.

REVENUE GROWTH STRATEGIES: PRICING, SALES, AND MARKETING

Revenue growth strategies are essential for organizations aiming to enhance their market position and drive profitability in a competitive landscape. These strategies encompass various aspects of pricing, sales, and marketing, each of which plays a pivotal role in maximizing revenue potential. By aligning these elements effectively, organizations can not only boost their top line but also ensure sustainable growth in the long term. A comprehensive approach to revenue growth requires a deep understanding of customer needs, market dynamics, and the overall value proposition of the organization's offerings. Pricing strategies are one of the most critical levers for driving revenue growth. The right pricing strategy can significantly impact consumer perception, demand elasticity, and ultimately, profitability. For instance, airlines and hotel chains often use these models to maximize occupancy rates and revenue per available room (RevPAR), demonstrating the effectiveness of responsive pricing strategies for sales outreach. For example, a B2B technology company might segment its market based on industry, tailoring its sales pitch to address the unique challenges faced by each sector (Paramasivam Selvakumar et al., 2024). Moreover, effective sales training and development programs are vital for empowering sales teams with the skills and knowledge needed to succeed. Training should focus on building consultative selling skills, product knowledge, and understanding customer pain points. Digital marketing offers unprecedented opportunities for organizations to engage with their audiences. Social media platforms enable brands to interact directly with customers, gather feedback, and build community. Paid advertising on platforms like Google Ads and social media allows for targeted outreach, ensuring that marketing efforts reach the most relevant audiences. Furthermore, marketing automation tools can streamline lead generation and nurturing processes, allowing organizations to maintain consistent communication with prospects and customers (Yadav et al., 2015). Customer retention strategies are also critical for sustained revenue growth. This includes personalized communications, responsive support, and loyalty programs that reward repeat business. Collaborative marketing efforts can also enhance brand visibility and credibility, ultimately driving sales. data analytics, customer retention initiatives, and strategic partnerships further amplifies these efforts, positioning organizations for success. As the business environment continues to evolve, those that prioritize a holistic approach to revenue growth will be better equipped.

RETURN ON INVESTMENT (ROI): MEASURING SUCCESS AND EVALUATING IMPACT

Return on Investment (ROI) is a fundamental metric that organizations use to measure the effectiveness and impact of their investments, whether in projects, marketing campaigns, new technologies, or human capital. By quantifying the, guiding strategic decision-making and resource allocation. In a business environment characterized by rapid change and increasing competition, understanding and accurately measuring ROI is crucial for organizations aiming to enhance profitability and sustain growth (Zhai et al., 2008). However, the simplicity of this calculation belies the complexity involved in accurately assessing ROI, particularly in contexts where benefits may not be immediately apparent or quantifiable. One of the significant challenges in measuring ROI is determining what constitutes the "final value" of an investment. For tangible investments, such as capital expenditures on equipment or facilities, calculating ROI may involve straightforward financial metrics, such as increased revenues or cost savings. However, for intangible investments—such as employee training programs, marketing initiatives, or research and development—the benefits can be more difficult to quantify. In these cases, organizations often rely on a combination of quantitative and qualitative metrics to assess impact. For example, while a marketing campaign may not lead directly to immediate sales, it could enhance brand awareness, customer engagement, and long-term loyalty, all of which contribute to future revenue (Paramasivam Selvakumar et al., 2024). In addition to traditional financial ROI calculations, organizations can benefit from a broader view that incorporates multiple performance indicators. For instance, the concept of Economic Value Added (EVA) assesses the true economic profit generated by an investment by considering the cost of capital. By focusing on the residual wealth created for shareholders, EVA provides a more comprehensive measure of performance that can inform investment decisions. These social ROI (SROI) metrics can enhance an organization's reputation and long-term viability, illustrating that a holistic view of ROI incorporates broader impacts beyond immediate financial gains., can help maintain data integrity. Additionally, adopting technology solutions—such as business intelligence tools—can facilitate data collection and analysis, enabling organizations to derive actionable insights from their ROI assessments. Moreover, continuous monitoring and reassessment of ROI should be embedded into the organizational culture. By adopting a dynamic approach to measuring ROI, organizations can adjust strategies in real-time based on performance data. This adaptability not only enhances the ability to respond to changing market conditions but also promotes a culture of learning and improvement within the organization. In summary, Return on Investment (ROI) is a vital metric for measuring success and evaluating the impact of investments within an organization. While calculating ROI involves straightforward financial metrics, a comprehensive understanding of ROI requires consideration of qualitative factors, time value, and broader impacts. Organizations that adopt a holistic approach to ROI measurement can better inform their strategic decisions, optimize resource allocation, and drive sustainable growth. By fostering a culture of continuous improvement and effective communication regarding ROI findings, businesses can enhance their overall performance and ensure long-term success in an increasingly competitive landscape.

LESSONS LEARNED: COMMON THEMES, BEST PRACTICES, AND KEY TAKEAWAYS

Lessons learned from various business experiences and initiatives serve as invaluable insights for organizations striving to improve their strategies, processes, and overall performance. By analyzing common themes, best practices, and key takeaways from both successes and failures, businesses can cultivate a culture of continuous improvement and innovation. These lessons not only inform future decision-making but also help organizations navigate challenges, capitalize on opportunities, and foster resilience in an ever-evolving marketplace (Sugumaran et al., 2024). One of the most prominent themes that emerges from lessons learned across industries is the importance of adaptability. This adaptability not only ensured business continuity but also revealed opportunities for enhanced employee productivity and engagement. Organizations that prioritize agility in their operations and decision-making processes are better equipped to thrive in uncertainty. Another critical theme is the necessity of data-driven decision-making, that integrate teams from development, marketing, and sales during product launches typically experience smoother rollouts and greater market success. Encouraging collaboration not only enhances creativity but also strengthens interpersonal relationships within the organization, contributing to a more cohesive and motivated workforce (Ramakrishnan et al., 2022). This commitment to employee development not only equips teams with the skills necessary to adapt to changing environments but also positions organizations for long-term success in a competitive landscape and machine learning—found new avenues for enhancing customer experiences and driving business growth. By fostering an innovative mindset, organizations can continuously explore new ideas, products, and services that resonate with evolving market demands For instance, organizations that implemented comprehensive risk management frameworks were able to weather economic downturns and crises more effectively, ensuring business continuity and minimizing disruptions. By fostering a culture of risk awareness, businesses can empower employees to make informed decisions that align with organizational objectives. increasingly seeking out companies that align with their values, making sustainability a crucial differentiator in the marketplace. Businesses that integrate sustainable practices into their operations—such as reducing waste, sourcing ethically, and supporting local communities—often see improved stakeholder relationships and increased brand loyalty (Sreenivasulu et al., 2022). This commitment to responsible business practices can lead to long-term financial success and a positive impact on society. In conclusion, the lessons learned from various business experiences reveal common themes, best practices, and key takeaways that are essential for driving success. Adaptability, data-driven decision-making, effective communication, collaboration, customer-centricity, continuous learning, technology adoption, risk management, sustainability, and performance measurement are all critical components of a successful organizational strategy (Zhai et al., 2009). By integrating these lessons into their operations,

APPLYING SUCCESS FACTORS TO ACHIEVE SUSTAINABLE GROWTH AND EXCELLENCE

Applying success factors to achieve sustainable growth and excellence is essential for organizations striving to navigate today's complex and competitive landscape. Sustainable growth is not merely about increasing revenues; it involves creating value for stakeholders, optimizing resources, and ensuring that organizational practices are environmentally and socially responsible. By identifying and leveraging key success factors—such as strong leadership, innovative culture, customer focus, operational efficiency, and strategic partnerships—organizations can develop a holistic approach that drives long-term performance and resilience and collaboration. Leaders who prioritize transparency and open communication encourage team members to share ideas, voice concerns, and engage in problem-solving. This inclusive approach not only enhances employee morale and engagement but also fosters a sense of ownership and commitment to organizational objectives. In practice, organizations led by visionary leaders tend to exhibit higher levels of innovation and adaptability, positioning themselves well to respond to market changes (Zhou et al., 2011). Innovation is another critical success factor for achieving sustainable growth. Additionally, organizations should invest in customer service excellence, ensuring that interactions are positive and meaningful. Training employees to understand the customer journey and address pain points can lead to higher satisfaction levels and repeat business (Ramakrishnan et al., 2022). Strategic partnerships and collaborations can also serve as powerful catalysts for sustainable growth. By forming alliances with complementary organizations, businesses can expand their reach, access new markets, and share resources. Partnerships can take various forms, including joint ventures, co-marketing initiatives, and supply chain collaborations. For instance, companies in the tech industry often partner with startups to access innovative solutions and accelerate product development. By leveraging the strengths of partner organizations, businesses can enhance their capabilities and drive mutual growth. Establishing clear communication channels and aligning goals with partners is essential for ensuring the success of collaborative efforts. In conclusion, applying success factors to achieve sustainable growth and excellence requires a multifaceted approach that encompasses strong leadership, innovation, customer focus, operational efficiency, strategic partnerships, sustainability, performance measurement, market awareness, and continuous learning.

CONCLUSION

Analyzing the factors that contributed to organizational success reveals a multifaceted landscape of strategies and practices that can be emulated across various sectors. Key elements such as visionary leadership, a strong organizational culture, customer-centricity, innovation, and operational efficiency consistently emerge as significant contributors to sustained growth and excellence. Operational efficiency, achieved through streamlined processes and the adoption of advanced technologies, enhances productivity and reduces costs, contributing directly to the bottom line. The integration of data-driven decision-making practices enables organizations to evaluate performance rigorously, ensuring that resources are allocated effectively and strategies are adjusted as necessary. Moreover, strategic partnerships and collaborations can amplify growth potential, providing access to new markets, resources, and expertise. the idea that long-term success is inextricably linked to positive societal and environmental impact. Conclusion, the analysis of successful organizations reveals that a comprehensive approach—rooted in strong leadership, an innovative culture, customer focus, operational efficiency, and strategic collaboration—can drive sustainable growth and excellence. The lessons learned emphasize the need for organizations to remain adaptable, prioritize customer engagement, and foster a culture of continuous learning and improvement. By integrating these elements into their strategic frameworks, businesses can position themselves for enduring success, ensuring they not only meet the demands of today but also pave the way for a prosperous future. Ultimately, the journey toward success is ongoing, requiring a commitment to evolve and grow in alignment with the changing dynamics of the market and society at large. However, for organizations to fully realize the benefits of data-driven decision-making, they must address several challenges. Additionally, organizations must prioritize data security and privacy, particularly in light of increasing regulations surrounding data protection. Building trust with customers regarding data usage is essential for fostering a positive relationship and encouraging data sharing. This cultural shift may require training and development programs to enhance employees' data literacy, equipping them with the skills needed to analyze and interpret data effectively. By cultivating a data-centric culture, organizations can empower their teams to embrace standard practice, leading to more informed choices and better outcomes. Tools like Tableau and Power BI enable teams to create interactive dashboards that visualize key performance indicators, facilitating real-time decision-making. By leveraging these technologies, organizations can enhance their analytical capabilities and ensure that insights are readily accessible to stakeholders. The integration of AI and ML further amplifies the potential of data-driven insights, enabling organizations to make informed decisions with greater accuracy and speed. However, organizations must prioritize data quality, governance, and cultural alignment to fully realize the benefits of this approach.

REFERENCES

Abhilasha, A., Sreenivasulu, A., & Manimozhi, T. KUMAR, P. S., Selvakumar, P., & Singh, P. (2022, April). The Model of Smart Sensing Device For Sensitive Nanoclusters Modification in Sensing Properties. In 2022 2nd International Conference on Advance Computing and Innovative Technologies in Engineering (ICACITE) (pp. 1043-1047). IEEE.

Aburas, W., & Alshammari, T. M. (2020). Pharmacists' roles in emergency and disasters: COVID-19 as an example. *Saudi Pharmaceutical Journal : SPJ : the Official Publication of the Saudi Pharmaceutical Society*, *28*(12), 1797–1816. DOI: 10.1016/j.jsps.2020.11.006 PMID: 33257901

Adhikari, B., Ozaki, A., Marahatta, S. B., Rijal, K. R., & Mishra, S. R. (2020). Earthquake rebuilding and response to COVID-19 in Nepal, a country nestled in multiple crises. *Journal of Global Health*, *10*(2), 1–4. DOI: 10.7189/jogh.10.020367 PMID: 33110561

Ahmed, S., Muhtasim, H., Yeasir, T., Farabi, I., Sarker, M., & Mithun, S. (2021). *Evaluation of flexible strategies to manage the COVID-19 pandemic in the education sector*. Global Journal of Flexible Systems Management., DOI: 10.1007/s40171-021-00267-9

Aschemann-Witzel, J., de Hooge, I. E., Rohm, H., Normann, A., Bossle, M. B., Grønhøj, A., & Oostindjer, M. (2017). Key characteristics and success factors of supply chain initiatives tackling consumer-related food waste—A multiple case study. *Journal of Cleaner Production*, *155*(July), 33–45. DOI: 10.1016/j.jclepro.2016.11.173

Bai, C., & Sarkis, J. (2013). A grey-based DEMATEL model for evaluating business process management critical success factors. *International Journal of Production Economics*, *146*(1), 281–292. DOI: 10.1016/j.ijpe.2013.07.011

Banik, A., Taqi, H. M. M., Ali, S. M., Ahmed, S., Garshasbi, M., & Kabir, G. (2020). Critical success factors for implementing green supply chain management in the electronics industry: An emerging economy case. International Journal of Logistics Research and Applications. .DOI: 10.1080/13675567.2020.1839029

Behl, A., & Dutta, P. (2019). Humanitarian supply chain management: A thematic literature review and future directions of research. *Annals of Operations Research*, *283*(1–2), 1001–1044. DOI: 10.1007/s10479-018-2806-2

Celik, E., & Taskin Gumus, A. (2016). An outranking approach based on interval type-2 fuzzy sets to evaluate preparedness and response ability of non-governmental humanitarian relief organizations. *Computers & Industrial Engineering*, *101*, 21–34. DOI: 10.1016/j.cie.2016.08.020

Chan, D. W. K. (2020). A reflection on the anti-epidemic response of COVID-19 from the perspective of disaster management. *International Journal of Nursing Sciences*, *7*(3), 382–385. DOI: 10.1016/j.ijnss.2020.06.004 PMID: 32817863

Craft, R. C., & Leake, C. (2002). The Pareto principle in organizational decision making. *Management Decision*, *40*(8), 729–733. DOI: 10.1108/00251740210437699

Dalalah, D., Hayajneh, M., & Batieha, F. (2011). A fuzzy multi-criteria decision making model for supplier selection. *Expert Systems with Applications*, *38*(7), 8384–8391. DOI: 10.1016/j.eswa.2011.01.031

Davis, I. (2014). Disaster risk management in Asia and the Pacific. In Disaster Risk Management in Asia and the Pacific. DOI: 10.4324/9781315761336

Ding, X. F., & Liu, H. C. (2018). A 2-dimension uncertain linguistic DEMATEL method for identifying critical success factors in emergency management. *Applied Soft Computing*, *71*, 386–395. DOI: 10.1016/j.asoc.2018.07.018

Dinter, B. (2013). Success factors for information logistics strategy—An empirical investigation. *Decision Support Systems*, *54*(3), 1207–1218. DOI: 10.1016/j.dss.2012.09.001

Fotopoulos, C., Kafetzopoulos, D., & Gotzamani, K. (2011). Critical factors for effective implementation of the HACCP system: A Pareto analysis. *British Food Journal*, *113*(5), 578–597. DOI: 10.1108/00070701111131700

Fuli, G., Foropon, C., & Xin, M. (2020). Reducing carbon emissions in humanitarian supply chain: The role of decision making and coordination. *Annals of Operations Research.* Advance online publication. DOI: 10.1007/s10479-020-03671-z

Gersons, B. P. R., Smid, G. E., Smit, A. S., Kazlauskas, E., & McFarlane, A. (2020). Can a 'second disaster' during and after the COVID-19 pandemic be mitigated? *European Journal of Psychotraumatology*, *11*(1), 2–5. DOI: 10.1080/20008198.2020.1815283 PMID: 33062215

Gunessee, S., Subramanian, N., Roscoe, S., & Ramanathan, J. (2018). The social preferences of local citizens and spontaneous volunteerism during disaster relief operations. *International Journal of Production Research*, *56*(21), 6793–6808. DOI: 10.1080/00207543.2017.1414330

Han, Y., & Deng, Y. (2018a). A hybrid intelligent model for assessment of critical success factors in highrisk emergency system. *Journal of Ambient Intelligence and Humanized Computing*, *9*(6), 1933–1953. DOI: 10.1007/s12652-018-0882-4

Han, Y., & Deng, Y. (2018b). An enhanced fuzzy evidential DEMATEL method with its application to identify critical success factors. *Soft Computing*, *22*(15), 5073–5090. DOI: 10.1007/s00500-018-3311-x

Ishiwatari, M., Koike, T., Hiroki, K., Toda, T., & Katsube, T. (2020). Managing disasters amid COVID-19 pandemic: Approaches of response to flood disasters. *Progress in Disaster Science*, *6*(April), 100096. DOI: 10.1016/j.pdisas.2020.100096 PMID: 34171012

Ivanov, D. (2020). Viable supply chain model: Integrating agility, resilience and sustainability perspectives—-Lessons from and thinking beyond the COVID-19 pandemic. *Annals of Operations Research.* Advance online publication. DOI: 10.1007/s10479-020-03640-6 PMID: 32836614

Kanipriya, M., Sugumaran, D., Pandiyarajan, V., Yogananda, B. S., Selvakumar, P., & Mohan, S. (2024, January). Analysis of Electromyography Signals for Control of Mechanical Prosthesis using Machine Learning Techniques. In 2024 2nd International Conference on Intelligent Data Communication Technologies and Internet of Things (IDCIoT) (pp. 1059-1067). IEEE.

Kaur, J., Sidhu, R., Awasthi, A., & Srivastava, S. K. (2019). A Pareto investigation on critical barriers in green supply chain management. *International JoUrnal of Management Science and Engineering Management, 14*(2), 113–123. DOI: 10.1080/17509653.2018.1504237

Lin, K. P., Tseng, M. L., & Pai, P. F. (2018). Sustainable supply chain management using approximate fuzzy DEMATEL method. *Resources, Conservation and Recycling, 128*, 134–142. DOI: 10.1016/j.resconrec.2016.11.017

Madgule, M., Vinayaka, N., Sonkhaskar, Y. M., Patel, D. R., Karthikeyan, R., & Selvakumar, P. (2023). Mechanical properties and microstructure of activated TIG welded similar joints of Inconel alloys by desirability approaches. *Materials Today: Proceedings, 77*, 528–533.

Ramakrishnan, T., Mohan Gift, M. D., Chitradevi, S., Jegan, R., Hency Jose, P. S., Nagaraja, H. N., & Hailegiorgis, S. M. (2022). Study of numerous resins used in polymer matrix composite materials. *Advances in Materials Science and Engineering, 2022*(1), 1088926.

Ramakrishnan, T., Mohan Gift, M. D., Chitradevi, S., Jegan, R., & Subha Hency Jose, P. Nagaraja, Rajneesh Sharma H.N., Selvakumar P., Sintayehu Mekuria Hailegiorgis, (2022). Study of Numerous Resins Used in Polymer Matrix Composite MaterialAdvances in Materials Science and Engineering, vol. 2022, Article ID 1088926, 8 pages, 2022. https://doi.org/DOI: 10.1155/2022/1088926

Selvakumar, P., Mariappan, P., Shunmugam, S., Paul, R., & Jabez, S. (2024). Removal of chemicals from effluent using photobioreactor technology to improve environmental and health impacts. *Zeitschrift für Physikalische Chemie, 2024*(7), 1295–1302. Advance online publication. DOI: 10.1515/zpch-2023-0450

Selvakumar, P., Palanisamy, S. K., Cinthaikinian, S., Palanisamy, V., Mariappan, R., & Selvakumar, P. K. (2024). Biosensors and its diverse applications in healthcare systems. *Zeitschrift für Physikalische Chemie, 2024*. Advance online publication. DOI: 10.1515/zpch-2023-0406

Vijayakumar, G., Rajkumar, M., Rajiv Chandar, N., Selvakumar, P., & Duraisamy, R. (2024). Muniyandi Rajkumar, Rajiv Chandar N, Selvakumar P and Ramesh Duraisamy, (2024). Environmentally friendly TDS removal from waste water by electrochemical ion exchange batch-type recirculation (EIR) technique. *Environmental Science. Water Research & Technology*, *10*(4), 826–835. DOI: 10.1039/D3EW00793F

Yadav, D. K., & Barve, A. (2015). Analysis of critical success factors of humanitarian supply chain: An application of Interpretive Structural Modeling. *International Journal of Disaster Risk Reduction*, *12*, 213–225. DOI: 10.1016/j.ijdrr.2015.01.008

Zhai, L. Y., Khoo, L. P., & Zhong, Z. W. (2008). A rough set enhanced fuzzy approach to quality function deployment. *International Journal of Advanced Manufacturing Technology*, *37*(5–6), 613–624. DOI: 10.1007/s00170-007-0989-9

Zhai, L. Y., Khoo, L. P., & Zhong, Z. W. (2009). Design concept evaluation in product development using rough sets and grey relation analysis. *Expert Systems with Applications*, *36*(3), 7072–7079. DOI: 10.1016/j.eswa.2008.08.068

Zhou, Q., Huang, W., & Zhang, Y. (2011). Identifying critical success factors in emergency management using a fuzzy DEMATEL method. *Safety Science*, *49*(2), 243–252. DOI: 10.1016/j.ssci.2010.08.005

Zhou, X., Shi, Y., Deng, X., & Deng, Y. (2017). D-DEMATEL: A new method to identify critical success factors in emergency management. *Safety Science*, *91*, 93–104. DOI: 10.1016/j.ssci.2016.06.014

Chapter 3
Scaling Up Women-Led Businesses:
A Critical Analysis of Crowdfunding and Alternative Financing Models

K. Balaji
https://orcid.org/0000-0002-3065-3294
Christ University, India

ABSTRACT

Women-led businesses have gained significant traction globally, yet many still face barriers to accessing traditional forms of financing. Crowdfunding and alternative financing models present new opportunities for these entrepreneurs to scale up and grow their ventures. This study critically examines how these models impact the growth, profitability, and long-term sustainability of women-led businesses. It identifies both the advantages and limitations of using crowdfunding and alternative financing mechanisms, such as peer-to-peer lending and microfinance, in fostering entrepreneurial success. The research further explores the challenges women entrepreneurs encounter in adopting these models, including the gender bias present in many crowdfunding platforms. This paper presents actionable solutions for improving the effectiveness of alternative financing in supporting women-led businesses. The study's findings contribute to both

DOI: 10.4018/979-8-3693-9193-8.ch003

academic research and practical business strategies, offering a roadmap for empowering women entrepreneurs in the evolving financial landscape.

INTRODUCTION

In recent years, women-led businesses have emerged as a powerful force in the global economy. Despite the considerable growth of women entrepreneurs across diverse industries, they continue to face significant obstacles when it comes to accessing capital, particularly through traditional financing channels like bank loans and venture capital. These challenges have intensified the need for alternative financing models, such as crowdfunding, peer-to-peer lending, and microfinance, which offer non-conventional avenues for securing funds. These financing models not only provide immediate capital but also enable women entrepreneurs to connect directly with their consumer base, gain market validation, and reduce dependency on traditional gatekeepers in the financial industry.

Crowdfunding platforms, such as Kickstarter, Indiegogo, and GoFundMe, have particularly gained popularity for their ability to democratize access to funds. These platforms allow women entrepreneurs to present their ideas directly to the public, bypassing traditional financial institutions that have historically been less supportive of female-led ventures. Furthermore, alternative financing methods like microfinance and peer-to-peer lending have become invaluable tools for women entrepreneurs in emerging economies where access to capital is even more constrained.

However, while these models provide promising solutions, they are not without their challenges. Many women entrepreneurs still face significant barriers in maximizing the potential of these platforms. Issues such as gender bias, market volatility, and lack of financial literacy limit the effectiveness of crowdfunding and alternative financing as viable long-term solutions for women-led businesses. This study aims to critically analyze the impact of crowdfunding and alternative financing models on the growth and profitability. By identifying both the opportunities and the limitations of these financing avenues, this paper seeks to offer actionable insights that can guide policy makers, platform developers, and entrepreneurs toward more inclusive and effective financing solutions.

Objectives of the Study

The primary objective of this study is to critically examine the role of crowdfunding and alternative financing models in scaling up women-led businesses. The study aims to:

1. Understand the influence of these financing methods on business growth and sustainability.
2. Identify the challenges and limitations faced by women entrepreneurs in utilizing these models.
3. Propose actionable solutions and recommendations for overcoming these challenges.
4. Assess the long-term viability of alternative financing in fostering sustainable entrepreneurship for women.

LITERATURE REVIEW

Alternative financing, particularly crowdfunding and microfinance, has gained increasing attention as a mechanism for promoting entrepreneurship, especially among women, since the 1980s. The relationship between women entrepreneurs and non-traditional financing has evolved, with scholars focusing on the gender-specific challenges and opportunities these mechanisms provide.

In one of the earliest works on entrepreneurship and finance, Scherr et al. (1993) explored the barriers small businesses face in accessing traditional financing.

Balaji, K. (2024). Study on The Nexus of Smart Contracts and Digital Twins Transforming Green Finance With Automated Transactions in Investment Agreements findings highlighted that women entrepreneurs were particularly disadvantaged when seeking capital from banks, which created a need for alternative financing mechanisms. This early work laid the foundation for future research into gender-based financial constraints.

Bygrave and Minniti (2000) extended this conversation by analysing entrepreneurial behaviors and how they differ across genders. Their study found that women were less likely to seek venture capital or angel investment, primarily because of structural barriers and societal expectations. This research underscored the importance of alternative financing models, which would later become essential tools for women entrepreneurs.

One of the most influential contributions to the discourse on women and microfinance is from Armendáriz and Morduch (2005). Their study, The Economics of Microfinance, focused on how microfinance institutions provide capital to women in developing countries, enabling them to become entrepreneurs and improve their socioeconomic status. Balaji, K. (2024). Charting the Path to Global Prosperity: Unveiling the Impact and Promise of Sustainable Development study's findings showed that women-led businesses benefited significantly from microfinance, although these benefits were often limited by the small scale of the loans.

Moving into the realm of crowdfunding, Belleflamme et al. (2010) examined the emerging concept of using online platforms to raise funds from a large number of people. Their study noted the democratizing potential of crowdfunding, especially for marginalized groups like women entrepreneurs who typically struggle with traditional financial institutions. Balaji, K. (2024). Harnessing AI for Financial Innovations: Pioneering the Future of Financial Services. cautioned that success on these platforms often depended on social networks and visibility, factors that can be influenced by gender dynamics.

Building on these ideas, Carter et al. (2003) investigated the role of gender in venture capital acquisition, finding that women were often perceived as less competent by investors. This gender bias persisted even when women-led ventures were equally or more promising than those led by men. Their findings emphasized the importance of alternative financial models, where the biases of traditional investors might not be as pervasive.

Brush et al. (2006) conducted one of the most comprehensive studies on women entrepreneurs and access to finance. Their research found that women entrepreneurs were systematically underfunded and often turned to informal networks or alternative financing models such as microloans and crowdfunding. They suggested that alternative financing models could help bridge the gap left by venture capital and bank loans, but emphasized that these models were still in their infancy at the time.

Mason and Harrison (2007) explored business angel investing and its impact on female entrepreneurs. Their research found that while women are less likely to receive funding from angel investors, they are more likely to turn to other forms of alternative financing, including peer-to-peer lending and crowdfunding. Balaji, K. (2025). Text Mining in Climate Change Communication and Corporate Sustainability Reporting study provided early evidence that women were more innovative in seeking non-traditional financing sources to overcome gender-based funding barriers. The role of alternative financing models in supporting women-led businesses has become increasingly relevant over the last decade. Researchers have explored various aspects of crowdfunding, peer-to-peer lending, and microfinance, shedding light on the potential and challenges of these mechanisms in promoting women entrepreneurship.

One of the earliest contributions to this discourse is by Belleflamme et al. (2014), who examined the role of crowdfunding as a financial tool for startups. Their study highlighted that while crowdfunding democratizes access to finance, women entrepreneurs often face challenges due to gender biases present in online platforms. Similarly, Mollick (2014) found that although crowdfunding offers women entrepreneurs a unique opportunity to bypass traditional finance gatekeepers, their campaigns often experience lower success rates compared to their male counterparts. This early research underscored the limitations women face even in non-traditional financing methods.

Subsequent research by Agier and Szafarz (2015) delved into the issue of gender disparities in peer-to-peer lending, finding that women entrepreneurs often pay higher interest rates than men in these lending models. The study emphasized the persistent gender biases that deter the full potential of women-led businesses. Conversely, Cumming, Leboeuf, and Schwienbacher (2015) explored the advantages of reward-based crowdfunding for women entrepreneurs. Balaji, K. (2024). Artificial intelligence for enhanced anti-money laundering and asset recovery: A new frontier in financial crime prevention research indicated that women-led campaigns tend to perform better in creative sectors such as arts and entertainment, though they still encounter challenges in high-tech sectors.

Building on these insights, Greenberg and Mollick (2017) focused on social networks and their role in crowdfunding success. K. Balaji, S. Karim and P. S. Rao (2024), "Unleashing the Power of Smart Chatbots: Transforming Banking with Artificial Intelligence," *2024* found that women entrepreneurs benefit more from social capital than financial capital, leveraging personal networks to achieve success. Similarly, research by Marom, Robb, and Sade (2016) emphasized that women are more likely to succeed in crowdfunding when their projects are aligned with traditionally female-oriented sectors, such as fashion or education.

Further emphasizing the challenges women face, Burtch, Ghose, and Wattal (2018) identified that women entrepreneurs face higher scrutiny from potential investors on crowdfunding platforms, leading to lower funding rates despite having equally viable business ideas. In contrast, Orser, Riding, and Weeks (2019) highlighted that alternative financing models such as microfinance and peer-to-peer lending are more accessible for women in developing countries, where traditional banking systems are less supportive. K. Balaji, (2023) "Unlocking the Potential of BI-Enhancing Banking Transactions Through AI&ML Tools," study emphasized that microfinance institutions in countries like Bangladesh and India have been pivotal in empowering women entrepreneurs.

A comprehensive study by Figueroa-Armijos and Johnson (2020) examined the sustainability of businesses funded through alternative models, concluding that while crowdfunding provides an initial boost, women-led businesses often struggle to achieve long-term profitability due to a lack of large-scale funding. K. Balaji, (2023), "Examining the Potential of Cryptocurrencies as An Asset Class concerns were raised by Courtney et al. (2021), who found that while women entrepreneurs who use crowdfunding achieve higher short-term growth, they face difficulties in scaling their businesses because alternative funding often lacks the consistency and volume of traditional financing.

More recent studies have continued to build on these findings. For example, Wang and Yang (2022) explored the relationship between women-led startups and equity crowdfunding, revealing that despite greater visibility, women continue to face challenges related to investor confidence, particularly in tech-based industries. Women entrepreneurs are often viewed as less capable of managing large-scale investments, leading to lower investor participation rates, a finding echoed by Eddleston et al. (2022), who examined the gendered perceptions of leadership in entrepreneurial ventures.

In a study focusing on peer-to-peer lending, Zhang et al. (2023) found that while these platforms provide greater access to capital for women, they also expose them to higher interest rates and repayment terms that can stifle business growth. This finding aligns with the work of González and Rivas (2023), who highlighted that microfinance, though widely celebrated as an enabler for women-led businesses in rural regions, often fails to provide sufficient capital for substantial business growth. These studies underscore the tension between access and sustainability in alternative financing models for women entrepreneurs.

Another study by Clark and Davis (2023) explored the regulatory aspects of crowdfunding, finding that platforms offering gender-neutral or female-targeted campaigns tend to perform better in terms of attracting women entrepreneurs. However, they also noted that regulatory support is crucial to ensuring that these platforms do not perpetuate existing gender biases. Meanwhile, Stewart and McGuire (2024) conducted a comparative analysis of crowdfunding platforms and found that women-led campaigns in emerging economies face additional challenges, including lower campaign visibility and less access to international investors. Adding a global perspective, Khalid et al. (2024) examined crowdfunding platforms in the Middle East and North Africa (MENA) region, finding that cultural barriers often exacerbate the challenges women face in securing alternative financing. This is particularly true in conservative societies where women's roles in business are often restricted by social norms.

The role of technology in alternative financing has also gained attention. A study by Cooper and Green (2024) explored the use of blockchain and decentralized finance (DeFi) in crowdfunding, suggesting that these technologies could democratize access further by providing women with more secure and transparent funding options. However, the study also warned of the technological literacy gap that may limit the participation of women in tech-driven alternative financing.

Finally, a notable contribution by Thornton and Lee (2024) focused on the psychological barriers that women entrepreneurs face when engaging in crowdfunding. They found that confidence, risk aversion, and perceived societal expectations play a significant role in women's decisions to pursue alternative financing. Addressing these psychological barriers, the authors argue, is as important as addressing the structural challenges within crowdfunding platforms.

The literature on crowdfunding and alternative financing models for women-led businesses reveals a complex landscape marked by both opportunities and persistent challenges. While alternative financing has undoubtedly democratized access to capital, women entrepreneurs continue to face significant barriers, from gender biases on platforms to limitations in scaling their businesses. The findings across the reviewed studies suggest that while these models provide a crucial lifeline for women entrepreneurs, they are insufficient in addressing the larger structural issues that hinder their business growth and sustainability. Future research should focus on enhancing the effectiveness of these platforms through technological innovations, regulatory reforms, and greater emphasis on gender equity.

RESEARCH METHODOLOGY

This study employs a mixed-methods approach, combining both qualitative and quantitative research techniques. The qualitative data were collected through in-depth interviews with women entrepreneurs who have successfully utilized crowdfunding and alternative financing models. Additionally, surveys were conducted to gather quantitative data on the financial performance and growth trajectories of businesses funded through these means. Secondary data from crowdfunding platforms, financial reports, and previous academic literature were also analyzed to complement the primary data. This multi-layered methodology provides a comprehensive understanding of how these models affect women-led businesses.

Innovative Tools and Technologies Supporting Crowdfunding and Alternative Financing Models

Crowdfunding and alternative financing models have seen significant advancements with the integration of innovative tools and technologies. These innovations are transforming how businesses, entrepreneurs, and individuals raise capital, making funding more accessible, transparent, and efficient. Among the most prominent technologies driving this evolution is blockchain, which enhances transparency and security in financial transactions. Blockchain-based platforms like KickICO and Coinstarter enable decentralized crowdfunding, where funds are tracked through immutable ledgers. Smart contracts, powered by blockchain, also automate the transfer of funds based on predefined conditions, fostering trust between backers and campaign creators. This is discussed in the Figure 1.

Figure 1. Innovative tools and technologies supporting crowdfunding and alternative financing models

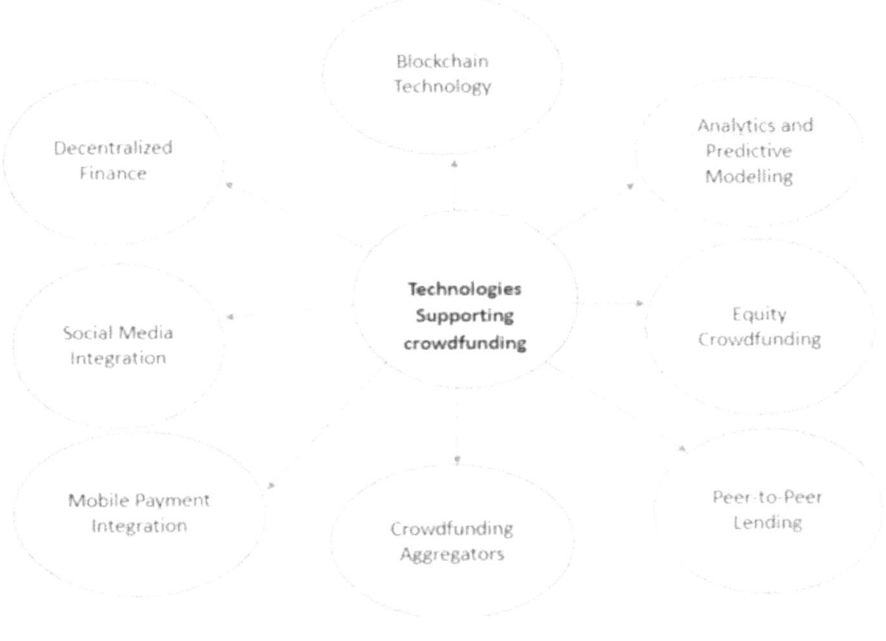

The detailed explanation of Innovative Tools and Technologies Supporting crowdfunding and alternative financing models (Figure 1) is as follows *Blockchain Technology*: Blockchain is revolutionizing crowdfunding by providing a secure and transparent way to manage transactions. Platforms like KickICO and Coinstarter leverage blockchain's decentralized ledger system, ensuring that all contributions are recorded immutably. This transparency fosters trust, as backers can track their funds and be assured that they are being used as promised. Furthermore, blockchain enables the use of smart contracts, which automatically release funds to campaign creators once certain predefined conditions are met. This automation reduces the need for intermediaries and provides assurance to contributors that their money will only be used if the campaign goals are achieved, adding an extra layer of accountability.

Artificial Intelligence and Machine Learning: AI and machine learning have significantly enhanced the crowdfunding process by providing data-driven insights that improve campaign success. By analysing historical campaign data, social media trends, and user behavior, AI tools can predict the likelihood of a campaign reaching its funding goals. Platforms like Kickstarter utilize AI for campaign optimization, helping creators adjust their strategies in real time based on predictive analytics. AI also aids in fraud detection by identifying suspicious patterns and activities, ensuring the platform remains trustworthy. Moreover, machine learning algorithms can suggest campaigns to potential backers based on their past interests, increasing the chances of successful funding.

Data Analytics and Predictive Modelling: Data analytics plays a vital role in shaping the success of crowdfunding campaigns. Platforms like Indiegogo use predictive modelling tools to help campaign creators understand the demand for their products or services. By analysing market data, these tools provide insights into potential funding targets, audience demographics, and pricing strategies, allowing creators to optimize their campaigns for maximum success. Additionally, real-time analytics can monitor campaign performance, offering suggestions on how to improve outreach or adjust funding goals dynamically. This data-driven approach helps campaigns stay on track and increases the likelihood of achieving or surpassing their funding targets.

Equity Crowdfunding Platforms: Equity crowdfunding has opened new opportunities for investors by allowing them to acquire stakes in startups and growing companies. Unlike traditional crowdfunding, where backers receive rewards or products, equity crowdfunding offers ownership in exchange for financial contributions. Platforms like Seedrs and Crowdcube facilitate these transactions while ensuring compliance with financial regulations through the use of regulatory technology (RegTech). These platforms perform due diligence on companies and provide investors with necessary legal and financial protections. Equity crowdfunding thus offers a more formal investment opportunity for backers, while allowing businesses to access capital from a broader pool of investors.

Peer-to-Peer Lending and Decentralized Finance (DeFi): Peer-to-peer (P2P) lending platforms, such as LendingClub and Funding Circle, have created an alternative to traditional bank loans by directly connecting borrowers with individual lenders. These platforms use sophisticated algorithms to assess borrower risk, match them with appropriate lenders, and automate the loan process, making borrowing more accessible and efficient. In a similar vein, decentralized finance (DeFi) platforms like Aave and Compound leverage blockchain technology to provide lending and borrowing services without intermediaries. DeFi platforms operate through smart contracts, offering an automated, transparent, and decentralized approach to lending, where lenders can earn interest on their contributions.

Crowdfunding Aggregators: Crowdfunding aggregators have simplified the investment process by compiling multiple campaigns across different platforms in one place. Tools like Crowdfundly allow investors to easily discover campaigns that match their interests, making the process more efficient. These aggregators use AI-powered search and filtering algorithms to provide personalized recommendations, helping backers find projects that align with their values or financial goals. For campaign creators, these platforms offer enhanced visibility and increased chances of attracting diverse groups of investors. By presenting a wide array of campaigns in one interface, aggregators help backers make more informed investment decisions.

Mobile Payment Integration: Mobile payment solutions have significantly streamlined the crowdfunding process by allowing contributors to make payments directly from their smartphones. Platforms like GoFundMe and Patreon have integrated mobile-friendly payment systems, making it easy for backers to contribute funds with just a few clicks. This convenience has broadened the reach of crowdfunding, as individuals who may not have access to desktop computers can still participate in campaigns through their mobile devices. Additionally, mobile payment solutions often come with built-in security features, providing backers with a safe and seamless way to support projects they believe in.

Social Media Integration: Social media integration has become a crucial tool for crowdfunding success. Platforms like Facebook and Instagram have built-in features that allow users to promote crowdfunding campaigns directly through social sharing, increasing visibility and engagement. Successful campaigns often go viral through social networks, driven by organic shares, likes, and endorsements from influencers. Social media integration tools enable campaign creators to reach a wider audience without significant advertising costs, as backers become promoters by sharing the campaign with their own networks. This increased exposure can dramatically enhance the chances of a campaign reaching its funding goals, particularly for smaller projects relying on grassroots support.

CASE STUDIES OF WOMEN-LED COMPANIES PROMOTING THROUGH CROWDFUNDING AND ALTERNATIVE FINANCING MODELS

Women entrepreneurs have increasingly turned to alternative financing methods, such as crowdfunding, microfinance, and peer-to-peer lending, to fund their businesses. These non-traditional models allow women to bypass institutional barriers and gain access to capital, which is often more difficult to obtain through conventional means like bank loans and venture capital. Below are five in-depth case studies of women-led companies around the world that have successfully raised funds through these models, showcasing the impact and potential of alternative financing.

1. Sara Blakely and Spanx (United States)

Sara Blakely, the founder of Spanx, is one of the most famous self-made female billionaires in the world. Spanx, known for its innovative shapewear, revolutionized the undergarment industry. What makes Blakely's story unique is her ability to launch and scale her business without traditional financing from banks or venture capitalists. Instead, Blakely used personal savings, demonstrating the power of self-funding and alternative finance for women entrepreneurs.

Blakely started Spanx in 2000 with $5,000 of her personal savings, despite being turned down by multiple potential investors and banks. This rejection was primarily due to gender biases and a lack of interest in her idea from male investors who dominated the venture capital scene. Blakely's resilience and ability to self-finance through her personal network allowed her to develop her first product and get it onto the shelves of department stores. Spanx quickly became a huge success. Blakely's product, which she initially sold door-to-door, was picked up by Neiman Marcus after a chance meeting with an executive. Her appearance on The Oprah Winfrey Show in 2000 skyrocketed the brand's visibility, leading to massive demand. With revenues steadily increasing, Blakely was able to avoid diluting ownership through venture capital or large bank loans. Instead, she used the profits generated from her sales to reinvest in the company.

Blakely's ability to leverage personal savings and her network is a lesson in how alternative financing methods, even without crowdfunding or peer-to-peer lending, can help women bypass traditional financial barriers. By avoiding the venture capital route, Blakely retained 100% ownership of Spanx, which gave her control over the company's direction and allowed her to focus on long-term growth without external pressure from investors. This independence enabled Spanx to grow into a billion-dollar company by 2012 when Blakely was featured on the cover of Forbes as the youngest self-made female billionaire. While Blakely didn't use crowdfunding in the modern sense, her story underscores how women entrepreneurs often need to look beyond conventional finance and adopt alternative models to succeed. Today, Spanx is a globally recognized brand with a valuation of over $1 billion, and Blakely has become a role model for women entrepreneurs around the world.

2. Tara Bosch and SmartSweets (Canada)

Tara Bosch is a Canadian entrepreneur who founded SmartSweets, a company specializing in low-sugar gummy candies, in 2016. Bosch's entrepreneurial journey began with a desire to provide healthier alternatives to traditional sweets. After realizing there was a gap in the market for candy with reduced sugar content, she decided to launch her own business. However, like many women entrepreneurs, Bosch encountered difficulties in securing funding through traditional means, which led her to explore alternative financing. In 2017, Bosch turned to crowdfunding via the Indiegogo platform. Her campaign sought to raise $50,000 to expand SmartSweets' production capabilities. Bosch's strategy was to market her product as part of a larger health-conscious movement, capitalizing on increasing consumer awareness of the negative effects of sugar. Her campaign video and marketing materials highlighted the product's benefits and its potential to disrupt the candy industry. The Indiegogo campaign was a resounding success, raising over $100,000, which allowed Bosch to increase production and secure retail partnerships.

Crowdfunding provided Bosch not only with capital but also with a loyal customer base. Many backers were early adopters of the brand and became long-term advocates, sharing their excitement for SmartSweets on social media and contributing to the company's viral success. The exposure Bosch gained from crowdfunding played a significant role in building her brand's credibility, attracting the attention of national retailers like Whole Foods and expanding her reach across North America. Following the success of her crowdfunding campaign, Bosch continued to scale SmartSweets, securing further investment from angel investors who were impressed by the company's early success and rapid growth. Within just three years, SmartSweets went from a small startup to a multi-million-dollar company, earning Bosch a spot on Forbes's "30 Under 30" list in 2019.

Bosch's use of crowdfunding is a testament to how women entrepreneurs can leverage alternative financing models to build successful businesses in highly competitive industries. The platform not only provided her with the capital she needed to grow but also allowed her to test the market, engage with her audience, and prove the viability of her business concept—all without relying on traditional financing mechanisms that might have been unavailable to her.

3. Emilia Villarroel and HOPE (Chile)

Emilia Villarroel, a social entrepreneur from Chile, founded HOPE (Helping Other People Evolve) in 2015 with the aim of providing sustainable employment opportunities for women artisans in rural Chile. HOPE is a socially responsible clothing brand that produces handwoven garments made by local women. Villarroel's mission was not only to create a profitable business but also to empower women and promote sustainable practices. Villarroel faced significant challenges in accessing traditional financing due to her business's small size and her lack of collateral. Recognizing the potential of alternative financing models, she turned to crowdfunding in 2018 to raise the capital necessary to expand her business. Using Kickstarter, she aimed to raise $100,000 to open a new workshop, purchase modern weaving equipment, and hire additional artisans.

Her crowdfunding campaign focused heavily on the ethical aspects of HOPE's mission. Villarroel created a series of videos and marketing materials that told the stories of the women artisans she employed, highlighting the positive social impact of the business. This resonated with an international audience, particularly consumers who were increasingly seeking out ethical and sustainable products. The Kickstarter campaign was a huge success, exceeding its target and raising over $120,000. The funds raised through crowdfunding allowed HOPE to significantly scale its operations. With the new workshop and equipment, the company was able to double its production capacity, increase the number of artisans employed, and secure contracts with international retailers interested in carrying HOPE's ethically produced garments. Moreover, the visibility gained from the campaign helped the brand establish itself as a leader in the sustainable fashion industry.

For Villarroel, crowdfunding was not just about raising money—it was about building a community around her brand. The backers of her campaign were deeply invested in the mission of HOPE, and many became long-term customers and advocates for the brand. This sense of community and shared purpose has been a driving force behind HOPE's continued growth and success. Villarroel's story demonstrates how women entrepreneurs, especially those focused on social impact, can use crowdfunding to access capital, build a loyal customer base, and scale their businesses. Crowdfunding allowed Villarroel to overcome the financial barriers she faced as a female entrepreneur in Chile, ultimately helping her to create a sustainable and socially responsible business that empowers women artisans and supports local communities.

4. Roberta Lucca and Bossa Studios (United Kingdom)

Roberta Lucca, co-founder of Bossa Studios, a London-based video game development company, has been a pioneer in using alternative financing to grow her business in a male-dominated industry. Bossa Studios is known for developing innovative and quirky video games that have garnered a loyal following. However, as a woman in the gaming industry, Lucca faced significant challenges in securing traditional venture capital funding, which is notoriously difficult for women to access. In 2017, Lucca turned to equity crowdfunding through the platform Seedrs to raise £1.5 million ($1.8 million). Equity crowdfunding differs from traditional crowdfunding in that backers receive a stake in the company in exchange for their investment. This model was particularly appealing to Lucca because it allowed her to retain control of the company while still raising the necessary capital for expansion.

The Seedrs campaign was a major success, exceeding its target and raising £1.75 million. The funds were used to expand Bossa Studios' development team, invest in new game projects, and enhance the company's marketing efforts. One of the key advantages of equity crowdfunding was that it allowed Lucca to tap into a broader investor base, many of whom were passionate about gaming but lacked access to traditional venture capital opportunities. Lucca's decision to use equity crowdfunding was strategic. By turning to her community of gamers and fans, she was able to raise the necessary capital while simultaneously building a deeper connection with her audience. The backers of her campaign were not just passive investors—they were active participants in the company's success, providing feedback on new game ideas and sharing their enthusiasm for Bossa Studios' projects.

The success of Lucca's equity crowdfunding campaign has had a lasting impact on Bossa Studios. The company has continued to grow and develop new games, and Lucca has become a prominent advocate for women in the gaming industry. She regularly speaks about the challenges women face in accessing venture capital and the importance of alternative financing models in leveling the playing field for female entrepreneurs. Lucca's story highlights the potential of equity crowdfunding for women-led businesses, particularly in industries like gaming and tech, where traditional financing options are often limited. By using alternative financing models, Lucca was able to overcome gender-based barriers and build a successful, innovative company that continues to thrive in a competitive market.

5. Lina Khalifeh and SheFighter (Jordan)

Lina Khalifeh is the founder of SheFighter, the first self-defense studio in the Middle East specifically designed for women. Based in Jordan, SheFighter trains women in self-defense techniques to empower them and reduce violence against women. Khalifeh's mission was not only to build a successful business but also to address a critical social issue in the region. However, as a woman entrepreneur in the Middle East, Khalifeh faced significant challenges in securing funding through traditional means. In 2016, Khalifeh turned to alternative financing by participating in the regional crowdfunding platform Zoomaal. Her campaign sought to raise $50,000 to expand SheFighter's operations, open new training centers, and develop an online platform to reach more women across the Middle East. The crowdfunding campaign was highly successful, raising over $75,000, which allowed Khalifeh to open new studios in Jordan and begin offering online self-defense courses.

Crowdfunding played a crucial role in SheFighter's growth. Not only did it provide the necessary capital, but it also helped Khalifeh raise awareness about the importance of self-defense for women in a region where such conversations are often taboo. The campaign attracted international attention, leading to partnerships with NGOs and women's rights organizations that further amplified SheFighter's impact. Khalifeh's success with crowdfunding has made her a role model for other women entrepreneurs in the Middle East. She has since expanded SheFighter to multiple countries and continues to advocate for women's empowerment through self-defense. Khalifeh's use of crowdfunding to overcome financial barriers and promote a socially impactful business demonstrates the power of alternative financing models in regions where women entrepreneurs face significant cultural and institutional obstacles.

These case studies illustrate the diverse ways in which women entrepreneurs around the world have used crowdfunding and alternative financing models to build and scale their businesses. Whether through equity crowdfunding, rewards-based platforms, or self-financing, these women have bypassed traditional financial barriers to achieve success and make a significant impact in their respective industries.

SUCCESS STORIES OF 10 WOMEN-LED COMPANIES PROMOTING THROUGH CROWDFUNDING AND ALTERNATIVE FINANCING MODELS

In recent years, crowdfunding and alternative financing models have emerged as vital tools for women entrepreneurs seeking to launch and grow their businesses. These innovative financing avenues not only provide capital but also create opportunities for women to engage directly with their consumer base, build community, and share their unique stories. Below are ten inspiring success stories of women-led companies that have utilized crowdfunding and alternative financing to achieve remarkable growth and impact.

1. Elvie by Tania Boler (United Kingdom)

Tania Boler is a visionary entrepreneur who founded Elvie, a health and wellness company focusing on women's intimate health. Launched in 2013, Elvie is best known for its innovative products like the Elvie Trainer, a smart device that helps women strengthen their pelvic floor muscles through guided exercises, and the Elvie Pump, a silent and wearable breast pump that allows mothers to express milk discreetly.

Despite the revolutionary nature of her products, Boler faced significant challenges in securing traditional funding. Investors were often hesitant to support a company focused on women's health, viewing it as a niche market with limited potential. To overcome these obstacles, Boler decided to pursue crowdfunding as a means of raising capital. In 2017, she launched a campaign on Crowdcube, aiming to raise £1.5 million. The campaign focused on the importance of women's health and empowerment, resonating with potential backers who were passionate about supporting innovative products that improved the lives of women. The crowdfunding campaign exceeded expectations, raising over £1.5 million from more than 1,200 investors. This influx of capital allowed Elvie to scale its production capabilities and expand its product line. The campaign also provided valuable visibility for the brand, leading to partnerships with major retailers and healthcare organizations. Boler's commitment to transparency and community engagement throughout the campaign helped foster a loyal customer base, as backers felt invested in the company's mission.

Since its launch, Elvie has garnered significant attention in the media and healthcare sectors, positioning itself as a leader in the femtech industry. The success of Elvie illustrates how women entrepreneurs can leverage crowdfunding to not only secure funding but also build a supportive community around their brand. Boler's journey exemplifies the potential of alternative financing models to disrupt traditional industries and promote social change.

2. Thinx by Miki Agrawal (United States)

Miki Agrawal is a trailblazer in the femtech industry, best known for co-founding Thinx, a revolutionary brand of period-proof underwear. Launched in 2013, Thinx aims to provide women with a sustainable and comfortable alternative to traditional menstrual products like pads and tampons. Agrawal's vision stemmed from her desire to empower women to embrace their bodies and break the stigma surrounding menstruation. Initially, Agrawal faced challenges in obtaining traditional funding due to the taboo nature of menstrual products. Investors were often reluctant to support a brand focused on such a sensitive subject. To navigate these challenges, Agrawal decided to turn to crowdfunding. In 2015, she launched a campaign on SeedInvest, where she successfully raised over $400,000. This crowdfunding campaign was not only a financial success but also a pivotal moment for the brand, as it helped validate the market demand for period-proof underwear.

The funds from the crowdfunding campaign were instrumental in expanding Thinx's product line and marketing efforts. Agrawal's bold and transparent approach to addressing menstrual health issues resonated with consumers, and the brand quickly gained traction among women looking for eco-friendly menstrual solutions. Thinx's unique marketing strategy challenged societal norms, encouraging open conversations about menstruation and female health. Thinx's success is a testament to the power of crowdfunding in breaking taboos and empowering women. The company has since grown into a multi-million-dollar brand, with a loyal customer base and recognition as a leader in the femtech industry. Agrawal's journey serves as an inspiration for women entrepreneurs looking to challenge the status quo and create impactful solutions in their respective fields.

3. Bee Love by Mikaila Ulmer (United States)

Mikaila Ulmer, a young entrepreneur from Texas, founded Bee Love when she was just 11 years old. After being stung by bees twice in one week, Ulmer developed a fascination with these essential pollinators and became determined to make a difference. Bee Love is a lemonade business that produces a unique blend of lemonade sweetened with local honey, with a mission to save bees and promote environmental sustainability. Ulmer initially funded her business through local fairs and small business competitions. However, her big break came when she appeared on the popular television show Shark Tank. During her pitch, she secured a $60,000 investment from Daymond John, which provided a crucial boost to her business. In addition to traditional funding, Ulmer also turned to crowdfunding. She launched a campaign on GoFundMe to support her bee conservation efforts and expand Bee Love.

The combination of funding from Shark Tank and crowdfunding allowed Ulmer to scale her production, secure distribution deals with major retailers like Whole Foods, and invest in educational initiatives about the importance of bees. Her business not only generates profits but also raises awareness about environmental issues and the need for bee conservation. Ulmer's success story exemplifies the power of combining traditional investment with crowdfunding. At such a young age, she has become a role model for aspiring entrepreneurs, demonstrating that passion and purpose can lead to significant impact. Bee Love continues to thrive, and Ulmer actively promotes her message of sustainability and environmental stewardship.

4. Peach and Lily by Alicia Yoon (United States)

Alicia Yoon, a Korean beauty expert, founded Peach and Lily in 2012 to bring high-quality Korean skincare products to the U.S. market. Recognizing the growing demand for innovative skincare solutions, Yoon aimed to create a platform that offered carefully curated products from Korea, emphasizing their efficacy and unique ingredients. Yoon faced challenges securing traditional funding, especially as a woman of color in the competitive beauty industry. To overcome these obstacles, she utilized alternative financing models, including equity crowdfunding. In 2017, Yoon launched a campaign on Republic, where she successfully raised over $1 million. The campaign not only provided essential funding for her business but also helped build a community of invested supporters who were passionate about Korean skincare.

The funds raised through crowdfunding allowed Peach and Lily to expand its product line, invest in digital marketing, and secure partnerships with major retailers like Ulta Beauty. Yoon's focus on education and transparency resonated with consumers, and her brand quickly gained traction in the beauty industry. By leveraging crowdfunding, Yoon was able to validate her product concept and create a loyal customer base that believed in her mission. Today, Peach and Lily is recognized as a leader in the K-beauty movement, with a strong online presence and a growing community of skincare enthusiasts. Yoon's journey illustrates how women entrepreneurs can successfully leverage crowdfunding to build a brand that challenges traditional beauty norms while fostering inclusivity and transparency.

5. TomboyX by Fran Dunaway and Naomi Gonzalez (United States)

TomboyX is a gender-neutral underwear brand founded by Fran Dunaway and Naomi Gonzalez in 2013. The company was created to address the lack of comfortable, inclusive underwear options for people of all genders and body types. Dunaway and Gonzalez wanted to challenge the traditional norms of the fashion industry by providing high-quality, comfortable underwear for everyone. Initially, Dunaway and Gonzalez struggled to secure traditional funding due to the niche nature of their product. To overcome these challenges, they launched a crowdfunding campaign on Kickstarter in 2014, aiming to raise $75,000 for their first production run. The campaign was a success, raising over $100,000 and allowing them to produce their first line of underwear. The success of the Kickstarter campaign also helped them validate their product concept and build an early customer base.

With the funds raised from crowdfunding, TomboyX was able to expand its product line and invest in marketing strategies that emphasized inclusivity and comfort. The brand quickly gained traction among consumers, resonating with those who sought gender-neutral clothing options. TomboyX's commitment to body positivity and inclusivity helped it stand out in a crowded market, and the company has since grown into a multi-million-dollar brand. Dunaway and Gonzalez continue to advocate for inclusivity and diversity in fashion, using their platform to promote body positivity and challenge societal norms. The success of TomboyX serves as a powerful example of how women entrepreneurs can leverage crowdfunding to create a meaningful impact while building a successful business.

6. Cuyana by Shilpa Shah and Karla Gallardo (United States)

Shilpa Shah and Karla Gallardo co-founded Cuyana in 2013, a fashion brand focused on the concept of "fewer, better things." Cuyana is dedicated to producing high-quality, sustainable clothing and accessories, encouraging consumers to invest in timeless pieces rather than fast fashion. The founders recognized the growing demand for ethical fashion and aimed to create a brand that prioritized quality, sustainability, and craftsmanship. To launch Cuyana, Shah and Gallardo initially funded their business through personal savings and small investments. However, they recognized the need for additional capital to expand their operations. In 2014, they turned to crowdfunding, launching a successful campaign on Indiegogo. The campaign emphasized the importance of sustainability and ethical production, resonating with consumers who were increasingly conscious of their purchasing decisions.

The funds raised through crowdfunding allowed Cuyana to expand its product line and enhance its marketing efforts. The brand quickly gained traction, attracting a loyal customer base that valued its commitment to quality and sustainability. Cuyana has since become a recognized name in the ethical fashion space, with partnerships with artisans around the world and a focus on reducing waste in the fashion industry. Shah and Gallardo's journey exemplifies the potential of crowdfunding to support socially conscious businesses. Cuyana's success demonstrates how women entrepreneurs can leverage alternative financing models to build brands that align with their values while making a positive impact on the world.

7. Girlboss by Sophia Amoruso (United States)

Sophia Amoruso is a well-known figure in the entrepreneurial landscape, initially gaining fame as the founder of Nasty Gal, an online fashion retailer that grew from a small eBay store to a multi-million-dollar company. After stepping down as CEO of Nasty Gal, Amoruso focused her efforts on empowering women through her media company, Girlboss, which aims to provide resources, community, and inspiration for women in business. Amoruso recognized the need for a platform that supports women entrepreneurs and addresses the challenges they face in the business world. In 2017, she founded Girlboss and began seeking alternative financing models to fund her new venture. The company launched an equity crowdfunding campaign on Republic in 2018, raising over $1 million from a diverse group of investors. This campaign allowed Girlboss to expand its platform, create original content, and launch events that fostered community and networking among women entrepreneurs.

The success of Girlboss demonstrates the power of crowdfunding in building a supportive community around a brand. Amoruso's focus on empowering women and promoting professional development resonated with investors and consumers alike. The platform has grown to include a podcast, online community, and various resources aimed at helping women navigate their careers and achieve their goals. Girlboss's success showcases how women entrepreneurs can leverage crowdfunding to create platforms that inspire and uplift others. Amoruso's journey emphasizes the importance of community and collaboration in the entrepreneurial ecosystem, making Girlboss a leading voice in the movement for women's empowerment in business.

8. Brewed by Leila Janah (United States)

Leila Janah founded Brewed, a socially conscious coffee company, with the mission to provide fair wages and sustainable livelihoods to coffee farmers in developing countries. Recognizing the challenges faced by smallholder farmers, Janah aimed to create a business model that prioritized social impact while delivering high-quality coffee to consumers. To launch Brewed, Janah initially relied on personal savings and small investments. However, she quickly realized that additional funding was necessary to expand her operations. In 2016, she turned to crowdfunding, launching a campaign on Kickstarter to raise funds for her first production run. The campaign highlighted the stories of the farmers behind Brewed's coffee and emphasized the importance of ethical sourcing and sustainable practices.

The crowdfunding campaign was a success, raising over $250,000 and allowing Janah to establish relationships with coffee farmers and invest in sustainable sourcing practices. Brewed's commitment to social responsibility and ethical production resonated with consumers, leading to a loyal customer base that valued the company's mission. Janah's journey with Brewed exemplifies how women entrepreneurs can leverage crowdfunding to create businesses that prioritize social impact. Her commitment to empowering smallholder farmers and promoting sustainability has made Brewed a leader in the ethical coffee space. Janah's story serves as an inspiration for aspiring entrepreneurs looking to make a difference while building successful businesses.

9. Zingerman's Bakehouse by Amy Emberling (United States)

Amy Emberling co-founded Zingerman's Bakehouse, a renowned bakery in Ann Arbor, Michigan, known for its artisanal bread and pastries. Established in 1992, Zingerman's Bakehouse has become a beloved destination for food lovers, emphasizing quality ingredients and traditional baking methods. Emberling's passion for baking and commitment to quality quickly set the bakery apart in a competitive market. To fund the launch of Zingerman's Bakehouse, Emberling initially relied on personal savings and loans. However, as the business grew, she recognized the need for additional capital to expand operations and enhance product offerings. In 2015, Emberling turned to crowdfunding, launching a campaign on Indiegogo to raise funds for a new baking facility and equipment upgrades.

The crowdfunding campaign was a success, raising over $500,000 from loyal customers and community supporters. The funds allowed Zingerman's Bakehouse to expand its production capabilities, introduce new product lines, and enhance its marketing efforts. The campaign also helped strengthen the bakery's connection with its community, as backers felt personally invested in its success. Emberling's journey with Zingerman's Bakehouse illustrates the potential of crowdfunding to support local businesses and foster community engagement. The bakery has since become a beloved institution in Ann Arbor, known for its commitment to quality and craftsmanship. Emberling's story serves as an inspiration for women entrepreneurs looking to build successful businesses rooted in community and quality.

10. Raising Girls by Elizabeth Duffy (United States)

Elizabeth Duffy founded Raising Girls, a platform dedicated to empowering young girls through education and mentorship. Recognizing the challenges faced by girls in underserved communities, Duffy aimed to create a program that provided resources, support, and opportunities for personal and professional development. To launch Raising Girls, Duffy initially relied on personal savings and small grants. However, she quickly realized that additional funding was necessary to expand her program and reach more girls. In 2018, she turned to crowdfunding, launching a campaign on GoFundMe to raise funds for educational materials, workshops, and mentorship opportunities.

The crowdfunding campaign was a success, raising over $100,000 from supporters who believed in Duffy's mission. The funds allowed Raising Girls to expand its reach, provide scholarships for girls to attend workshops, and create a network of mentors who could support their personal and professional development. Duffy's journey with Raising Girls exemplifies the power of crowdfunding in supporting social initiatives that empower young women. Her commitment to creating opportunities for girls has made a significant impact in her community, and her story serves as an inspiration for women entrepreneurs looking to make a difference through their work. These ten women-led companies demonstrate the power of crowdfunding and alternative financing models in fostering innovation and social impact. By harnessing these innovative financing methods, these entrepreneurs have created successful businesses that not only generate profits but also promote positive change in their communities and industries. Their journeys serve as a testament to the resilience, creativity, and determination of women entrepreneurs worldwide.

ETHICAL CONSIDERATIONS OF CROWDFUNDING AND ALTERNATIVE FINANCING

Transparency and Accountability: One of the key ethical considerations in crowdfunding and alternative financing models is ensuring transparency and accountability. Campaign creators have an ethical obligation to be clear about their funding goals, project timelines, and how they plan to use the funds.

Exploitation of Vulnerable Populations: Crowdfunding platforms often attract individuals and causes that evoke strong emotional responses, such as medical treatments, emergency relief, or charitable projects. While these campaigns can do immense good, there is an ethical concern regarding the potential exploitation of vulnerable populations.

Equity and Access: While crowdfunding democratizes access to capital by allowing anyone with internet access to raise funds, not all individuals or businesses have equal access to these opportunities. There are ethical concerns about the digital divide and whether those without access to technology, social networks, or marketing resources are left behind.

Investor Rights and Fairness: In equity crowdfunding, ethical considerations extend to the protection of investor rights. Investors who provide capital for startups or businesses through crowdfunding often face higher risks than they would with traditional investments, as these ventures are typically early-stage and more prone to failure.

Reward and Compensation Ethics: Reward-based crowdfunding often promises contributors products, services, or perks in exchange for their financial support. However, many campaigns experience delays or fail to deliver the promised rewards, leaving backers empty-handed. This raises ethical concerns about the fairness of compensation and whether creators are fulfilling their obligations.

Social Impact and Responsibility: Crowdfunding campaigns and alternative financing models can have significant social impacts, both positive and negative. On one hand, they can empower individuals, support charitable causes, and foster innovation. On the other hand, campaigns that promote harmful or controversial products, services, or ideologies can raise ethical concerns.

CHALLENGES FOR CROWDFUNDING AND ALTERNATIVE FINANCING MODELS

Regulatory and Compliance Issues: One of the significant challenges facing crowdfunding and alternative financing models is navigating complex regulatory environments. Different countries have varying rules regarding financial securities, investor protections, and tax implications. For equity crowdfunding, in particular, regulatory requirements can be stringent, with companies needing to meet strict disclosure and reporting standards. Inconsistent regulations across jurisdictions can limit the global expansion of crowdfunding platforms and make it difficult for businesses to raise funds from international backers. Ensuring compliance with local and international laws requires significant resources, which can be a burden for startups and small businesses relying on these platforms for capital.

Fraud and Scams: Crowdfunding platforms are often vulnerable to fraudulent campaigns or scams, which can erode trust between backers and creators. Fake campaigns that never deliver promised products or services can damage the credibility of crowdfunding as a legitimate financing model. Although many platforms use artificial intelligence and fraud detection tools to combat these issues, sophisticated scams still manage to slip through. For backers, the lack of a robust refund mechanism or legal recourse in the event of fraud makes it a risky investment. As a result, potential investors may be hesitant to support new campaigns, especially on platforms with a history of fraudulent activity.

Market Saturation: As crowdfunding becomes more popular, the number of campaigns on platforms has skyrocketed, leading to increased competition for backers' attention and funds. This market saturation can make it difficult for individual campaigns to stand out, particularly for smaller or less-known creators. Campaign creators must invest more in marketing and promotion to distinguish themselves, which can be costly and reduce the net funds raised. Additionally, backers are becoming more selective, often gravitating towards high-profile or well-marketed projects, which can leave smaller or niche campaigns struggling to reach their funding goals.

Platform Fees and Costs: While crowdfunding offers an alternative to traditional financing, it is not without costs. Most crowdfunding platforms charge fees that can range from 5% to 10% of the total funds raised, plus additional payment processing fees. For businesses operating on tight margins, these fees can significantly reduce the amount of capital available after a successful campaign. Furthermore, there are hidden costs such as marketing, campaign management, and rewards fulfillment, which can further eat into profits. These financial barriers may deter some small businesses or creators from using crowdfunding as a viable funding option.

Lack of Investor Protection: Unlike traditional financing models, crowdfunding often lacks formal investor protections. Many crowdfunding platforms operate on a rewards-based or donation model, where backers contribute money with no guarantee of receiving a return or even the promised product. In equity crowdfunding, while investors acquire shares, the risk of failure is high, especially with startups, and many investors are not experienced enough to evaluate these risks properly. Without mechanisms in place to ensure that funds are used as intended, backers can lose money with no legal recourse, which can discourage future participation in crowdfunding campaigns.

Scalability and Sustainability: Another challenge for crowdfunding and alternative financing models is scalability. While these models can be effective for raising initial capital, they are often not sustainable for long-term growth. Once a company grows beyond a certain size, it may require more substantial investment than what can be raised through crowdfunding. Moreover, the one-time nature of many crowdfunding campaigns means that businesses must continually seek new sources of funding or transition to more traditional financing models like venture capital or bank loans, which can undermine the very purpose of using alternative financing in the first place.

SOLUTIONS AND RECOMMENDATIONS

To address the challenges women entrepreneurs face in accessing alternative financing, this study recommends the development of more inclusive crowdfunding platforms that actively address gender bias. Financial literacy programs tailored specifically for women entrepreneurs should be widely implemented to help them better understand the complexities of these financing models. Additionally, regulatory frameworks need to be strengthened to ensure that alternative financing mechanisms remain sustainable and supportive of long-term business growth. Finally, partnerships between crowdfunding platforms and traditional financial institutions could provide a hybrid solution that combines the accessibility of alternative financing with the stability of traditional funding sources.

Implications of the Study

Academic Implications: This study contributes to the growing body of literature on gender and entrepreneurship by providing critical insights into the intersection of alternative financing and women-led businesses. It fills a gap in research by focusing specifically on how these models can scale up women-led ventures, thus broadening the scope of entrepreneurial finance studies.

Industry Implications: For the business community, the findings offer practical strategies for improving the accessibility and sustainability of alternative financing for women entrepreneurs. Crowdfunding platforms, in particular, can use the insights to redesign their platforms in a way that minimizes gender bias and maximizes the potential for business growth.

Future Research Directions

Future research could explore the role of emerging technologies such as blockchain and AI in optimizing alternative financing models for women entrepreneurs. Studies could also investigate the impact of government policies and regulations on the success of women-led businesses utilizing these models. Additionally, cross-cultural comparisons between developed and developing economies could provide a more global perspective on the efficacy of these financing mechanisms.

Conclusion

Crowdfunding and alternative financing models hold great promise for empowering women-led businesses, but they are not without their limitations. While these models provide much-needed capital and market exposure, they must be coupled with systemic reforms to overcome the challenges women entrepreneurs face. By enhancing financial literacy, addressing gender bias, and strengthening regulatory frameworks, these financing models can become more effective in fostering long-term growth and sustainability for women-led businesses. Ultimately, a combination of innovative financing and supportive policies will be necessary to truly scale up women-led ventures and drive meaningful change in the entrepreneurial landscape.

REFERENCES

Agier, I., & Szafarz, A. (2015). Microfinance and gender: Is there a glass ceiling on loan size? *World Development*, *47*, 61–72.

Armendáriz, B., & Morduch, J. (2005). *The economics of microfinance*. MIT Press.

Balaji, K. (2023, June). Unlocking the Potential of BI-Enhancing Banking Transactions Through AI&ML Tools. In *2023 International Conference on Applied Intelligence and Sustainable Computing (ICAISC)* (pp. 1-6). IEEE.

Balaji, K. (2023, June). Blockchain Based Banking Transactions Enabled by Big Data. In 2023 5th International Conference on Energy, Power and Environment: Towards Flexible Green Energy Technologies (ICEPE) (pp. 1-6). IEEE.

Balaji, K. (2024). The Nexus of Smart Contracts and Digital Twins Transforming Green Finance With Automated Transactions in Investment Agreements: Leveraging Smart Contracts for Green Investment Agreements and Automated Transactions. In Jafar, S., Rodriguez, R., Kannan, H., Akhtar, S., & Plugmann, P. (Eds.), *Harnessing Blockchain-Digital Twin Fusion for Sustainable Investments* (pp. 287–315). IGI Global., DOI: 10.4018/979-8-3693-1878-2.ch012

Balaji, K. (2024). Charting the Path to Global Prosperity: Unveiling the Impact and Promise of Sustainable Development. In Ordóñez de Pablos, P., Anshari, M., & Almunawar, M. (Eds.), *Harnessing Green and Circular Skills for Digital Transformation* (pp. 1–22). IGI Global., DOI: 10.4018/979-8-3693-2865-1.ch001

Balaji, K. (2024). Harnessing AI for Financial Innovations: Pioneering the Future of Financial Services. In Jermsittiparsert, K., Phongkraphan, N., & Lekhavichit, N. (Eds.), *Modern Management Science Practices in the Age of AI* (pp. 91–122). IGI Global., DOI: 10.4018/979-8-3693-6720-9.ch004

Balaji, K. (2024). Artificial intelligence for enhanced anti-money laundering and asset recovery: A new frontier in financial crime prevention. In *2024 Second International Conference on Intelligent Cyber Physical Systems and Internet of Things (ICoICI)* (pp. 1010-1016). DOI: 10.1109/ICoICI62503.2024.10696100

Balaji, K. (2025). Text Mining in Climate Change Communication and Corporate Sustainability Reporting. In Bansal, R., Rabby, F., Sharma, R., Parwani, D., & Gupta, A. (Eds.), *Text Mining and Sentiment Analysis in Climate Change and Environmental Sustainability* (pp. 385–418). IGI Global., DOI: 10.4018/979-8-3693-7230-2.ch021

Balaji, K., & Babu, M. K. (2017). A study on the affect of technology on unplanned purchase behaviour among the customers across selected corporate retail chains of Andhrapradesh, India. *International Journal of Economic Research*, *14*(4), 277–288.

Balaji, K., Karim, S., Naidu, N. G., Venkatesh, T., & Ranjitha, P. V., & ChandraSekhar, S. (2023, June). Examining the Potential of Cryptocurrencies as An Asset Class-An Empirical Study. In 2023 International Conference on Applied Intelligence and Sustainable Computing (ICAISC) (pp. 1-6). IEEE.

Balaji, K., Karim, S., & Rao, P. S. (2024, May). Unleashing the Power of Smart Chatbots: Transforming Banking with Artificial Intelligence. In *2024 International Conference on Advances in Computing, Communication and Applied Informatics (ACCAI)* (pp. 1-7). IEEE.

Belleflamme, P., Lambert, T., & Schwienbacher, A. (2010). Crowdfunding: Tapping the right crowd. *Journal of Business Venturing*, *29*(5), 585–609. DOI: 10.1016/j.jbusvent.2013.07.003

Belleflamme, P., Lambert, T., & Schwienbacher, A. (2014). Crowdfunding: Tapping the right crowd. *Journal of Business Venturing*, *29*(5), 585–609. DOI: 10.1016/j.jbusvent.2013.07.003

Brush, C. G., Carter, N. M., Gatewood, E. J., Greene, P. G., & Hart, M. M. (2006). *The Diana Project: Women entrepreneurs and the venture capital myth*. Edward Elgar Publishing.

Burtch, G., Ghose, A., & Wattal, S. (2018). An empirical examination of the antecedents and consequences of contribution patterns in crowd-funded markets. *Information Systems Research*, *24*(3), 499–519. DOI: 10.1287/isre.1120.0468

Bygrave, W. D., & Minniti, M. (2000). The social dynamics of entrepreneurship. *Entrepreneurship Theory and Practice*, *24*(3), 25–36. DOI: 10.1177/104225870002400302

Carter, N. M., Brush, C. G., Greene, P. G., Gatewood, E. J., & Hart, M. M. (2003). Women entrepreneurs who break through to equity financing: The influence of human, social and financial capital. *Venture Capital*, *5*(1), 1–28. DOI: 10.1080/1369106032000082586

Clark, S., & Davis, R. (2023). Regulatory frameworks in crowdfunding: How gender-focused platforms perform. *Journal of Financial Regulation*, *10*(2), 132–150.

Cooper, J., & Green, M. (2024). Blockchain and decentralized finance in crowdfunding: The next frontier for women entrepreneurs. *FinTech Journal*, *11*(1), 22–35.

Cumming, D. J., Leboeuf, G., & Schwienbacher, A. (2015). Crowdfunding models: Keep it all vs. all-or-nothing. *Financial Management*, *44*(2), 387–408.

Eddleston, K., Ladge, J. J., Mitteness, C., & Balachandra, L. (2022). Do female entrepreneurs face greater constraints in raising equity capital? *Entrepreneurship Theory and Practice*, *46*(3), 655–684.

Figueroa-Armijos, M., & Johnson, T. (2020). Crowdfunding and business sustainability: The case of women entrepreneurs. *Journal of Small Business Management*, *58*(4), 565–584.

González, L., & Rivas, D. (2023). Microfinance and the scalability of women-led businesses in rural areas. *Development Studies Quarterly*, *15*(2), 99–115.

Greenberg, J., & Mollick, E. (2017). Activist choice homophily and the crowdfunding of female entrepreneurs. *Administrative Science Quarterly*, *62*(2), 343–369. DOI: 10.1177/0001839216678847

Khalid, A., El Sayed, H., & Mansour, K. (2024). Crowdfunding for women entrepreneurs in the MENA region: Cultural barriers and solutions. *Middle East Economic Review*, *21*(1), 12–28.

Marom, D., Robb, A., & Sade, O. (2016). Gender dynamics in crowdfunding: Evidence on entrepreneurs, investors, deals, and taste-based discrimination. *Journal of Economics & Management Strategy*, *25*(2), 453–471.

Mason, C. M., & Harrison, R. T. (2007). Business angel investment activity in the financial crisis: Is there a gender effect? *Venture Capital*, *9*(4), 313–334. DOI: 10.1080/1369106042000286471

Mollick, E. (2014). The dynamics of crowdfunding: An exploratory study. *Journal of Business Venturing*, *29*(1), 1–16. DOI: 10.1016/j.jbusvent.2013.06.005

Mollick, E. (2014). The dynamics of crowdfunding: An exploratory study. *Journal of Business Venturing*, *29*(1), 1–16. DOI: 10.1016/j.jbusvent.2013.06.005

Orser, B., Riding, A., & Weeks, J. (2019). The case for inclusive microfinance. *Journal of International Development*, *31*(4), 554–572.

Scherr, F. C., Sugrue, T. F., & Ward, J. B. (1993). Financing the small firm start-up: Determinants of debt use. *The Journal of Entrepreneurial Finance*, *3*(1), 17–36. DOI: 10.57229/2373-1761.1141

Stewart, R., & McGuire, A. (2024). Crowdfunding challenges for women-led businesses in emerging economies. *International Journal of Entrepreneurial Finance*, *18*(2), 39–55.

Thornton, B., & Lee, H. (2024). Psychological barriers to crowdfunding for women entrepreneurs. *Journal of Entrepreneurial Psychology*, *9*(1), 53–68.

KEY TERMS AND DEFINITIONS

Blockchain Technology: Blockchain enhances transparency and security in crowdfunding by recording all transactions on an immutable ledger and automating fund transfers through smart contracts.

Artificial Intelligence and Machine Learning: AI tools analyze data to predict campaign success, optimize strategies, and detect fraud, while machine learning suggests campaigns to potential backers based on past behavior.

Data Analytics and Predictive Modelling: Data analytics provides insights into market demand, audience targeting, and campaign performance, enabling creators to optimize funding goals and outreach efforts dynamically.

Equity Crowdfunding Platforms: Equity crowdfunding platforms allow backers to acquire stakes in businesses, offering investment opportunities with the support of regulatory technology (RegTech) for compliance.

Peer-to-Peer Lending and Decentralized Finance (DeFi): P2P lending platforms connect borrowers with individual lenders, while DeFi platforms use blockchain and smart contracts to offer decentralized lending without intermediaries.

Crowdfunding Aggregators: Aggregators compile campaigns from various platforms, using AI to offer personalized recommendations, helping backers discover and support projects that match their interests.

Mobile Payment Integration: Mobile payment tools streamline contributions by enabling backers to fund campaigns through their smartphones, providing convenience and accessibility with built-in security features.

Social Media Integration: Social media integration helps campaigns gain visibility, as platforms like Facebook and Instagram allow for easy sharing, boosting engagement and campaign success through viral reach.

Chapter 4
A Systematic and Bibliometric Analysis of Venture Capital Exit Strategies

Poonam Singh
https://orcid.org/0000-0003-1113-6096
Manav Rachna International Institute of Research and Studies, India

Nupur Mishra
Galgotias University, India

Mohd Shamshad
Galgotias University, India

ABSTRACT

the study aimed to explore and synthesize the current knowledge clusters in the venture capital exit strategies or routes. The paper adopted a robust and scientific protocol to retrieve the 436 journal articles published in the Scopus-indexed journals from 2002-2022. Then, bibliometric analysis is carried out using the VOS viewer, Science of Science (Sci2), and Gephi. Keyword co-occurrence, prestige analysis, bibliographic coupling, and citation analysis are performed to merge knowledge clusters. The results of keyword co-occurrence and co-citation analysis suggest that there exist

DOI: 10.4018/979-8-3693-9193-8.ch004

mainly two prominent exit strategies in venture capital which are Initial public offering (IPO) and M&A. These clusters have significant relation with other parameters but limited research observed on them. The findings also indicate that, of all the tactics employed, secondary sales and strategic sale are the technique that has received the least research. Also, at the same time IPO and Merges and acquisitions are the most prevailed exit tactics of venture capitalists to retain investment.

1. INTRODUCTION

The worldwide growth and opportunities on account of globalization enabled the venture capital (VC) sector to gain significant importance. Many developed nations may witness the advantages of VC financing in the form of significant industrial growth, improved employment possibilities, higher turnover, and revenue creation for the government. However, VC finance initially rose due to liberalization but then began to decline (Torres J, 2020). The venture capital investment has been greatly admired and received preference in the United States during the period 2016-2021. However, research by IVCA-EY, highlights India's performance "Investment by Private Equity and Venture Capital Firms in Indian Companies Touch High of $77 billion in 2021, over 60% greater than 2020,".

The long-term relationships between business owners and their investors are governed by venture capital (VC) contracts, which define cash flow and control rights. The long-term nature of VC-entrepreneur partnerships leaves VCs exposed to expropriation by entrepreneurs (Gompers, 1998; Casamatta, 2003) and entrepreneurs subject to exploitation by VCs (Fried and Ganor, 2006). As a result, it is only natural for contracts to be influenced by the entrepreneurs' and venture capitalists' negotiating positions as well as the legal framework that oversees their interactions. Furthermore, contracts are set up so that control rights are distributed over exit decisions because high-tech start-up entrepreneurial firms lack the cash flows to pay interest on debt or dividends on equity (Sahlman 1990; Schwienbacher, 2007).

For small and expanding businesses, venture capital (VC) funds are a crucial source of funding since they invest money entirely based on an entrepreneur's promising idea and probable return on investment (Harris and Bovaird 1996). According to Black and Gilson (1998), the expansion of the venture capital business depends on venture capital exits. Venture capitalists (VCs) can reuse non-financial contributions by quitting and investing in fresh investee firms. It also makes it easier to get additional funding and builds the reputation of successful venture capitalists.

The most important stage of venture capitalists' operations can be thought of as a process (Bygrave and Timmons 1992). As this offers a way to cash-out profits to earn a return on their investments, venture capitalists actively participate in guiding investees towards the exit. VCs can reuse their non-financial contributions in subsequent rounds of investment thanks to the exit mechanism. Additionally, it makes contractual arrangements between venture capital managers and the lenders of their funds easier (Black and Gilson 1998). The latter can evaluate the profitability of venture capital in comparison to other investment mechanisms and the relative expertise of VCs. Berlin (1998) claims that the exit is the "home run" that establishes a venture capitalist's reputation since it allows for the calculation of the venture fund's success and return on investment.

Numerous research on VC departures have been conducted over the past ten years in both the US and Europe (Barry et al. 1990). There are, however, surprisingly few research on VC exits in developing nations like India.

The VC supported startups have emerged fast and consequently demand of venture capital funds increased significantly due to expected attractive yields. The term "Exit" in this study means simply a chance for an investor to withdraw the investment or venture capitalists recognize and comprehend to drive returns from investments. Also, a venture capitalist can exit from venture at different stages as well as various available routes of exit strategy (Dugar & Basant, 2021; Honorine & Emmanuelle, 2019). However various routes are significantly prominent and prevailing in venture capital, those include IPOs (initial public offerings), mergers and acquisitions, share buybacks, sales to other strategic investors, sales in the over-the-counter market, and management buyouts. Through these exit plans, a business owner can maximize or fully exploit the worth of his company at a lower risk, influence investors, and create the best possible future prospects. According to the PE-VC roundup report, exit strategy routes worth $43.2 billion in 2021 were made on 280 deals in the Indian context.

There are various research studies available on conceptual evaluation of venture capital investment and methodologies. However, not much research was found on venture capitalists' exit strategies. The present study emphasizes on the Exit route in VC to address the following issues.

(i) To explore about the most significant research paper on venture capital's exit strategy?
(ii) To evaluate the most popular keyword used to combat the most widely used venture capital exit strategies globally?
(iii) To analyse which of the venture capital exit strategy research publication has received the most citations?

This paper explores the current knowledge clusters in the venture capital exit strategies by analysing 436 articles published from 2002-2022 in the Scopus indexed journals. The further is divided as follows: after introduction the paper discusses the methodology used, results, academic and managerial implications, limitations, conclusion and references.

2. METHODOLOGY

This review of the literature is organised systematically and bibliometric on various Exit routes and policies of Venture Capital. A comprehensive framework has been created to achieve a substantial study outcome. In their literature review-based study, Benzouai & Djeffal (2021) used the Web of Science database platform to review research papers and articles on venture capital. Out of 2,607 total publications, 1,840 were useful research papers, and authors from 518 journals contributed to the review. Further refinement is search limited the most relevant data to 436.

The Scopus database was used for the current study since it includes high-quality research papers that have undergone peer assessment. The period of publications considered is 2002 to 2020. Afterwards, keywords chosen according to the domain were used to find quality-reviewed research articles, yielding a total of 2930 papers. The search was then refined using a number of parameters to extract research publications on venture capital exit strategies that were title-specific. The information was then extracted, imported, and collated for a thorough evaluation and analysis to streamline important venture capital exit options.

Afterwards, the database was subjected to a thorough bibliometric analysis. Initially, it was focused on country-wise, author-wise, year-wise, journal-wise and keyword-wise information to form tables and figures. Further, the focus of Bibliometric, however, is on author citations, co-citations, bibliometric coupling of authors and keywords, and citation through network-building graphs. Knowing the dry research area and the one that receives the most citations within a certain Domain is the overarching goal. Knowing the dry research area and the one that receives the most citations in a given domain is the overarching goal.

Figure 1. Search mechanism adopted in the study (Author compilation)

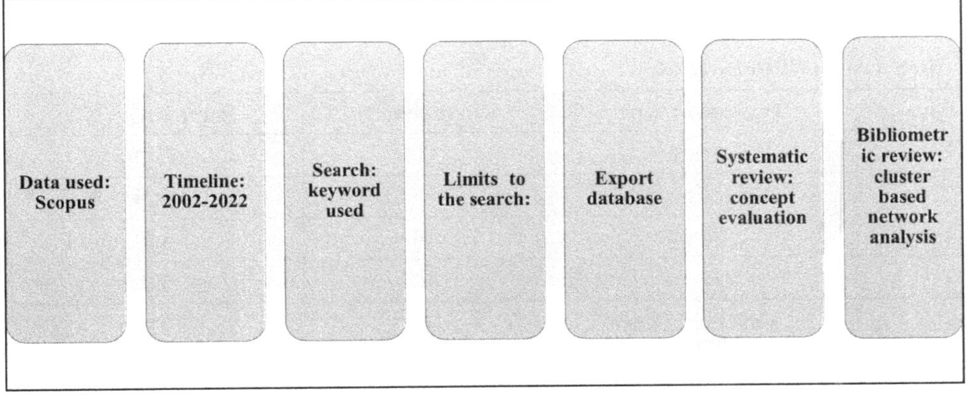

(i) Search mechanism

Since Scopus database (located at scopus.com) handles the quality component of scientific peer review, it was chosen for the study. In this case, the database was extracted in order to measure expertise in a specific area of the study's topic.

(ii) Document retrieved from search Engine

Around 2970 research papers were extracted using the term "venture capital," and then the search was further filtered using the keyword "Exit policy." There have been almost 967 research publications submitted. Further, the search was refined limiting research papers by excluding Subject area, "engi", envi", "arts", "medi", "psyc", "bioc", "eart", "multi", agri", "ceng", "heal", "mate" and "neur". Further, limitation on Publication stage "aip,', document type "ed", "tb" and language excluded keyword "Russian". Thereafter, received 436 significant research papers specific to venture capital exit strategy.

3. SYSTEMATIC REVIEW OF LITERATURE

I. Nature of Document

Table 1. Document type

S.no	Document type	No of article	Percentage (%)
1	Article	337	77.0
2	Book Chapter	63	14.0
3	Book	16	3.7
4	Review	16	3.7
5	Conference Paper	4	0.9

Source: Scopus, author compilation

The majority (77%) of the documents found were research articles, followed by book chapters (14%), books (3.7%), review papers (3.7%), and conference papers (0.9%). The database is then further filtered with the restriction of the study period from "2002-2020." As a result, Table 1 lists the five kinds of document types that were taken into account for this study on venture capital and its exit plan to retain earning after stage of financing to start-ups.

II. Subject Area of Document

Table 2. Document by broad area of study

S.no	Document by Subject	Document	Percentage %
1	Business management and accounting	310	48
2	Economics, econometrics, and social science	313	48
3	social science	27	4

Source: Scopus, author compilation

Table 2 expressed that the only three of the 24 thematic areas of knowledge, out of the 650 research papers that were retrieved from the Scopus database were considered to be core knowledge. These focus of these 650 articles were specifically on venture capital's exit strategy. Economics, econometrics, and social science 313 with 48%, business management and accounting 310 with 48%, and social science 27 with 4% are all clearly counted in the table above. As a result, the primary three subject areas show an evolution of research interest in the venture capital domain.

III. Documents by Year

Figure 2. Documents by year (Scopus)

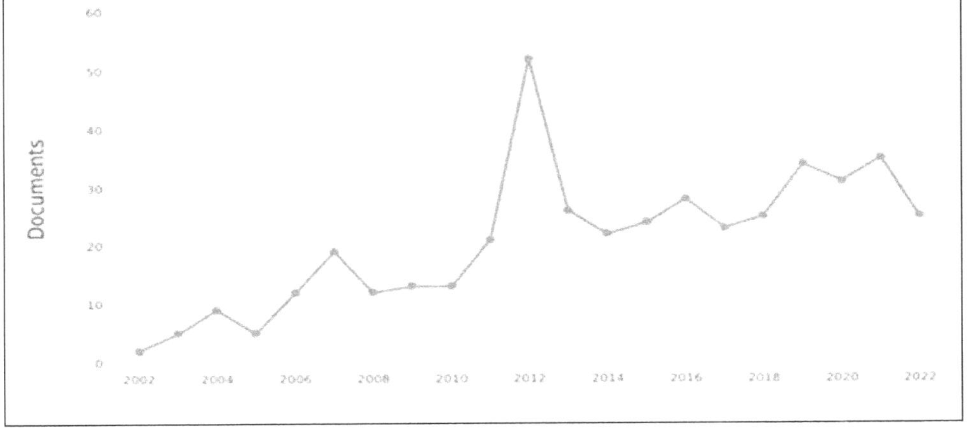

In addition, the papers that were extracted from year to year are explained in Figure 2. The years 2002 through 2022 make up the time frame of the study, with 2012 being the year in which the most documents were published in Scopus. Nevertheless, an upward trend can be seen throughout the course of the years, despite some fluctuations in the figure. Small and medium-sized businesses continue to see value in venture capital. Nonetheless, a decline was observed in recent 2022. There has been a significant fluctuation in the number of documents received by Scopus about exit strategies for venture capital, but on the whole, the trend is upwards.

IV. Documents by Country

Figure 3. Documents by country (Scopus)

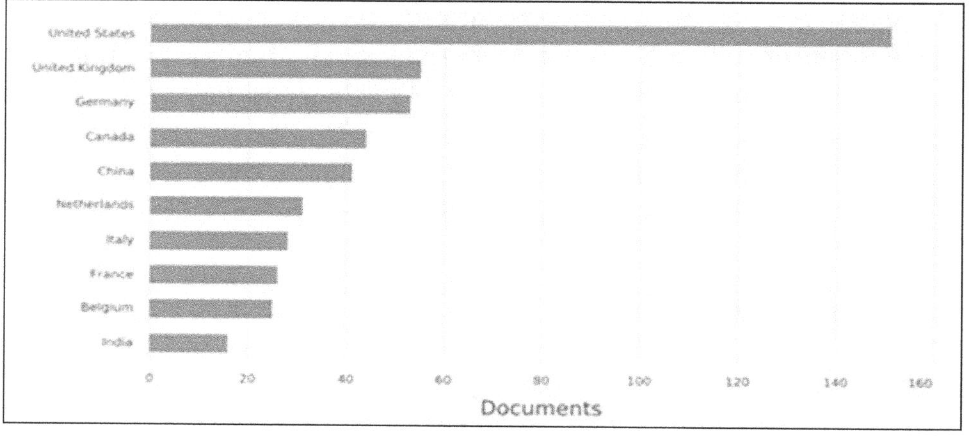

Table 3 shows that only 10 of the 15 nations were well-represented in the venture capital studies cited above. The United States has the most articles published on the topic of venture capital (150 total), while India has the least (18 Documents). The disparity is substantial, suggesting there is considerable need for further study in this area within the Indian setting, more so if compared with developed and developing countries. The range of documents examining venture capital is large, from 25 to 45 different sources in countries including Germany, Canada, China, the Netherlands, and others. Table 2 and 3, simultaneously describes during the years 2002-2022 maximum no of document over venture capital have been served by US Country only.

IV. Analysis by Author

Table 3. Authors and no. of citations

S.No	Author	Documents	Citations	Total link strength
1	cumming d.	21	1337	223
2	schwienbacher a.	13	629	140
3	hellmann t.	5	546	34
4	wright m.	9	519	92
5	cumming d.j.	9	516	113
6	nahata r.	6	498	91
7	dai n.	5	467	75
8	fleming g.	5	331	77
9	block j.h.	5	185	19
10	manigart s.	9	159	94
11	vanacker t.	5	138	60
12	li y.	5	125	25
13	wang l.	5	110	60
14	tykvová t.	5	104	48
15	johan s.	6	93	38
16	mohamed a.	6	57	39

Source: Scopus, author compilation

The emphasis in Table 3 above is on authors and the number of citations they have in research domain of venture capital and its exit plans. Cumming D has produced the most research articles on venture capital exit strategies with 21 documents and received 1337 citations over it. In contrast, Mohamed A have only 6 research papers with 57 citations which means their studies have been used by other researchers, Followed by Iohans, S. with 6 no of documents and 97 citations on his work. In leading direction, Figure 4 have expressed on cluster formed by authors have significantly worked venture capital strategies.

Figure 4. Clusters of authors

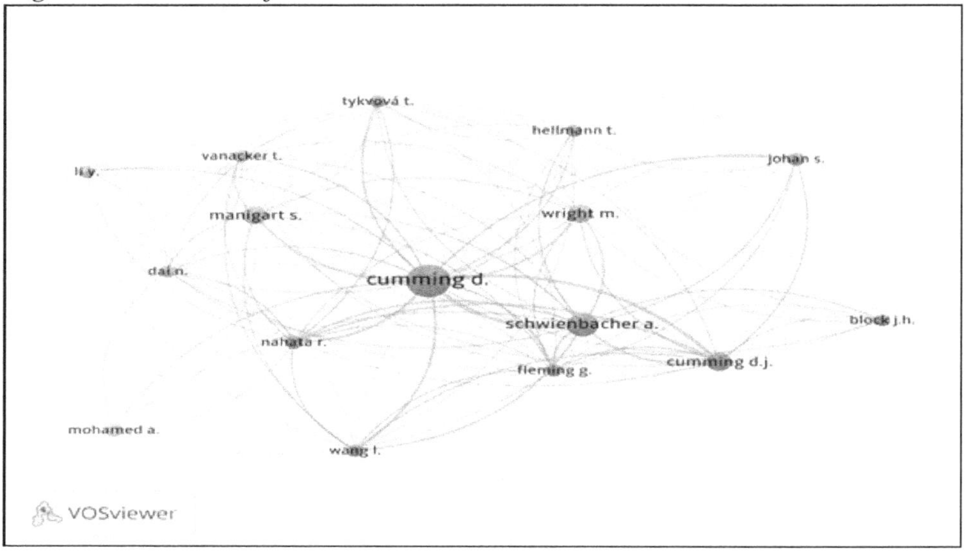

The range of research on Venture capital exit strategies is depicted in Figure 4 above, which brings together five cluster to draw attention to the topic. Comparable to the red team of Cumming d.j., Schwienbacher a., and Cummming d. those have done plenty of research on (corporate venture capital with technology and innovation area) same or similar area of study. Others are also making steady progress in (venture capital and IPOs) similar area reflected with green cluster by authors li y., dai. n., wright. m., and blue cluster with authors hellmann t., johan. S.,. (Mixed methods in venture capital) To contrast, Mohamed a. is tied for last place (with yellow cluster) (Venture capital and buyout backed IPO and international Syndicates) in terms of total contributions with 6 documents and 57 citations, this reflects, much of the work has not been done on study pursued by this author.

Figure 5. Analysis by affiliation of author

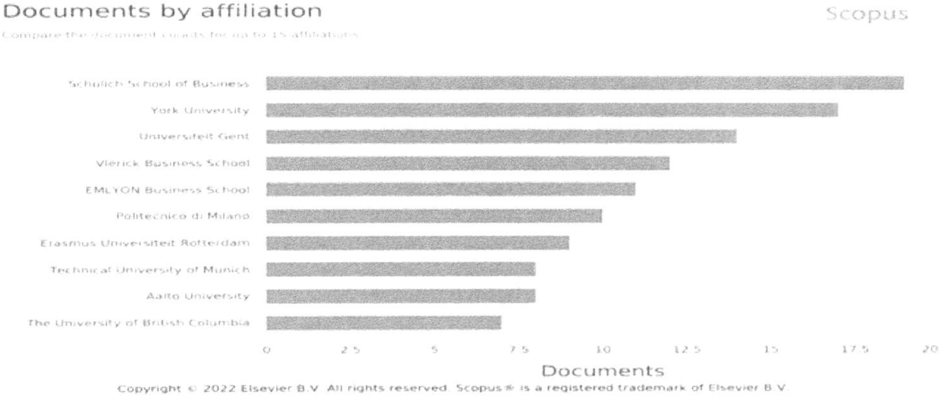

Figure 5 is provided to show the author affiliations of those who bring research on the exit strategies for venture capital. A maximum of 18 research papers published on this topic from the Schulich School of Business, however, 16 served by York University. In contrast, only 6 research papers on venture capital-related articles were submitted to British Columbia University.

The Cust of above all is, much research done by authors name(Chahine et al., 2021; D. Cumming et al., 2017; D. J. Cumming & Schwienbacher, 2018), citation no is 1337 with (D. Cumming et al., 2017; D. J. Cumming & Schwienbacher, 2018), country name is United states, affiliation to Schulich School of Business, broad area of research is Business management and accounting.

4. BIBLIOMETRIC ANALYSIS

This Section deals with the bibliometric analysis of venture capital exit policy. Bibliometric analysis pact with word cloud, network and cluster outcome based on citation, occurrence of keywords and coupling.

I. Co-Occurrence

The term "co-occurrence" is used to describe the recurrence of certain terms or pieces of information in studies that are related to or coincide with venture capital. A recurrence of these terms in the context of venture capital has been noted and serves to highlight their significance for linked industries (word). A large number of connections among words network indicates extensive research in that area, while a small number of networks indicates only preliminary investigation. Now, using the Vos viewer in present study, we performed Co-occurrence to locate a pronounced concentration of colour variants. The overall prevalence of these words has been seen in research on venture capital.

Figure 6. Co-occurrence of all keywords

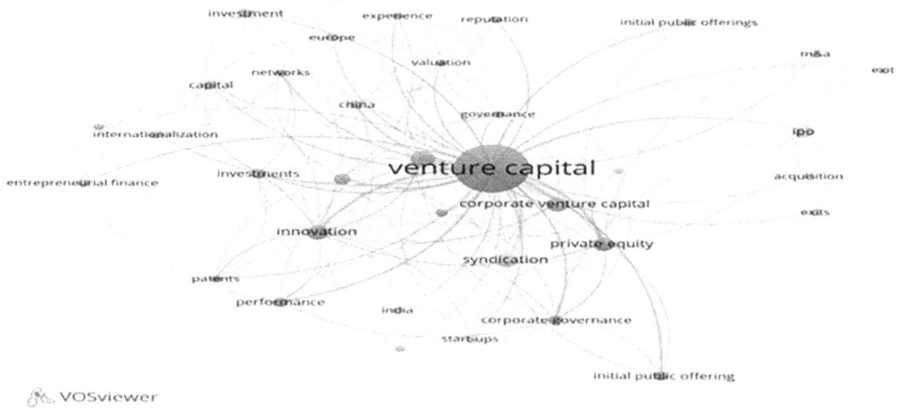

The above Figure 6, obtained six clusters on venture capital exit policies; the most noticeable network within this network is highlighted in red and represents the maximum amount of work that venture capital has done in relation to innovation, private equity, corporate governance performance, IPOs, and patents, among this innovation, IPO, buyback were much cited exit strategy of Venture capital.

Significant work has been done by these authors (Kato & Germinah, 2022; N. Khan et al., 2021; Kim & Park, 2017; J. Y. Lin, 2020; Maxin, 2020; Park & Bae, 2018; Pradhan et al., 2017; Que & Zhang, 2020; Rossi et al., 2020; Shinkle & Suchard, 2019; Wang et al., 2019) over involvement and impact of Innovation and technology in venture capital and much prevailing area to explore on it. In contrast, the yellow colour cluster is associated with the least amount of work in exits, mergers and acquisitions, and IPOs. Authors worked on IPO exit strategy of venture capital are (Amor & Kooli, 2020; Andrieu & Peter Groh, 2021; Dominic, 2020; Ginsberg & Marcus, 2018; Montanaro et al., 2022; Shin, 2019).

Internationalization, investment, China, value, reputation, and capital with green and purple colour clusters are further important subjects for venture capital study. But the light blue colour cluster also represented specialised areas of venture capital, where less work had been done in India context (Dominic, 2020; Dominic & Gopalaswamy, 2019; Dugar & Basant, 2021; Dugar & Pandit, 2017; K. Joshi et al., 2019; K. A. Joshi, 2019; Katti & Raithatha, 2020; A. M. Khan et al., 2019) and in start-ups context (Barg et al., 2021; Nigam et al., 2020; Zhang et al., 2019). Seeing Lesser no of research then much insights are available to cover in it.

Figure 7. Co-occurrence of author keywords

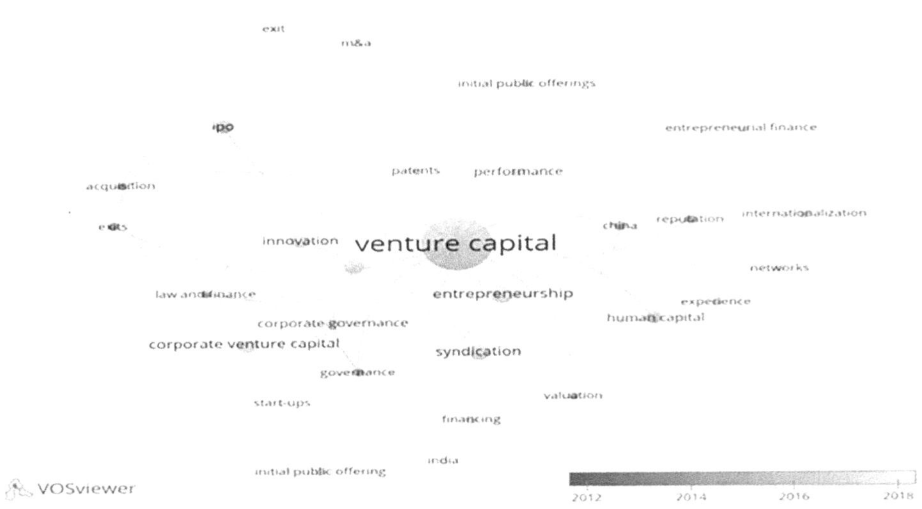

This illustration in Figure 7 illustrates as how the author's limited keywords was repeatedly employed in a study on venture capital exit options by various other authors. The preceding Table 3, however, focused on all keywords associated to venture capital overall domain. Further, we have narrowed the field by evaluating only specific author's keywords over period of time classified in clusters of various colours with blue green and yellow. The transition in colour from blue to yellow represented the past to present efforts done in this area.

There was an average of 3 publications containing the Author keyword "M&A". The average year of publication by author keyword for the terms "Startups," "Patents," and "India" was in 2018. Such start-up studies with venture capital were like (Barg et al., 2021; Nigam et al., 2020; Zhang et al., 2019), on Indian venture capital studies were (Dominic, 2020; Dominic & Gopalaswamy, 2019; Dugar & Basant, 2021; Dugar & Pandit, 2017; K. Joshi et al., 2019; K. A. Joshi, 2019; Katti & Raithatha, 2020; A. M. Khan et al., 2019) and on patent with venture capital study was (Zhang et al., 2019). The significant no of studies on "venture capital" work was observed in 2017 (D. Cumming et al., 2017; Dugar & Pandit, 2017; Hain & Jurowetzki, 2018; Jia & Wang, 2017; Kang, 2019; Kim & Park, 2017; Klonowski, 2017; Lee, 2019; R. Lin et al., 2017; Pradhan et al., 2017; Torres, 2020). Further, further exploration in venture capital with specific to exit strategies in year 2020 are(Amor & Kooli, 2020; Dominic, 2020). Refer to Table 4.

The amount of research done on a connected field of venture capital may be easily determined because the number of author keywords used are filtered as per time frame.

Table 4. Clusters classified as per author keywords

Cluster1	**Corporate Governance, IPO, Innovation, patent, performance, private equity and venture capital**
Cluster-2	China, Experience, Human capital, internationalization, network, reputation, syndication
Cluster-3	Corporate venture capital, entrepreneurship, Financing, Governance, valuation
Cluster-4	Acquisition, exits, IPO, law and Finance
Cluster-5	Exit, IPOS, mergers and acquisitions
Cluster-6	India, start-ups
Cluster-7	Entrepreneurship Finance

On concreate basis such observation have been made by research as per given Table 4 that the Cluster 4, 5, 6 and 7 there are keywords lesser used in research studies and much studies are not available on venture capital exit routes, keyword "start-up" only 3 studies (Barg et al., 2021; Nigam et al., 2020; Zhang et al., 2019)

Limited studies observed on Indian start-ups considering at Idea or Seed stage of financing, Also IPO as exit route again limited studies on recent years however, in recent past such were available are (Buchner et al., 2019; Cormier et al., 2018; Honorine & Emmanuelle, 2019; Que & Zhang, 2019). Another route of exit for venture capitalist is M &A such author has worked on it (Amor & Kooli, 2020; Cormier et al., 2018; Jin et al., 2021). Therefore, much wide scope is present to pursue further research on venture capitalist

Citation

In this sector, there is a discussion on citation and numbers of citation of Journals. There is renowned journal have published studies extracted by Vos viewer on venture capital exit strategy area.

Figure 8. Prestigious journals on venture capital

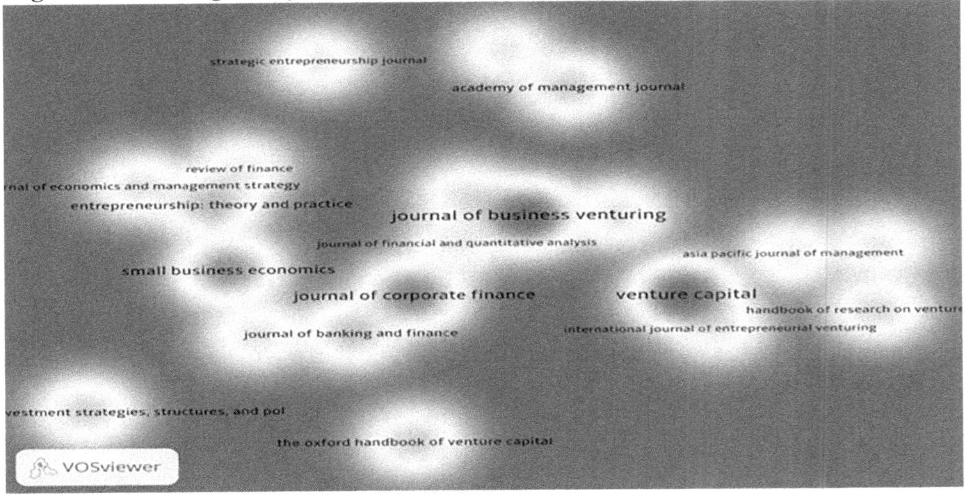

Figure 8 clearly show how many research articles on venture capital exit strategy have been published in journals worldwide. Journals named "Journal of Business Venturing,"((Andrieu & Peter Groh, 2021; Belderbos et al., 2018; Domurath et al., 2020; Kim & Park, 2021; Pan et al., 2020; Tumasjan et al., 2021)) "Venture Capital," (Bonini & Capizzi, 2019; Glücksman, 2020; Kim & Park, 2021; Tennert et al., 2018) and "Journal of Corporate Finance"(Block et al., 2019a, 2019b; Butticè et al., 2020; Chemmanur et al., 2021; Chircop et al., 2020; Hasan et al., 2018; Jia & Wang, 2017; Nahata, 2019; Nguyen & Vo, 2021) have published the most research articles on venture capital and its valuation on its determinant. The density of orange dots in the previously provided graphic made this very clear. Journals that have featured venture capital articles less frequently include "Review of Finance," "Asia Pacific Journal of Management," and "Strategic Entrepreneurship Journals." The lowest have been observed in "Journal of Financial and Quantitative Analysis" author worked (Bayar et al., 2020; D. Cumming et al., 2017)

Further, analysis continue to evaluate countries published or publishing enough studies on venture capital exit strategy, as indicated in Figure 9.

Figure 9. Country wise research on venture capital

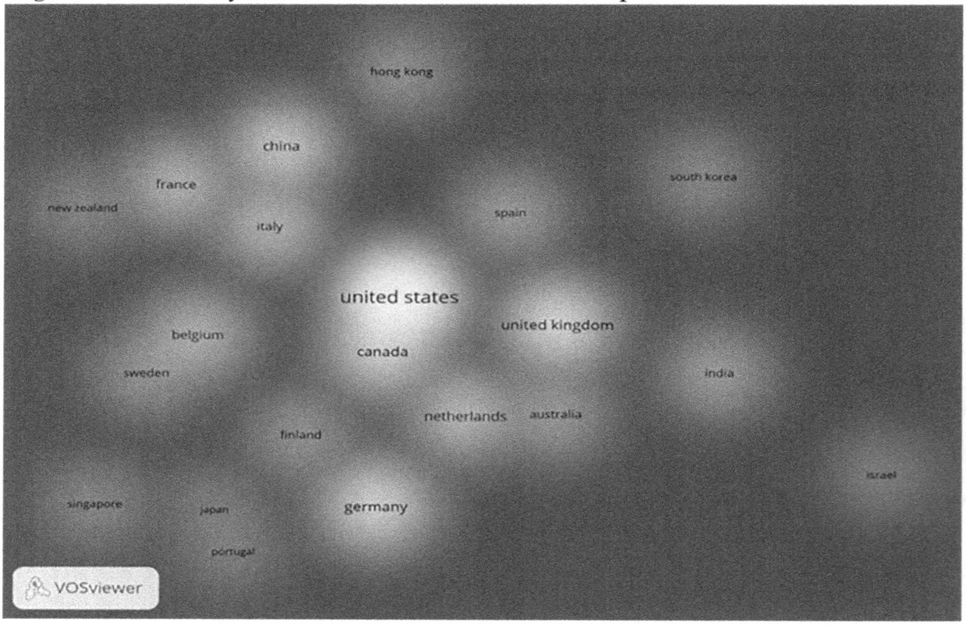

Figure 9 above describes a nation that receives a lot of venture money. The United States is the most frequently mentioned country when discussing venture capital and clearly visible in above Figure 8, followed by the United Kingdom, Canada, Germany, and China. However, nations like India, Israel, South Korea, Japan, and New Zealand have noted that there has been relatively little research done in the field of venture capital as per above given figure.

Because of this, it can be inferred that the United States and the United Kingdom have sufficiently investigated venture capital and its exit options. The Journal of Business Venturing, Venture Capital, and Journal of Corporate Finance all belong to the United States, whereas Netherlands owns the Journal of Corporate Finance. There is plenty of scope to publish in the same field in near future because the "Asia Pacific Journals of Management Studies" is associated with the Asia-Pacific region and hasn't yet published many articles on venture capital.

Bibliometric Coupling

The underlying meaning of bibliometric coupling is that the authors 1 and 2 used the same research paper in their study to bring authenticity and to continue with tale of research in one domain of study. Numerous authors cite other authors effective work in their literature review papers and in empirical papers, this makes bibliometric coupling crucial. Much cited work in research field has great significance and authors known for their research work only. In this present study on venture capital exit route also have few prevailed authors whose work is cited (used by) other authors. For same refer given below Figure 10.

Figure 10. Bibliometric coupling of authors on venture capital

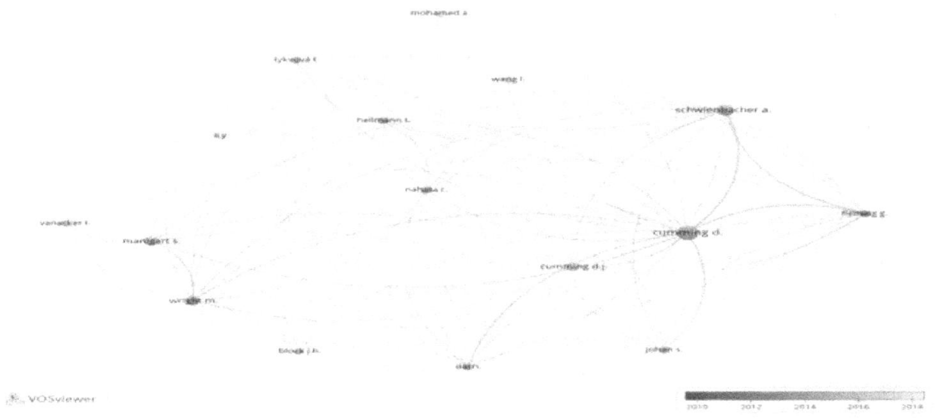

While referring given Figure 10, several authors who have written about venture capital are shown in the illustration, along with instances where other authors have simultaneously cited their writings. The study by(D. Cumming et al., 2017; D. J. Cumming & Schwienbacher, 2018) examined Fintech venture capital and Entrepreneurial Litigation and Venture Capital Finance. It was part of a series of documents by the same author on the same subject over the years. Our study is limited to time period, however, same authors have linked their results over time and referenced in related previous studies also. The aforementioned figures result in the development of four clusters that are represented by blue, green, and yellow colors. (Capizzi et al., 2022) illuminate the business investment angels and venture capital funding" indicates that the yellow shade network of writers has just recently taken up this area of study (citation-3). Other authors include (Chahine et al., 2021, (Buchner et al., 2019; Khurshed et al., 2020), (Block et al., 2019a), (Ke & Wang, 2021; Wang et al., 2019) As a result, researchers from various countries have examined venture capital and the elements that are associated to it.

The author "cumming d." has served 21 documents and received 1337 citations to date by working on venture capital exit strategies. Author "Schwienbacher a." has received 629 citations in the same field of study, according to a systematic examination of the authors in Table 3.

Further, Table 5 reflects Countries where much of the work is done in these countries along with no. of citation received by authors of Individual country.

Table 5. Country wise no of citation

S.no	Country	documents	citations	total link strength
1	United states	151	6932	157586
2	Canada	44	2332	76009
3	United Kingdom	55	1743	76405
4	Netherlands	31	1441	60978
5	Germany	53	898	73194
6	Italy	28	817	41256
7	Finland	12	764	20371
8	Australia	15	689	24454
9	Belgium	25	672	43962
10	France	26	475	39836
11	China	40	456	46054
12	Hong Kong	12	439	16989
13	Spain	16	213	22044
14	Singapore	8	202	5212
15	Sweden	12	179	9872
16	Japan	5	93	5953
17	India	16	68	15247
18	South Korea	9	58	10670
19	New Zealand	7	47	11562
20	Israel	6	35	5799

The preceding Table 5 makes it obvious that the United Nations serves the majority of research articles with 151 documents and 6932 citations worldwide. This indicates that the United States, followed by Canada with 44 Documents (2332 citation) and the United Kingdom with 55 Document (1743 citation), examine and analyse the majority of the angles and related elements related to venture capital, virtually reaching saturation level. The table also expresses that there is still much to learn about venture capital and its exit methods in India over 16 documents with 68 citations, Japan with 5 documents with 93 citations, Sweden 12 documents with 179 citations, South Korea 9 documents with 58 citations, and New Zealand 7 documents with 47 citations. Further, there are significant research has already been conducted in nations like Germany, China, Australia, and the Netherlands

Moreover, the total link strength is expressed on relationship between authors, considering above Table 5, reflects strong co-authorship among authors of United states with 1,57,586 TLS over 151documents. However, least co-authorship among authors have been observed between Israel Co-authors 5799, over 6 Documents.

5. ACADEMIC AND MANAGERIAL IMPLICATIONS

The country's venture capital industry has promising possibilities thanks to increased support for professional entrepreneurship, the use of cutting-edge technologies, and an integration of Indian businesses with the worldwide market. The industry and service sectors, in particular, provide this. Greater trust and transparency between the entrepreneur and the investor are required for the venture fund investment to become more professional.

From an academic standpoint, this study will add to the knowledge of venture capital at worldwide. Insights into venture capital and the many exit options that corporations pursuing it will be used and benefited by various researchers, academicians, and students. Additionally, this investigation over venture capital has uncover a variety of research strands that could serve as future study objectives like Effectiveness of IPO and mergers and acquisition as exit strategy of venture capital, sustainable finance in venture capital, stage financing with exit route, strategic sale much can be investigated on it.

Limitations

These limitations are a result of the nature of the bibliometric investigation. This study's findings were limited by its period-based design (2012-2020). Therefore, it did not incorporate previous studies over venture capital. As the changing trend over venture capital also influence and put various keyword restrictions are also employed to extract important research papers. Additionally, this is restricted to venture capital exit options, and the current study does not contain any additional venture capital parameters. Venture capital are financed by various financial institutions and Banks, dive into it to further explore int it to reach specified findings.

6. CONCLUSION

An entrepreneur's idea is supported for a while by a venture capitalist. The venture capitalist then made their exit using a number of exit options (IPO, M&A, strategic sale). The two topics of venture capital investment and their exit options from a specific endeavour were addressed in this essay. The piece also creates a journal analysis that identifies the top researchers in the area (D. Cumming et al., 2017; D. J. Cumming & Schwienbacher, 2018). We specifically point out that compared to other journals, some specialist publications publish more research on venture capital. Even if they publish a lot of articles in VC research, other journals that have a high number of citations (D. Cumming et al., 2017; D. J. Cumming & Schwienbacher, 2018), also highlighted that US Country have explored venture capital area over period of time with initial stage of financing till exit stage of venture capital.(Dugar & Basant, 2021; Honorine & Emmanuelle, 2019) This essay also looks at the gaps in the literature about venture capitalists' departure strategy and the stages at which they leave a certain start-up in Indian context and Asian Countries(Nigam et al., 2020). The findings indicate that, of all the tactics employed, secondary sales and strategic sale are the technique that has received the least research. Also, at the same time IPO and Merges and acquisitions are most prevailed exit tactics of venture capitalist to retain investment. This also establishes venture capital relation with sustainable Finance context. In conclusion, venture capitalist investments carry a high level of risk and have brighter chances of making a profit.

REFERENCES

Amor, S., & Kooli, M. (2020). Do M&A exits have the same effect on venture capital reputation than IPO exits? *Journal of Banking & Finance, 111*, 105704. Advance online publication. DOI: 10.1016/j.jbankfin.2019.105704

Andrieu, G., & Peter Groh, A. (2021). Strategic exits in secondary venture capital markets. *Journal of Business Venturing, 36*(2), 105999. Advance online publication. DOI: 10.1016/j.jbusvent.2019.105999

Barg, J. A., Drobetz, W., & Momtaz, P. P. (2021). Valuing start-up firms: A reverse-engineering approach for fair-value multiples from venture capital transactions. *Finance Research Letters, 43*, 102008. Advance online publication. DOI: 10.1016/j.frl.2021.102008

Barry, C. B., Muscarella, C. J., Peavy Iii, J. W., & Vetsuypens, M. R. (1990). The role of venture capital in the creation of public companies: Evidence from the going-public process. *Journal of Financial Economics, 27*(2), 447–471. DOI: 10.1016/0304-405X(90)90064-7

Bayar, O., Chemmanur, T. J., & Tian, X. (2020). Peer monitoring, syndication, and the dynamics of venture capital interactions: Theory and evidence. *Journal of Financial and Quantitative Analysis, 55*(6), 1875–1914. DOI: 10.1017/S0022109019000218

Belderbos, R., Jacob, J., & Lokshin, B. (2018). Corporate venture capital (CVC) investments and technological performance: Geographic diversity and the interplay with technology alliances. *Journal of Business Venturing, 33*(1), 20–34. DOI: 10.1016/j.jbusvent.2017.10.003

Berlin, M. (1998). That thing venture capitalists do. *Business Review (Federal Reserve Bank of Philadelphia), 1*, 15–26.

Black, B. S., & Gilson, R. J. (1998). Venture capital and the structure of capital markets: Banks versus stock markets. *Journal of Financial Economics, 47*(3), 243–277. DOI: 10.1016/S0304-405X(97)00045-7

Block, J., Fisch, C., Vismara, S., & Andres, R. (2019a). Private equity investment criteria: An experimental conjoint analysis of venture capital, business angels, and family offices. *Journal of Corporate Finance*, *58*, 329–352. DOI: 10.1016/j.jcorpfin.2019.05.009

Block, J., Fisch, C., Vismara, S., & Andres, R. (2019b). Private equity investment criteria: An experimental conjoint analysis of venture capital, business angels, and family offices. *Journal of Corporate Finance*, *58*, 329–352. DOI: 10.1016/j.jcorpfin.2019.05.009

Bonini, S., & Capizzi, V. (2019). The role of venture capital in the emerging entrepreneurial finance ecosystem: future threats and opportunities. In *Venture Capital* (Vol. 21, Issues 2–3, pp. 137–175). Routledge. DOI: 10.1080/13691066.2019.1608697

Buchner, A., Mohamed, A., & Wagner, N. (2019). Are venture capital and buyout backed IPOs any different? *Journal of International Financial Markets, Institutions and Money*, *60*, 39–49. DOI: 10.1016/j.intfin.2018.12.002

Butticè, V., di Pietro, F., & Tenca, F. (2020). Is equity crowdfunding always good? Deal structure and the attraction of venture capital investors. *Journal of Corporate Finance*, *65*, 101773. Advance online publication. DOI: 10.1016/j.jcorpfin.2020.101773

Bygrave, W. D., & Timmons, J. (1992). *Venture capital at the crossroads*. University of Illinois at Urbana-Champaign's Academy for Entrepreneurial Leadership Historical Research Reference in Entrepreneurship.

Capizzi, V., Croce, A., & Tenca, F. (2022). Do Business Angels' Investments Make It Easier to Raise Follow-on Venture Capital Financing? An Analysis of the Relevance of Business Angels' Investment Practices. *British Journal of Management*, *33*(1), 306–326. DOI: 10.1111/1467-8551.12526

Casamatta, C., & Haritchabalet, C. (2003). Learning and syndication in venture capital investments. *Available atSSRN* 413401.

Chahine, S., Filatotchev, I., Bruton, G. D., & Wright, M. (2021). "Success by Association": The Impact of Venture Capital Firm Reputation Trend on Initial Public Offering Valuations. *Journal of Management*, *47*(2), 368–398. DOI: 10.1177/0149206319847265

Chemmanur, T. J., Hu, G., Wu, C., Wu, S., & Yan, Z. (2021). Transforming the management and governance of private family firms: The role of venture capital. *Journal of Corporate Finance, 66*, 101828. Advance online publication. DOI: 10.1016/j.jcorpfin.2020.101828

Chircop, J., Johan, S., & Tarsalewska, M. (2020). Does religiosity influence venture capital investment decisions? *Journal of Corporate Finance, 62*, 101589. Advance online publication. DOI: 10.1016/j.jcorpfin.2020.101589

Cormier, D., Coulombe, D., Gomez Gutierrez, L., & Mcconomy, B. J. (2018). Firms in Transition: A Review of the Venture Capital, IPO, and M&A Literature. In *Accounting Perspectives* (Vol. 17, Issue 1, pp. 9–88). Canadian Academic Accounting Association. DOI: 10.1111/1911-3838.12162

Cumming, D., Haslem, B., & Knill, A. (2017). Entrepreneurial Litigation and Venture Capital Finance. *Journal of Financial and Quantitative Analysis, 52*(5), 2217–2250. DOI: 10.1017/S0022109017000758

Cumming, D. J., & Schwienbacher, A. (2018). Fintech venture capital. *Corporate Governance, 26*(5), 374–389. DOI: 10.1111/corg.12256

Dominic, J. (2020). Decoding venture capital exit patterns: An indian perspective. In *Asian Economic and Financial Review* (Vol. 10, Issue 9, pp. 956–969). Asian Economic and Social Society. DOI: 10.18488/journal.aefr.2020.109.956.969

Dominic, J., & Gopalaswamy, A. K. (2019). Is the venture capital market liquid? Evidence from India. *Global Finance Journal, 41*, 146–157. DOI: 10.1016/j.gfj.2019.04.002

Domurath, A., Patzelt, H., & Liebl, A. (2020). Does negative feedback impact new ventures' organizational identity? The role of founding teams' human capital and feedback source. *Journal of Business Venturing, 35*(3), 105987. Advance online publication. DOI: 10.1016/j.jbusvent.2019.105987

Dugar, P., & Basant, R. (2021). Antecedents of Stage-wise Investment Preferences of Venture Capital and Private Equity Firms in India: An Empirical Exploration. *Journal of Emerging Market Finance, 20*(3), 264–289. DOI: 10.1177/09726527211022900

Dugar, P., & Pandit, N. (2017). Growth of Venture Capital and Private Equity in India. *Journal of Private Equity*, *21*(1), 79–93. DOI: 10.3905/jpe.2017.21.1.079

Fried, J. M., & Ganor, M. (2006). Agency costs of venture capitalist control in startups. *NYUL rev.*, *81*, 967.

Ginsberg, A., & Marcus, A. (2018). Venture capital's role in creating a more sustainable society: The role of exits in clean energy's investment growth. In *Advances in Strategic Management* (Vol. 38, pp. 145–168). Emerald Group Publishing Ltd., DOI: 10.1108/S0742-332220180000038011

Giot, P., & Schwienbacher, A. (2007). IPOs, trade sales and liquidations: Modelling venture capital exits using survival analysis. *Journal of Banking & Finance*, *31*(3), 679–702. DOI: 10.1016/j.jbankfin.2006.06.010

Glücksman, S. (2020). Entrepreneurial experiences from venture capital funding: Exploring two-sided information asymmetry. *Venture Capital*, *22*(4), 331–354. DOI: 10.1080/13691066.2020.1827502

Gompers, P., & Lerner, J. (1998). Venture capital distributions: Short-run and long-run reactions. *The Journal of Finance*, *53*(6), 2161–2183. DOI: 10.1111/0022-1082.00086

Hain, D. S., & Jurowetzki, R. (2018). Local competence building and international venture capital in low-income countries: Exploring foreign high-tech investments in Kenya's Silicon Savanna. *Journal of Small Business and Enterprise Development*, *25*(3), 447–482. DOI: 10.1108/JSBED-03-2017-0092

Harris, S., & Bovaird, C. (1996). *Enterprising Capital: A Study of Enterprise Development and the Institutions which Finance it*. Avebury.

Hasan, I., Khurshed, A., Mohamed, A., & Wang, F. (2018). Do venture capital firms benefit from a presence on boards of directors of mature public companies? *Journal of Corporate Finance*, *49*, 125–140. DOI: 10.1016/j.jcorpfin.2017.04.018

Honorine, A. N., & Emmanuelle, D. (2019). Stage financing and syndication in the IPO underpricing of venture-backed firms: Venture capital and IPO underpricing. *International Journal of Entrepreneurship and Innovation*, *20*(4), 289–300. DOI: 10.1177/1465750318795083

Jia, N., & Wang, D. (2017). Skin in the game: General partner capital commitment, investment behavior and venture capital fund performance. *Journal of Corporate Finance*, *47*, 110–130. DOI: 10.1016/j.jcorpfin.2017.09.008

Jin, Y., Xu, M., Wang, W., & Xi, Y. (2021). Venture capital network and the M&A performance of listed companies. *China Finance Review International*, *11*(1), 92–123. DOI: 10.1108/CFRI-02-2020-0016

Joshi, K., Chandrashekar, D., Brem, A., & Momaya, K. S. (2019). Foreign venture capital firms in a cross-border context: Empirical insights from India. *Sustainability (Basel)*, *11*(22), 6265. Advance online publication. DOI: 10.3390/su11226265

Joshi, K. A. (2019). Specialisation and syndication as risk management strategies for venture capital firms in India. In *Int. J. Entrepreneurial Venturing* (Vol. 11, Issue 6). DOI: 10.1504/IJEV.2019.103740

Kang, S. (2019). The impact of corporate venture capital involvement in syndicates. *Management Decision*, *57*(1), 131–151. DOI: 10.1108/MD-01-2017-0024

Kato, A. I., & Germinah, C. P. E. (2022). Empirical examination of relationship between venture capital financing and profitability of portfolio companies in Uganda. *Journal of Innovation and Entrepreneurship*, *11*(1), 30. Advance online publication. DOI: 10.1186/s13731-022-00216-5

Katti, S., & Raithatha, M. (2020). Impact of Venture Capital Investment on Firm Performance: An Indian Evidence. *Global Business Review*, *21*(4), 1011–1024. DOI: 10.1177/0972150918779165

Ke, B., & Wang, L. (2021). Mixed ownership and firm performance: Evidence from the Chinese venture capital industry. *Emerging Markets Review*, *49*, 100759. Advance online publication. DOI: 10.1016/j.ememar.2020.100759

Khan, A. M., Arafat, M. Y., Raushan, M. A., Saleem, I., Khan, N. A., & Khan, M. M. (2019). Does intellectual capital affect the venture creation decision in India? *Journal of Innovation and Entrepreneurship*, *8*(1), 1–15. DOI: 10.1186/s13731-019-0106-y

Khan, N., Qu, H., Qu, J., Wei, C. M., & Wang, S. (2021). Does Venture Capital Investment Spur Innovation? A Cross-Countries Analysis. *SAGE Open*, *11*(1), 21582440211003087. Advance online publication. DOI: 10.1177/21582440211003087

Khurshed, A., Mohamed, A., Schwienbacher, A., & Wang, F. (2020). Do venture capital firms benefit from international syndicates? *Journal of International Business Studies*, *51*(6), 986–1007. DOI: 10.1057/s41267-019-00296-8

Kim, J. Y., & Park, H. D. (2017). Two faces of early corporate venture capital funding: Promoting innovation and inhibiting IPOs. *Strategy Science*, *2*(3), 161–175. DOI: 10.1287/stsc.2017.0032

Kim, J. Y., & Park, H. D. (2021). The influence of venture capital syndicate size on venture performance. *Venture Capital*, *23*(2), 179–203. DOI: 10.1080/13691066.2021.1893933

Klonowski, D. (2017). The venture capital deformation: Value destruction throughout the investment process. In *The Venture Capital Deformation: Value Destruction throughout the Investment Process*. Springer International Publishing., DOI: 10.1007/978-3-319-70323-7

Lee, B. (2019). Human capital and labor: The effect of entrepreneur characteristics on venture success. *International Journal of Entrepreneurial Behaviour & Research*, *25*(1), 29–49. DOI: 10.1108/IJEBR-10-2017-0384

Lin, J. Y. (2020). What affects new venture firm's innovation more in corporate venture capital? *European Management Journal*, *38*(4), 646–660. DOI: 10.1016/j.emj.2020.01.004

Lin, R., Li, Y., Peng, T., & Zhang, H. (2017). Venture capital reputation and portfolio firm performance in an emerging economy: The moderating effect of institutions. *Asia Pacific Journal of Management*, *34*(3), 699–723. DOI: 10.1007/s10490-016-9500-1

Maxin, H. (2020). Corporate venture capital and the nature of innovation. *Economics of Innovation and New Technology*, *29*(1), 1–30. DOI: 10.1080/10438599.2019.1571673

Montanaro, B., Cavallo, A., Giudici, G., & Ghezzi, A. (2022). Determinants of the exit value in European venture capital-backed technology startups. *Competitiveness Review*, *32*(7), 62–84. DOI: 10.1108/CR-03-2021-0032

Nahata, R. (2019). Success is good but failure is not so bad either: Serial entrepreneurs and venture capital contracting. *Journal of Corporate Finance*, *58*, 624–649. DOI: 10.1016/j.jcorpfin.2019.07.006

Nguyen, G., & Vo, V. (2021). Asset liquidity and venture capital investment. *Journal of Corporate Finance*, *69*, 101963. Advance online publication. DOI: 10.1016/j.jcorpfin.2021.101963

Nigam, N., Benetti, C., & Johan, S. A. (2020). Digital start-up access to venture capital financing: What signals quality? *Emerging Markets Review*, *45*, 100743. Advance online publication. DOI: 10.1016/j.ememar.2020.100743

Pan, L., Li, X., Chen, J., & Chen, T. (2020). Sounds novel or familiar? Entrepreneurs' framing strategy in the venture capital market. *Journal of Business Venturing*, *35*(2), 105930. Advance online publication. DOI: 10.1016/j.jbusvent.2019.02.003

Park, J. H., & Bae, Z. T. (2018). When are 'sharks' beneficial? Corporate venture capital investment and startup innovation performance. *Technology Analysis and Strategic Management*, *30*(3), 324–336. DOI: 10.1080/09537325.2017.1310376

Pradhan, R. P., Maradana, R. P., Zaki, D. B., Dash, S., Jayakumar, M., & Gaurav, K. (2017). Venture Capital and Innovation: Evidence from European Economic Area Countries. *International Journal on Management of Innovation & Technology*, *14*(6), 1750031. Advance online publication. DOI: 10.1142/S0219877017500316

Que, J., & Zhang, X. (2019). Pre-IPO growth, venture capital, and the long-run performance of IPOs. *Economic Modelling*, *81*, 205–216. DOI: 10.1016/j.econmod.2019.04.005

Que, J., & Zhang, X. (2020). The role of foreign and domestic venture capital in innovation: Evidence from China. *Accounting and Finance*, *60*(S1), 1077–1110. DOI: 10.1111/acfi.12401

Rossi, M., Festa, G., Fiano, F., & Giacobbe, R. (2020). To invest or to harvest?: Corporate venture capital ambidexterity for exploiting/exploring innovation in technological business. *Business Process Management Journal*, *26*(5), 1157–1181. DOI: 10.1108/BPMJ-05-2019-0204

Sahlman, W. A. (1990). The structure and governance of venture-capital organizations. *Journal of Financial Economics*, *27*(2), 473–521. DOI: 10.1016/0304-405X(90)90065-8

Shin, S. Y. (2019). Network advantage's effect on exit performance: Examining venture capital's inter-organizational networks. *The International Entrepreneurship and Management Journal*, *15*(1), 21–42. DOI: 10.1007/s11365-018-0545-0

Shinkle, G. A., & Suchard, J. A. (2019). Innovation in newly public firms: The influence of government grants, venture capital, and private equity. *Australian Journal of Management*, *44*(2), 248–281. DOI: 10.1177/0312896218802611

Tennert, J., Lambert, M., & Burghof, H. P. (2018). Moral hazard in high-risk environments: Optimal follow-on investing in venture capital finance. *Venture Capital*, *20*(4), 323–338. DOI: 10.1080/13691066.2018.1491095

Torres, J. P. (2020). The Venture Capital Feedback Cycle: A Critical Review and Future Directions. *Entrepreneurship Research Journal*. Advance online publication. DOI: 10.1515/erj-2017-0205

Tumasjan, A., Braun, R., & Stolz, B. (2021). Twitter sentiment as a weak signal in venture capital financing. *Journal of Business Venturing*, *36*(2), 106062. Advance online publication. DOI: 10.1016/j.jbusvent.2020.106062

Wang, L., Zhou, F., An, Y., & Yang, J. (2019). Corporate venture capital: Technological innovation or value creation? A comparative study of CVC- and IVC-invested Chinese listed companies. *Asian Journal of Technology Innovation*, *27*(3), 257–279. DOI: 10.1080/19761597.2019.1669470

Zhang, L., Guo, Y., & Sun, G. (2019). How patent signals affect venture capital: The evidence of bio-pharmaceutical start-ups in China. *Technological Forecasting and Social Change*, *145*, 93–104. DOI: 10.1016/j.techfore.2019.05.013

Chapter 5
Women Technopreneurship in a Developing Economy:
Understanding the Growth Prospects and Barriers

Zelda Arku
https://orcid.org/0000-0001-8045-9804
University of Mines and Technology, Ghana

Sheena Lovia Boateng
https://orcid.org/0000-0002-4512-4555
University of Ghana, Ghana

Stephen Boateng
https://orcid.org/0000-0003-4040-1442
University of Mines and Technology, Ghana

Desmond Kwadjo Kumi
University of Ghana, Ghana

ABSTRACT

This study examines the growth prospects and barriers for women techno-

DOI: 10.4018/979-8-3693-9193-8.ch005

preneurs in Ghana, focusing on their landscape, challenges, and key growth drivers. Using data from 60 women technopreneurs in Ghana and Nigeria, it explores four critical factors—Entrepreneurial Culture, Technopreneurship Capabilities, Staged Financing, and Business Support Mechanisms—and evaluates the moderating role of the regulatory environment. Partial Least Squares Structural Equation Modeling (PLS-SEM) was used to analyze causal relationships. Findings show women-led technopreneurs are profit-driven, leveraging technologies like social media and cloud computing but face barriers such as taxation, limited financing, and cultural biases. The regulatory environment moderated Technopreneurship Capabilities, Entrepreneurial Culture, and Staged Financing but did not significantly moderate Business Support Mechanisms. These results are thoroughly discussed, and relevant recommendations made.

BACKGROUND

In light of the emergence of the digital economy and globalization, technology with entrepreneurship have become the driving agents of the economy (Soekarno & Setiawati, 2020; Usman et al., 2024). Technologies such as the internet of things, big data, cloud computing, artificial intelligence, blockchain, and digital multiple transformations are influencing entrepreneurship (Nambisan et al., 2020). An entrepreneur is an individual who can convert a vision, idea, or invention into a successful business (Ovharhe, 2024). Again, entrepreneurs are individuals who innovate new products/services, create new processes, open new markets, and organize new industries (Modgil et al., 2022). The concept of entrepreneurship therefore encompasses efforts to bring about new economic, social, institutional, and cultural environments through the actions of an individual or group of individuals (Abubakre & Mkansi, 2022). When entrepreneurship meets technology, capital, and a supportive environment, it moves on to a more advanced level of technopreneurship as technology has the most important role in transforming the world, especially since the late 20th-century environment (Abbas, 2018; Ingram Bogusz et al., 2019; Katjiteo, 2024).

Technopreneurship is simply entrepreneurship applied in a technology-intensive context (Koe, 2020). There is a strong connection between Technological development, Innovations, and entrepreneurship (Amante & Ronquillo, 2017), hence is it noteworthy that, entrepreneurship forms the substructure upon which the technology is built. The difference between technopreneurship and entrepreneurship is that Technopreneurship is either involved in delivering an innovative hi-tech product (e.g. Microsoft) or making use of hi-tech in an innovative way to deliver its product to the consumer (e.g. eBay), or both (e.g. most pharmaceutical companies) while entrepreneurship is not mainly technology-centered. (Fowosire et al., 2017). Technopreneurs have a protagonist role in promoting and creating new information and communication technologies (ICTs) goods and services for the local and global markets to satisfy the customer demand in the digital economy (Soomro & Shah, 2020; Bhat & Gulzar, 2020). Soomro and Shah, (2020, p 502) defined a technopreneur as “a new age entrepreneur who utilizes the technology to produce or make something unique or to create innovations”. They contribute to economic growth by creating employment and the technology used aids them to gain a competitive advantage (Mefteh et al., 2015; Yeganegi et al., 2021). However, there are some disadvantages they experience including the government policy, human capacity, development, lack of facilities, and lack of a standard for confirmation, capital, market, and energy (Fowosire et al., 2017).

Extant literature exists on Technopreneurship. Majority of these studies have examined factors influencing Technopreneurship development (Nikraftar, Hosseini & Mohammadi 2022), technopreneurship capabilities (Petti & Zhang, 2011), technopreneurship impact on economic development (Huggins et al., 2015; Soekarno & Setiawati, 2020), impact on consumer (Bhardwaj, 2021) and technopreneurship intention through academic education (Salhieh & Al-Abdallat, 2022). For instance, Nikraftar et al., (2022) found that organizational, environmental, institutional, individual, and technology factors influence technopreneurship intention. Most of the authors also consider the Technopreneurship phenomenon in the context of stable developed economies (Amante & Ronquillo, 2017) while the specifics of technopreneurship in developing economies are still under-represented (Simuka & Masunda, 2023). There is therefore limited research on the growth prospects and barriers for women technopreneurs in a developing economy context. To bridge this gap in the literature, this research aims to understand the growth prospects and barriers for women technopreneurs in a developing country. The study employs a conceptual framework with constructs from TOE (Regulatory environment), dynamic capability theory (Technopreneurship Capabilities), Entrepreneurial Culture, Staged Financing, and Business Support Mechanisms from literature. The research questions are *(1) What is the nature of women's Technopreneurship landscape in Ghana? (2) What are the barriers faced by women technopreneurs in Ghana? and (3) What are the factors that shape the growth of women technopreneurs in Ghana?*

The outline of the paper is as follows: section 2 presents the literature review and hypothesis development, section 3 presents the research methodology, section 4 presents the data analysis and results, section 5 presents the discussion and finally, section 6 presents the conclusion and future research directions.

LITERATURE REVIEW

Technopreneurship

Technopreneurship was coined from technology and entrepreneurship. Technopreneurship is concerned with the transformation of theoretically feasible technological ideas and knowledge into prosperous ventures (Singhry, 2015). Therin (2007) argued that Technological entrepreneurship could be used as technology entrepreneurship, technical entrepreneurship, and techno-entrepreneurship and hence have received much attention in the literature (Nikraftar et al., 2022). Technopreneurship is not a commodity that can be easily traded but it's a composition of a group of skills, scientific expertise, and intelligence possessed by an individual or several individuals which represents the first building blocks of the digital society, smart cities, and space technology (Abbas, 2018). It requires a high level of intelligence and expertise, and it provides sophisticated programs to create strategic thinkers with the required skills to achieve success in a competitive dynamic environment. In the concept of technopreneurship, development starts from innovation in the field of technology and is not just focused on high-tech but also on the application of knowledge to the work of the (human work) such as the application of accounting, economic order quantity, online and offline marketing (Hariyono & Andrini, 2020).

Technopreneurship is an innovative application of science and technical knowledge by a person or a group of people who create and lead a business (Rafiana, 2024). It is a combination of technology and commercial enterprise, which represents the future engineering of the individual, organization, nation, and science (Musa et al., 2017). The following subsection presents the hypothesis development of this research to examine the factors that influence women's Technopreneurship growth.

HYPOTHESIS DEVELOPMENT

Entrepreneurial Culture

Fritsch and Wyrwich (2016, p. 1–2) define entrepreneurial culture as "a culture of entrepreneurship can be understood as norms, values, and codes of conduct that promote social acceptance and approval of entrepreneurial activities resulting in high self-employment rates which persist over time." Entrepreneurial culture encompasses the mental, physical, intellectual, and emotional characteristics of a group of entrepreneurs, including lifestyle, values, traditions, and beliefs (Nguyen, 2016). Buccieri et al. (2021) found that entrepreneurial culture positively influences firm performance in international new ventures. Similarly, Hassan et al. (2021) highlighted the significant role of empowerment in cultivating entrepreneurial culture, and Khadhraoui et al. (2016) identified positive correlations between entrepreneurial culture dimensions and entrepreneurial intention. A favorable regulatory environment can influence how entrepreneurial culture drives technopreneurship growth by providing supportive legal frameworks, reducing bureaucratic barriers, and encouraging innovation. When the regulatory environment is conducive, entrepreneurial norms and values are more likely to translate into sustainable growth. Therefore, the following hypotheses are proposed:

H1: Entrepreneurial culture has a significant influence on women technopreneurship growth.
H1a: The regulatory environment moderates the relationship between entrepreneurial culture and women technopreneurship growth.

Technopreneurship Capabilities

Technological capabilities are critical for firm performance, growth, innovation, and competitive advantage. These capabilities emanate from the structural component of dynamic capability theory (Lamin & Dunlap, 2011). Zahra (2022) defines technopreneurship capabilities as the ability of entrepreneurs to recognize, create, and exploit opportunities using technology. Individuals with strong technological capabilities can generate more value from technology investments and achieve higher collaborative gains (Garcia, Avella, & Farnandez, 2012). However, entities without sufficient IT expertise may face challenges in adopting and leveraging new technologies (Singhry, 2015). The regulatory environment can amplify or hinder the effectiveness of technopreneurship capabilities by shaping technology adoption policies, intellectual property rights, and compliance requirements. A supportive regulatory environment may enhance the ability of technopreneurs to leverage their capabilities effectively. Hence, the following hypotheses are postulated:

H2: Technopreneurship capabilities have a significant influence on women technopreneurship growth.
H2a: The regulatory environment moderates the relationship between technopreneurship capabilities and women technopreneurship growth.,

Staged Financing

Financing is a fundamental building block for all businesses, including technopreneurs. Sources of financing are broadly categorized into personal (e.g., self-financing) and external sources (e.g., bank loans, angel investors, and venture capital) (Gartner et al., 2011). Cowling et al. (2012) found that women-led firms generally have lower demand for external finance, which persists during recessionary periods. Additionally, Gartner et al. (2011)

noted that nascent entrepreneurs with greater net worth and resources are more likely to secure external funding. Manolova et al. (2007) suggested that women could enhance access to financing by forming networks with financial institutions, government agencies, and trade associations. The regulatory environment plays a critical role in access to financing, as favorable policies, tax incentives, and reduced bureaucratic barriers can encourage financial institutions and investors to support technopreneurs. In restrictive regulatory settings, however, financing may become a significant hurdle. Based on these arguments, the authors of this research hypothesized that:

> **H3**: Staged financing has a significant influence on women technopreneurship growth.
> **H3a**: The regulatory environment moderates the relationship between staged financing and women technopreneurship growth.

Business Support Mechanisms

Business support mechanisms for technopreneurs include government programs (Baumol, 2014), business incubators (Ratinho et al., 2020; Jamil et al., 2016), and accelerators (Lange & Johnston, 2020). These mechanisms provide resources such as access to funding, management consulting, and support for business development. Informal support, including assistance from family and friends, has been linked to entrepreneurial wellbeing (Rogers, 2005). Ratinho et al. (2020) found that the survival of incubated firms depends on the fit between resources provided and the incubator's location. Nwankwo et al. (2010) highlighted the inadequacies of public business support programs, emphasizing the need for tailored interventions. A favourable regulatory environment can enhance the effectiveness of business support mechanisms by providing clear policies, streamlined processes, and incentives for business support organizations. Conversely, regulatory bottlenecks can diminish the impact of such mechanisms. Therefore, the following hypotheses are proposed:

> **H4**: Business support mechanisms have a significant influence on women technopreneurship growth.

H4a: The regulatory environment moderates the relationship between business support mechanisms and women technopreneurship growth.

Figure 1. Conceptual framework

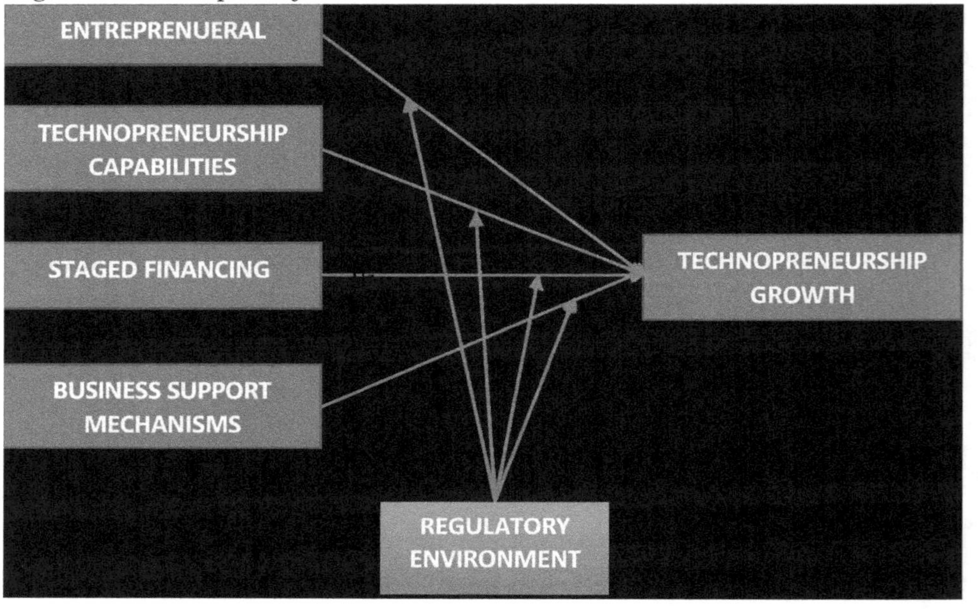

The model below (Table 1) explains the growth stages of technopreneurs, the types of technologies they use, their entrepreneurial capabilities and the forms of barriers they face.

Table 1. Technopreneurship model

STAGES	TYPE OF TECHNOPRENEUR	CAPABILITIES	TECHNOLOGIES and EXAMPLES	
Idea Development	**Ground-breaker (Idea generation)**	**Internet Research, E-learning, Self-Learning**	**Wiki, Tech News Platforms, Self-learning Platforms, Social Media (e.g. Udemy, LinkedIn Learning, YouTube, Coursera.)**	
Start-up	**Business Model Developer (Idea Refinement)**	**Incubation, Acceleration, Funding, Mentorship**	**Website, Social Media, Email Client (e.g. Gmail, Facebook, YouTube, Personal Website, etc.)**	
Growth Stage	**Executor (Model Activation)**	**Teamwork, Networking, Marketing**	**Website, Social Media, Email Client, Video Conferencing. (e.g. Zoom, Facebook, Twitter, Gmail, etc.)**	
Expansion / Scale	**Innovator (Integrate New Technologies)**	**Partnership, Networking, Marketing (Local)**	**Website, Social Media, Email Client, e-CRM, e-SCM, Video Conferencing, e-Procurement (e.g. Zoom, Facebook, Twitter, Gmail, etc.)**	
Maturity Stage	**Global Player (Global Brand & Reach)**	**Partnership, Networking, Marketing (Foreign)**	**Website, Social Media, Email Client, e-CRM, e-SCM, Video Conferencing, e-Procurement, ERP (e.g. Zoom, Facebook, Twitter, Gmail, SAP ERP, etc.)**	
WOMEN TECHNOPRENEURSHIP BARRIERS/DETERMINANTS				
Technopreneural Capabilities	**Access to Finance**	**Market Conditions**	**Regulatory Framework**	**Culture**
Internet Usage	Access to Equity (Venture Capital, Angel Investor etc.)	Competition	Legal Entry & Growth Burden	Societal Ownership Mindset
Communication Skills	Access to Debt Financing	Access to Local Market	Product and Service Regulation	Normative Pressure
Marketing Skills	Incubators and Accelerators	Access to Foreign Market	Taxes (Income, Capital, Business)	Trust Dimensions

RESEARCH METHODOLOGY

This study adopts a quantitative research method, specifically a survey. A survey gives a quantitative description of the opinions of a population by studying a sample of that population (Creswell, 2009). According to Creswell (2009), a survey provides a numeric description of trends, or opinions of a population by studying a sample of the population. This study adopted a non-probability sampling technique, specifically purposive sampling in the administration of the questionnaire. The purposive sampling technique, also known as judgment sampling, is "the deliberate choice of an informant due to the qualities the informant possesses" (Tongco, 2007). A survey questionnaire was employed to acquire the response from the chosen participants. However, the items of the survey questionnaire were adopted from the literature. To confirm the questionnaire in our study's context, a pilot survey was conducted to gain the response from 5 respondents. An online survey was created via Google forms using closed-ended questions from May 2022 to June 2022. Female technopreneurs in Ghana and Nigeria were given a link to the online survey; they subsequently shared the links with their respective colleagues to complete the survey. A total of 60 responses were received.

Data Analysis

The study used descriptive statistics using graphs and tables to investigate the nature of women's technopreneurship landscape in a developing economy. To achieve sample adequacy, the tenets of PLS-SEM were adhered to. SEM is a multivariate data analysis technique that has been widely adopted by IS research for construct validation and testing causal relationships between constructs (Gefen et al., 2000). Unlike covariance-based structural equation modeling (CB-SEM), PLS-SEM is a SEM approach with no assumptions about data distribution (Vinzi et al., 2010). PLS-SEM is useful in research projects where there are limited respondents, and data distribution is skewed (Wong, 2011). As recommended by Hair, Ringle, & Sarstedt, Hair, Ringle, & Sarstedt, (2011), the minimum sample size required to carry out this study was 60 based on the 10 times rule on the constructs with the maximum number of indicators (i.e., 10*6). In addition, the researcher adopted PLS-SEM because the objective of the study is to examine the causal relationship between dependent constructs and the independent constructs using the effect size and predictive relevance which is not offered by using CBSEM (Astrachan et al., 2014). The first step in PLS-SEM requires examination of the measurement models. "Model estimation delivers empirical measures of the relationships between the indicators and the constructs (measurement models) as well as between the constructs (structural model)" (Hair et al., 2016, p. 105). Essentially, the measurement model's assessment helps the researcher compare the theory adopted for the study with the real data collected.

In this study, indicator reliability, internal consistency, convergent validity, and discriminatory validity were assessed by ensuring that the standard decision rules are applied (Hair et al., 2019). After the measurement model was validated, the researchers further assessed the structural model (Hair et al., 2019; Urbach & Ahlemann, 2010). The following five essential steps were followed to assess the structural model, as suggested by Hair et al. (2019), and Urbach and Ahlemann (2010). These are assessment of the structural model for collinearity issues, an assessment of the significance and relevance of structural model relationships, an assessment of the goodness of fit (GOF), an assessment of the effect size (f-square), and an assessment of the predictive relevance (q-square). After the assessment of the measurement and structural model was completed, a multi-group analysis was performed to examine the effect of the moderating variables on the relationship between independent constructs and dependent constructs.

DATA ANALYSIS AND RESULTS

Demographic Characteristics of Technopreneurship Firms

This section discusses the demographic profile of the sampled technopreneurship firms used in the study. They have been profiled according to their; country of origin, year of establishment, educational qualification of founders, legal ownership type, founders and employees, and technological factors among others. This information is described below.

Figure 2. Technopreneurship distribution by year of formation

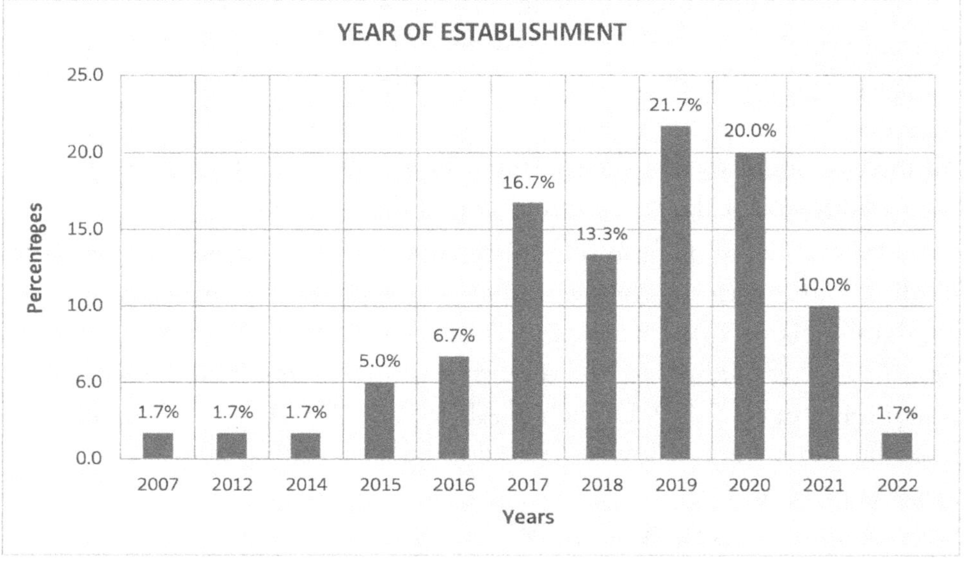

From Figure 2 above, out of the 60 technopreneurship firms studied, 21.7% were established in 2019, 20.0% in 2020, 16.7% were established in 2017, 13.3% in 2018, 10.0% each in 2021, 6.7% in 2016, 5.0% in 2015 and 1.7% for 2007, 2012, 2014 and 2022.

Figure 3. Technopreneurship firms distribution by country of origin

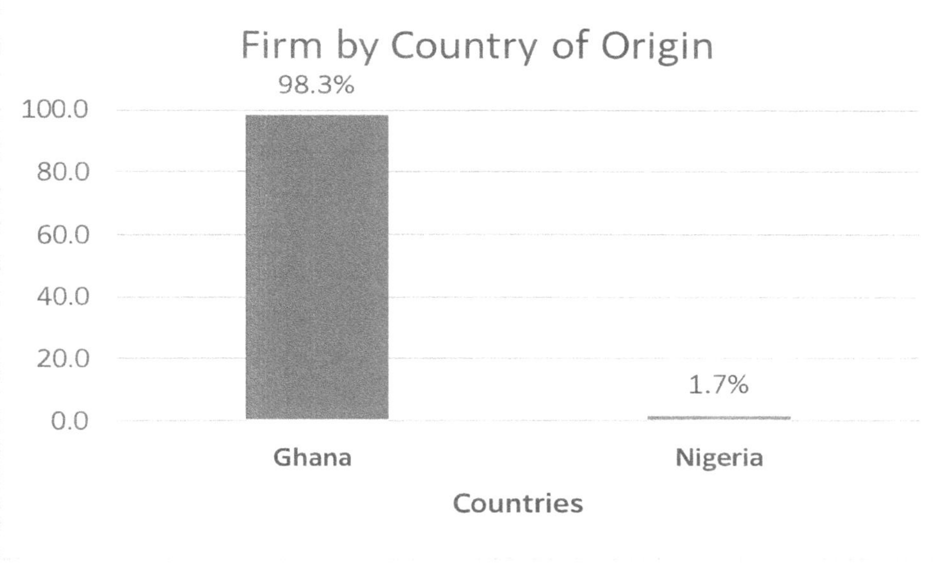

The technopreneurship firms used in this study originate from Ghana and Nigeria. Most of the firms representing 98.3% originate from Ghana whilst 1.7% have Nigeria as their country of origin. This result is illustrated in Figure 3.

Table 2. Distribution per no. of founders, age & education of founders, and no. of employees

Firm Demographic	Characteristics	Frequency	%
	One	14	23.3
No. of Founders	Two	21	35.0
	Three to Five	25	41.7
	Total	60	100
Founders Age	Under 25	14	23.3
	26-35	38	63.3
	36-45	16	26.7
	Above 45	1	1.7

continued on following page

Table 2. Continued

Firm Demographic	Characteristics	Frequency	%
	Total	60	100
Founder(s') Education	Vocational/High School	6	10
	Diploma	10	16.7
	First Degree	40	66.7
	Master's Degree	21	35
	Doctoral Degree	2	3.3
	Total	60	100
No. of Employees	Under 10	44	73.3
	10-20	13	21.7
	21-40	3	5.0
	Above 40	0	0.0
	Total	60	100

Concerning the number of founders, the results in Table 2 indicate that most of the women technopreneurship firms had founders within the range of 3 - 5 representing (41.7%) followed by those with two (2) founders (35%). Firms with individual or single female founders were 23.3%. There were none with founders beyond 5.

From Table 2, the age of the founders at the time of this study was accessed. From the results, the dominant age range is 26-35 representing 63.3%. The next age bracket is 26 -35 representing 26.7%, followed by those under 25years (23.3%). Only 1 firm had a founder above 45years (1.7)

On the issue of the educational qualification of Founders, 66.7% representing the majority have a First degree. Next are those with a master's degree (35%), followed by diploma holders (16.7%). Those with vocational or secondary level educational qualifications make up 10% of the founders. The minority in this classification is Doctoral degree holders who represent 3.3%.

Also, the number of employees in these firms was assessed. 73.3% had employees under 10, 21.7% had employed from 10 to 20 workers, and 5% employed 21 to 40 workers. None of the technopreneurship firms assessed had above 40 employees

Figure 4. Legal ownership type

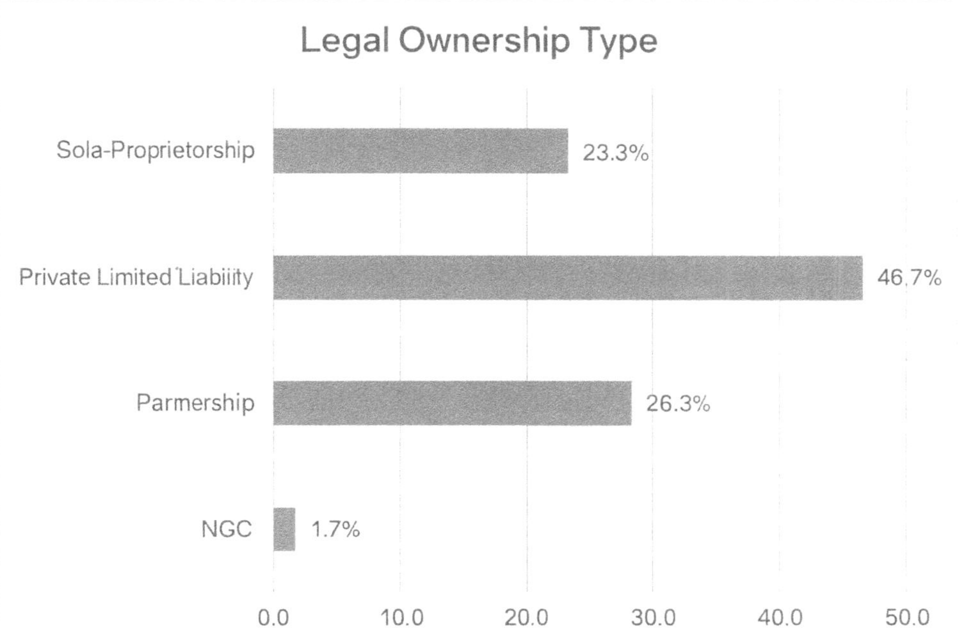

Figure 4 also indicates the type of ownership over the technopreneurship under study. Private Limited Liability recorded the highest (46.7%) concerning firm ownership. Followed by Partnership (28.3%), Sole proprietorship (23.3%), and lastly NGO (1.7%).

Table 3. Distribution per industry or primary business activity

Industry	**Frequency**	%
E-commerce & Digital Marketing	12	20.0
Education	3	5.0
Fashion	5	8.3
Financial Services	4	6.7
Health Care, Food and Social Welfare	6	10.0
IT and Technical Services	22	36.7
Tourism & Transportation	6	10.0

continued on following page

Table 3. Continued

Industry	Frequency	%
Others	2	3.3
Total	**60**	**100**

In assessing the industry or primary business of the technopreneurship firms, 36.7% are into IT and Technical Services, followed by 20% that are into eCommerce and Digital Marketing. Health Care, Food and Social Welfare, as well as Tourism & Transportation firms, formed 10% each. Next is the fashion industry representing (8.3%). 6.7% of the firms were in the Financial Services industry and 5% operated within the educational sector. About 3.3% belonged to other industries. Results are presented in Table 3.

Assessment of Measurement Model

The reliability indicator, as depicted in the loading, shows the strength of the indicators used to measure or represent latent variables. To ensure indicator reliability, indicator loadings should be at least 0.708 (Hair et al., 2019). All indicator loadings scored the minimum of 0.708 as depicted in Figure 2 below and thus indicate indicator reliability. Composite Reliability was used to determine internal consistency reliability. Researchers (Hair et al., 2019; Joreskog, 1971) suggest measuring internal consistency reliability using composite reliability instead of Cronbach's Alpha because Cronbach's Alpha tends to undervalue the reliability scale. Composite reliability values should be at least 0.70 to indicate sufficient internal consistency reliability. Composite reliability values presented in Table 4 below indicate adequate internal consistency reliability in our model. The Average Variance Extracted (AVE) is a method for determining convergent validity. AVE values should be at least 0.50 (Chin, 1998). AVE values presented in Table 4 below show a minimum value of 0.758, indicating sufficient convergent validity in our model.

Table 4. Reliability and validity

	Cronbach's Alpha	Composite reliability (rho_a)	Composite reliability (rho_c)	Average Variance Extracted (AVE)
Business Support Mechanism	0.746	0.748	0.887	0.798
Entrepreneurial Culture	0.864	0.909	0.916	0.785
Regulatory Support	0.794	1.002	0.900	0.818
Staged Financing	0.842	0.870	0.904	0.758
Techno Capabilities	0.921	0.929	0.944	0.810
Technopreneurship _Growth	0.921	0.937	0.942	0.766

We assessed discriminant validity using the Heterotriat-Monotrait ratio of correlations (HTMT). Henseler, Ringle, and Sarstedt (2015) recommend the use of HTMT in assessing discriminant validity because other methods for evaluating discriminant validity such as the Fornell – Larcker criterion underperforms in cases when indicator loadings differ slightly. As a rule of thumb, HTMT values should not exceed 0.90, to ensure discriminant validity. HTMT values presented in Table 5 below depict discriminant validity in our model. The fulfillment of the indicator reliability, internal consistency reliability, convergent validity, and discriminant validity requirements paves the way for the evaluation of the structural model.

Table 5. Heterotrait-Monotrait ratio (HTMT)

	Business Support Mechanism	Entrepreneurial_ Culture	Regulatory Support	Staged Financing	Techno Capabilities	Technopreneurship _Growth
Business Support Mechanism	0.893					
Entrepreneurial_ Culture	0.245	0.886				
Regulatory Support	0.397	0.187	0.904			
Staged Financing	0.394	0.246	0.160	0.871		
Techno Capabilities	0.307	0.794	0.195	0.190	0.900	
Technopreneurship _Growth	0.489	0.585	0.346	0.422	0.598	0.875

Assessment of Structural Model

The results of the structural model assessment provide significant insights into the relationships between the constructs (Hair et al., 2019). The coefficient of determination (**R2**) indicates that the exogenous constructs—Business Support Mechanisms, Entrepreneurial Culture, Regulatory Environment, Staged Financing, and Technopreneurship Capabilities—explain 61.5% of the variance in Technopreneurship Growth. This highlights the substantial predictive power of the model. Among the direct relationships as indicated in Table 6, Technopreneurship Capabilities emerged as the strongest predictor of Technopreneurship Growth with a path coefficient of 0.454 ($t = 5.206$, $p < 0.001$). Business Support Mechanisms (0.222, $t = 4.500$, $p < 0.001$), Staged Financing (0.188, $t = 4.252$, $p < 0.001$), and Entrepreneurial Culture (0.162, $t = 2.012$, $p < 0.05$) also demonstrated significant positive effects.

Figure 5. Reflective loadings

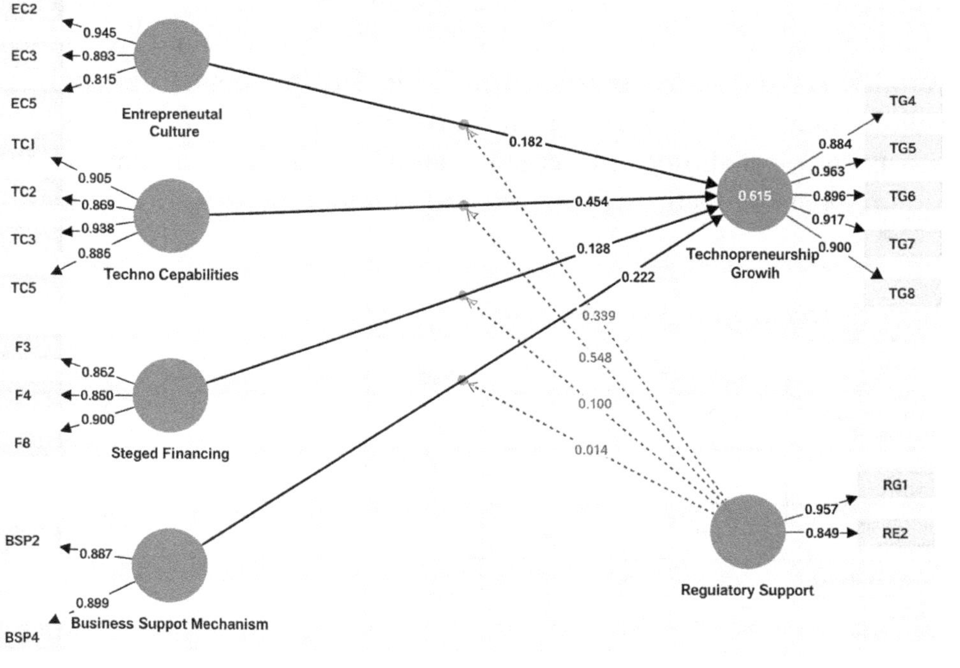

Table 6. Hypothesis testing results

	Hypothesized Path	Path Coefficient	T statistics (|O/STDEV|)	P values	Results
H1	Business Support Mechanism -> Technopreneurship _Growth	0.222	4.500	0.000	Supported
H2	Entrepreneurial_ Culture -> Technopreneurship _Growth	0.162	2.012	0.044	Supported
H3	Staged Financing -> Technopreneurship _Growth	0.188	4.252	0.000	Supported
H4	Techno Capabilities -> Technopreneurship _Growth	0.454	5.206	0.000	Supported
H1a	Regulatory Support x Business Support Mechanism -> Technopreneurship Growth	0.014	0.503	0.615	Not Supported
H2a	Regulatory Support x Staged Financing -> Technopreneurship Growth	-0.100	2.523	0.012	Supported
H3a	Regulatory Support x Techno Capabilities -> Technopreneurship Growth	0.548	5.798	0.000	Supported
H4a	Regulatory Support x Entrepreneurial_ Culture -> Technopreneurship Growth	-0.389	4.086	0.000	Supported
	R2 (Technopreneurship Growth) = 61.5%				

The moderating effects of the regulatory environment reveal nuanced interactions between the predictors and Technopreneurship Growth. Regulatory Support significantly moderates the relationships between Technopreneurship Capabilities (0.548, $t = 5.798$, $p < 0.001$), Entrepreneurial Culture (-0.389, $t = 4.086$, $p < 0.001$), and Staged Financing (-0.100, $t = 2.523$, $p < 0.05$) on Technopreneurship Growth. The positive moderating effect on Technopreneurship Capabilities indicates that a favorable regulatory environment enhances the ability of technopreneurs to leverage their capabilities for growth. Conversely, the negative interaction with Entrepreneurial Culture suggests that restrictive regulatory conditions may dampen the positive impact of cultural entrepreneurial norms. Similarly, the negative moderation of Staged Financing highlights potential regulatory barriers that could limit access to or the effectiveness of financial support. Notably, the regulatory environment did not significantly moderate the relationship between Business Support Mechanisms and Technopreneurship Growth ($p = 0.615$), suggesting that the influence of these mechanisms may be relatively independent of regulatory conditions. These results emphasize the critical role of regulatory policies in shaping the effectiveness of key determinants of technopreneurship growth.

Figure 6. **Model path coefficients**

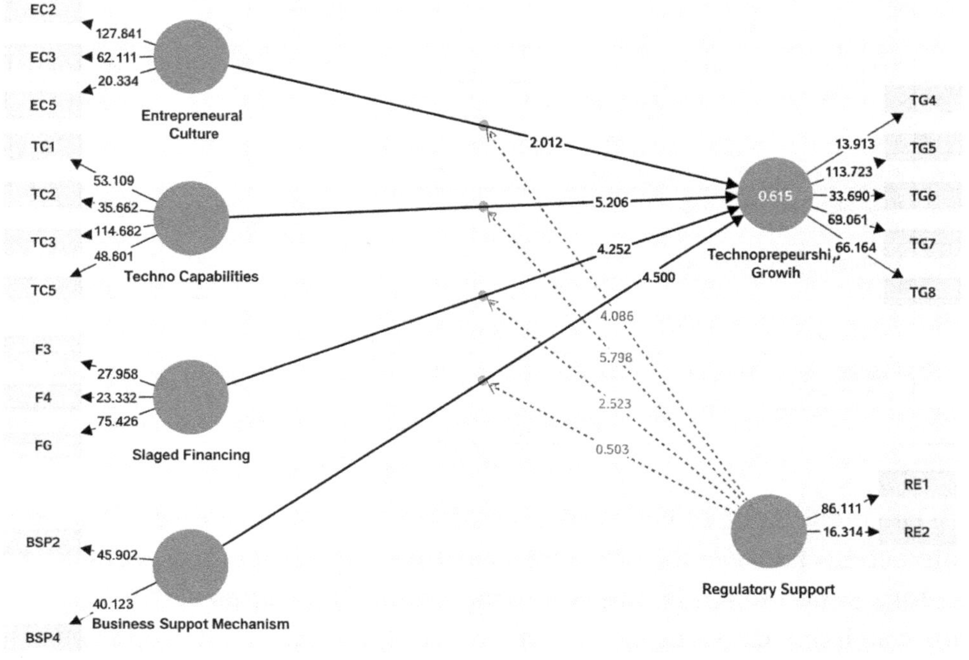

DISCUSSION

Nature of Women Technopreneurship landscape in Ghana?

The first research question sought to understand the nature of the women's technopreneurship landscape in Ghana. To that end, the technopreneurship firms sampled were classified according to their business incentive, growth stages, IT innovations utilized, and funding sources.

Women Technopreneurs Business Incentive

Technopreneurship firms are birthed based on different motivations. York, O'Neil, and Sarasvathy, (2016) postulated that environmental entrepreneurs are motivated by identities based on both commercial and ecological logic. Indeed, the core drive for a business or its primary incentives "can be expected to influence the competitive dynamics between entrants and incumbents" (Berglund & Sandström, 2017, p. 145). The findings revealed that most women technopreneurs are motivated by the need to improve their financial status (50.0%). This next incentive is related to idea exploration (43.3%), followed by Market Gap recognition (38.3%). The least incentive was to impact lives (1.7%). The predominance of economic motivation is reflected in the assertion by Xheneti, Madden, & Thapa Karki, (2019) that women must be considered as rational actors with a capacity to respond freely to economic incentives. Figure 7 presents a chart on Women Technopreneurs Business Incentive.

Figure 7. Women technopreneurs business incentive

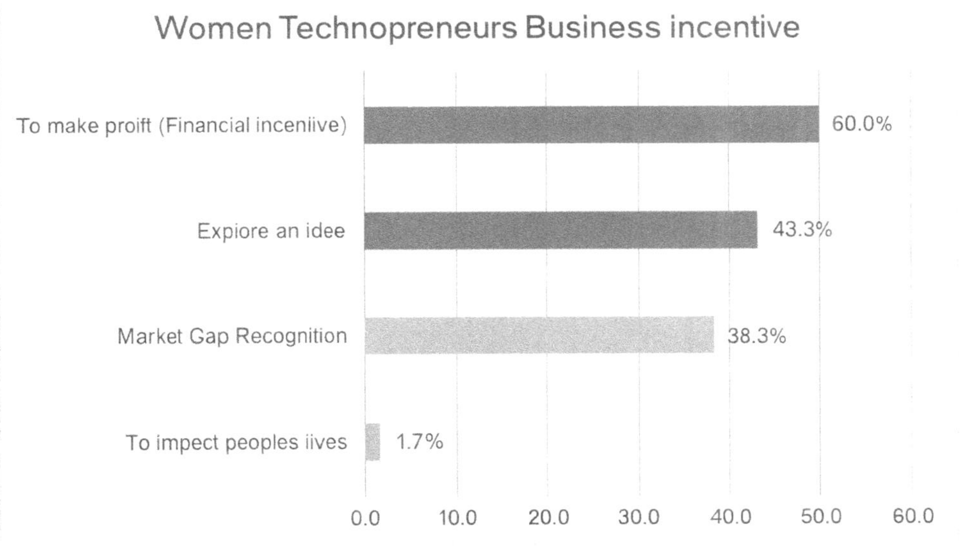

IT Innovations Utilized by Women Technopreneurship Firms

The potential for emerging technopreneur businesses has been expanded substantially by new-generation technologies that are expanding the frontiers for their rapid growth. This research focused on four key technologies that are accelerating the growth of women's technopreneur businesses namely social media, cloud computing, data analytics, and enterprise applications. Figure 8 illustrated the results of the women technopreneurship firm with regards to the technologies utilized in their business operations. The results show that all the technopreneurship firms (100%) studied are leveraging social media channels perhaps for marketing, promotions, and customer engagement. Again, 58.2 percent of the firms sampled use cloud computing services, followed by the least utilized technology, data analytics tools representing 23.5%.

Figure 8. Technology utilized by women-led technopreneurship firms

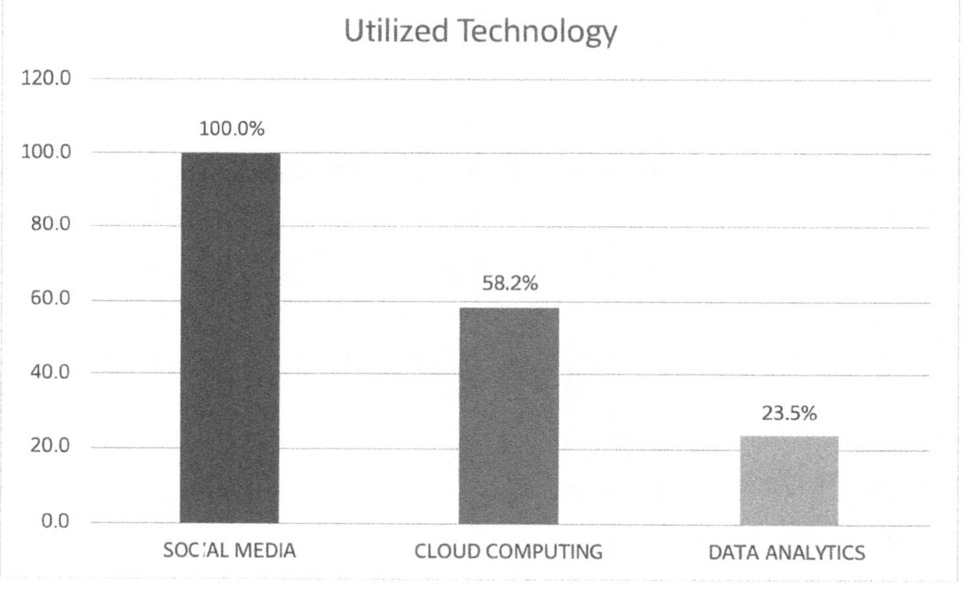

In a social media mapping study, Nascimento and da-Silveira (2016) discovered that social media is used for customer engagement, business promotion, and product or service assessment. Some social media channels leveraged used by the technopreneurship firms include Facebook, Twitter, LinkedIn, Instagram, and TikTok. Yamin (2013) affirms that cloud computing gives new businesses with little money the chance to get access to data storage, software, infrastructure, and services. Technopreneurship firms in developing economies are increasingly leveraging cloud services because they offer businesses scalable and agile infrastructure at affordable prices (Allan, 2012).

The findings show that Data analytics was the least (23.5%) used technological innovation among women-led technopreneurship firms in Ghana. Big Data technologies aren't used as much in developing economies. This could be because they don't have as much experience with data mining to deal with the volume, variety, and speed of data. Park, Chung, Zhao, & Supakkul, (2017, p.1), in their study, identified that the "biggest challenges for transforming hidden insights into business value lie in the fact that data analytics is not aligned with business goals. Also, there is a lack of business context around the data and a lack of expertise to connect the dots." This finding also backs up a study by Villars et al. (2011), who found that businesses can't do good data analysis without a lot of computing power because the process is usually slow and hard.

Growth Stages of Women Technopreneurship Firms in Ghana

The results show that the firms sampled identified with different growth stages. Figure 9 indicates that the majority of the technopreneurship firms sampled are at the technopreneurship firm stage, representing 41.7% of the sample. This is the stage where firms have refined their business model with a potentially scalable idea for a product or service targeting a market that is poised to generate value. The growth stage ranked second among the firms representing 30%, followed by the expansion stage (11.7%). Next is the maturity stage (10%) and finally the idea development stage (6.7%).

Figure 9. Technopreneurship growth stages

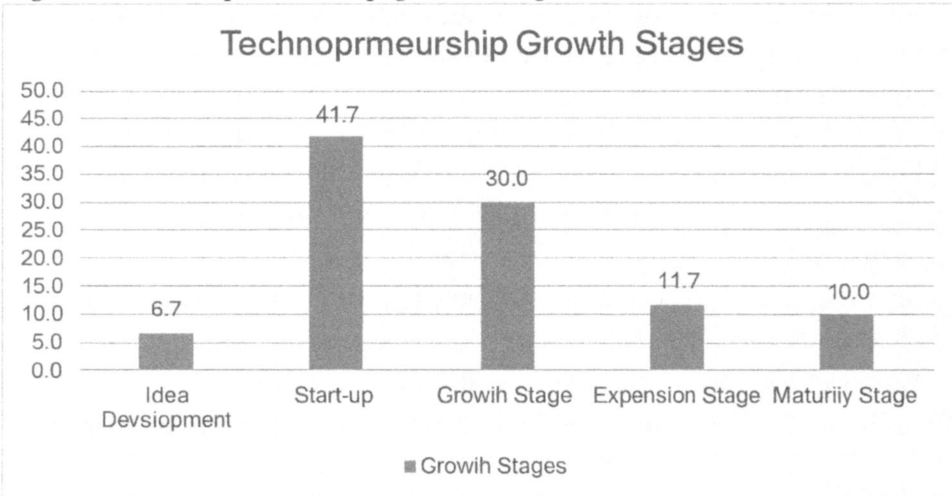

Table 7. Cross-tabulation of technopreneurship growth stages and funding

		Firm Funding Sources						
		Self-Funding	**Family & Friends**	**Angel Investor**	**Venture Capitalist**	**Bank Loan**	**Government Scheme**	**Total**
Firm Growth Stage	**Idea Development N=4**	**6.7%**; 4	**5.0%**; 3	**1.7%**; 1	**0%**; 0	**0%**; 0	**0%**; 0	**13.3%**; 8
	Start-up N=25	**35.0%**; 21	**23.3%**; 14	**5.0%**; 3	**11.7%**; 7	**3.3.0%**; 3	**0%**; 0	**73.3%**; 44
	Growth Stage N=18	**20.0%**; 12	**15.0%**; 9	**6.7%**; 4	**23.3%**; 14	**10.0%**; 6	**0%**; 0	**66.7%**; 40
	Expansion / Scale N=7	**8.3%**; 5	**5.0%**; 3	**8.3%**; 5	**10.0%**; 6	**3.3%**; 2	**0%**; 0	**33.3%**; 20
	Maturity Stage N=6	**3.3%**; 2	**1.7%**; 1	**5.0%**; 3	**8.3%**; 5	**5.0%**; 3	**0%**; 0	**23.3%**; 14
	Total	**73.3%**; 44	**50.0%**; 30	**26.7%**,16	**53.3%**; 32	**21.7%**; 13	**0%**; 0	**NA**

In exploring the nature of technopreneurship firms in Ghana, Table 7 presents a cross-tabulation of technopreneurship growth stages, and the sources of financing utilized at each stage. Before discussing the stages as juxtaposed against the funding sources, Table 7 shows that the sources of funding for the samples firms in descending order are self-financing (73.3%), Venture Capital (53.3%), Family and Friends (50%), Angel investors (26.7%) and Bank Loan (21.7%). None of the firm's samples are beneficiaries of crowd-funding and government funding sources.

At the ideation stage, technopreneurs mainly rely on self-funding (6.7%) as well as family and friends (5.0%). The ideation stage is critical to subsequent stages. This is the stage where the technopreneur brainstorms for that innovative, market viable, and scalable product or service. However, very few can attract some angel investment at this stage with the majority relying on either bootstrapping or family and friends. Overall, 4 out of 60 firms classified themselves as being in the idea development stage.

Funding dynamics for technopreneurship firms at the start-up stage are still dominated by bootstrapping (self-funding-35%) and social circles (family and friends-23.3%). Few technopreneurship firms can secure funding from sources such as Venter Capitalist (11.7%), Angel Investors (5%), and Bank Loan (3.3%). It appears that women technopreneurs have some challenges with access to external sources of financing, especially at the start-up stage. Businesses are established with personal funds and funds borrowed from their family or friends. Overall, 25 out of 60 firms classified themselves as being in the startup stage.

Table 7, the growth stage, is the point where the firm has begun a rapid execution of its business model and generating a consistent income stream. It is at this stage that they begin to attract more external sources of funding from venture capitalists (23.3%), bank loans (10%), and angel investors (6.7%). It is important to point out that some technopreneurship firms still depend on self-funding (20.0%) as well as family and friends (15.0%) even at the growth stage. This implies that external funding of technopreneurship firms is more likely when investors come to the understanding that the firm has a great product or service with the potential to scale. Due to the rate of failure of technopreneurship firms, many investors remain skeptical until they can see positive indicators for a good return on investment (Sun, Chen, Sunny, & Chen, 2019). Overall, 18 out of 60 firms classified themselves as being in the growth stage. With a total of 7 out of 60 firms at the expansion stage, a majority have received funding from venture capitalists (10.0%), followed by angel investors and self-funding (both 8.3%). Next is Family and friends (5.0%) before bank loans (3.3%).

Finally, very few technopreneurship firms classified themselves to be at the Maturity stage. Firms at this stage gain easier access to more external sources such as venture capitalists (8.3%), followed by Angel investors and Banks Loan (both 5.0%). Even at this stage some firms still relied on self-funding (3.3) as well as family and friends (1.7%).

Barriers Faced by Women Technopreneurs in Ghana?

Women technopreneurs are confronted with several socio-economic barriers which form part of the main purpose of those studies. Figure 10 indicated that out of the 60 women-led technopreneurship firms sampled 55% identified taxation barriers as the leading barrier to their growth and development, followed by Access to Funding (50%) and then Bureaucratic Barriers (45%). The next barriers in descending order are Access to Foreign Markets (38.3%), Wining customer Trust and Access to support programs (Both 36.7%), Cultural Biases and Access to Local Market (Both 18.3%), IT skill Development (16.7%) and finding qualified staff (13.3%). On the issue of barriers faced by women in technopreneurship, it is evident that Taxation, Funding, and Bureaucratic processes remain dominant buttressing the need for revised Tax structures for emerging technopreneurship firms as well as the creation of an enabling environment for firms to access funding devoid of needless bureaucratic and legal barriers.

Figure 10. Women technopreneurship growth barriers

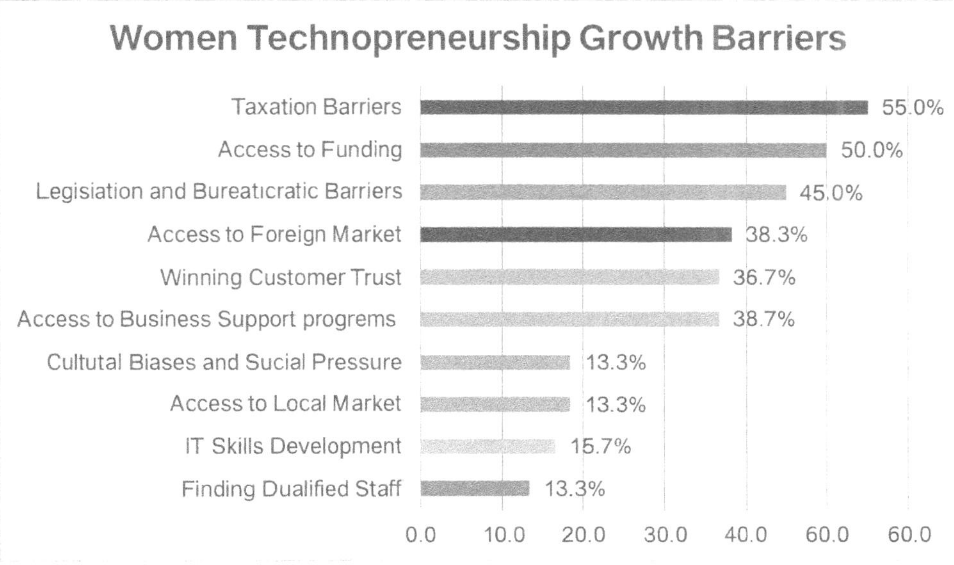

Factors That Shape the Growth of Women Technopreneurs in Ghana?

This study explored the factors influencing the growth of women technopreneurs in Ghana and developed a conceptual model grounded in technopreneurship literature. Five hypotheses were tested, focusing on Entrepreneurial Culture, Technopreneurship Capabilities, Staged Financing, Business Support Mechanisms, and the moderating role of the Regulatory Environment. The findings provide nuanced insights into the relationships between these constructions and Technopreneurship Growth.

Entrepreneurial Culture was positively associated with Technopreneurship Growth, confirming its role as a critical success factor. The results indicate that entrepreneurial values, norms, and behaviors significantly influence the ability of technopreneurs to achieve substantial growth. This aligns with prior studies (Buccieri et al., 2021; Hassan et al., 2021; Khadhraoui et al., 2016), which highlight the importance of fostering an entrepreneurial mindset to drive business performance. The findings emphasize that cultivating entrepreneurial culture can provide women technopreneurs with the resilience and strategic orientation needed to navigate competitive markets in Ghana.

Technopreneurship Capabilities, defined as the ability to develop and leverage technical know-how, also significantly influenced growth. This suggests that women technopreneurs with the skills to identify, develop, and exploit opportunities are better positioned for sustained success. The results resonate with the literature (Lockett et al., 2015; Vu, 2020), which underscores the centrality of technological expertise and strategic adaptability to technopreneurship success. These capabilities empower women technopreneurs to innovate and respond effectively to changing market dynamics.

Staged Financing was another significant factor, emphasizing the importance of access to sustainable financial resources for technopreneurs. The study found that women technopreneurs in Ghana often rely on self-financing and support from family and friends during the early stages of their ventures, with limited access to external funding. This finding aligns with prior research (Denis & McKeon, 2021; Panda & Gopalaswamy, 2020), which highlights the critical role of financing in the survival and growth of businesses. Success stories like Jetstream and BezoMoney demonstrate the transformative potential of securing equity funding for scaling operations and bridging market gaps.

Business Support Mechanisms were found to play a pivotal role in promoting Technopreneurship Growth. These mechanisms—such as incubators, accelerators, and government support programs—provide essential resources, mentorship, and networking opportunities. The findings align with Masenya (2019) and Jamil et al. (2016), who highlight the importance of structured support systems in creating an enabling environment for business growth. Programs that connect technopreneurs to funding, technical equipment, and strategic guidance were particularly impactful for women technopreneurs.

The Role of the Regulatory Environment as a Moderating Variable

The regulatory environment emerged as a critical moderating factor, shaping the relationships between the independent variables and Technopreneurship Growth. Specifically, the findings indicate that:

Technopreneurship Capabilities benefit significantly from a supportive regulatory environment, with the interaction showing the strongest positive effect. This suggests that policies that encourage technology adoption, protect intellectual property, and reduce compliance costs amplify the impact of technopreneurship capabilities on growth. The interaction between Staged Financing and the regulatory environment revealed a negative effect. This may indicate that overly restrictive or complex financial regulations can deter access to external funding, limiting the effectiveness of staged financing strategies. The relationship between Entrepreneurial Culture and growth was negatively moderated by the regulatory environment, suggesting that certain cultural entrepreneurial norms may face challenges in overly regulated contexts. Business Support Mechanisms were not significantly moderated by the regulatory environment, implying that the impact of support programs may be relatively independent of external regulatory conditions.

CONCLUSION

The study sought to explore the growth prospects and barriers for women technopreneurs in Ghana by addressing three key questions: *(1) What is the nature of the women technopreneurship landscape in Ghana? (2) What are the barriers faced by women technopreneurs in Ghana? and (3) What factors shape the growth of women technopreneurs in Ghana?* The findings provide valuable insights into the current state, challenges, and growth drivers of women-led technopreneurship firms in Ghana.

The results show that women-led technopreneurship firms are largely profit-driven, though some aim to fill market gaps or bring innovative ideas to life. Social media emerged as a key enabling technology for business operations, alongside other tools like cloud computing and data analytics.

Most firms are at the start-up stage, with self-financing identified as the predominant funding source in the early phases of growth. Also, barriers to growth include taxation, limited access to financing, legislative and bureaucratic constraints, and other challenges such as access to foreign markets, customer trust, support programs, cultural biases, and limited access to local markets. These barriers underscore the structural and systemic challenges that women technopreneurs face in their business journey.

The study found that four key factors—Entrepreneurial Culture, Technopreneurship Capabilities, Staged Financing, and Business Support Mechanisms—significantly influence the growth of women technopreneurs in Ghana. Technopreneurship Capabilities emerged as the strongest predictor, highlighting the critical role of technical expertise and strategic decision-making. Entrepreneurial Culture, Staged Financing, and Business Support Mechanisms also contribute meaningfully to growth by fostering innovation, ensuring financial sustainability, and providing essential resources and mentorship. The regulatory environment emerged as a key moderating factor in the study, significantly shaping the relationships between growth determinants and Technopreneurship Growth. A supportive regulatory environment enhanced the impact of Technopreneurship Capabilities, highlighting the importance of policies that encourage technology adoption and reduce compliance costs. However, restrictive financial regulations negatively influenced the effectiveness of Staged Financing, while overly regulated contexts dampened the positive effects of Entrepreneurial Culture. Interestingly, the impact of Business Support Mechanisms appeared independent of regulatory conditions, suggesting their effectiveness may not rely heavily on external policy frameworks.

Implications for Future Research

This study contributes to the body of knowledge on women-led technopreneurship by offering a nuanced perspective on their growth prospects and barriers in a developing country context. It provides a foundation for further research into sector-specific dynamics, especially the interactions between regulatory frameworks and entrepreneurial growth factors. Additionally, this study serves as a practical guide for aspiring and current women technopreneurs by highlighting prevailing technologies, challenges, and growth factors essential for business success.

From a policy perspective, the findings emphasize the need for a supportive regulatory environment tailored to the unique challenges of women technopreneurs. Governments and policymakers should prioritize reforms that reduce bureaucratic barriers, provide tax incentives, and establish accessible funding schemes. Targeted initiatives, such as incubators and accelerators, should focus on mentorship, networking opportunities, and access to advanced technologies to empower women technopreneurs.

Future research could further enrich this understanding by focusing on sector-specific dynamics within technopreneurship, exploring how unique challenges and growth opportunities vary across industries like fintech, agritech, and edtech. Additionally, examining the influence of societal and cultural factors, including gender biases and family dynamics, would provide deeper insights into the non-structural barriers faced by women technopreneurs. Lastly, documenting success stories of women technopreneurs who have navigated significant barriers could offer practical strategies and inspiration for aspiring entrepreneurs.

REFERENCES

Abbas, A. A. (2018). The Bright Future of Technopreneurship. *International Journal of Scientific and Engineering Research, 9*(December), 563–566.

Abubakre, M., & Mkansi, M. (2022). How do technologists do "ICT for development"? A contextualised perspective on ICT4D in South Africa. *European Journal of Information Systems, 31*(1), 7–24. DOI: 10.1080/0960085X.2021.1978343

Adam, I. O., & Dzang Alhassan, M. (2021). The mediating role of ICT regulation on the effects of ICT access and ICT use on e-participation: Evidence from structural equation modelling and necessary condition analysis. *African Journal of Science, Technology, Innovation and Development, 0*(0), 1–12. DOI: 10.1080/20421338.2021.1937815

Afzal, M. N. I., Siddiqui, S., & Dutta, S. (2018). Determinants of entrepreneurial capability (EC) environment in ASEAN-05 economies - a log-linear stochastic frontier analysis. *Journal of Global Entrepreneurship Research, 8*(1), 14. Advance online publication. DOI: 10.1186/s40497-018-0101-y

Amante, A. D., & Ronquillo, T. A. (2017). Technopreneurship as an outcomes-based education tool applied in some engineering and computing science programme. *Australasian Journal of Engineering Education, 22*(1), 32–38. DOI: 10.1080/22054952.2017.1348186

Bhardwaj, B. R. (2021). Adoption, diffusion and consumer behavior in technopreneurship. *International Journal of Emerging Markets, 16*(2), 179–220. DOI: 10.1108/IJOEM-11-2018-0577

Bhat, I. S., & Gulzar, F. (2020). An Insight into the Factors Affecting Women Technopreneurs. *International Journal of Knowledge Management and Practices, 8*(1), 33–40. http://proquest.umi.com/login/athens?url=https://www.proquest.com/scholarly-journals/insight-into-factors-affecting-women/docview/2540764815/se-2?accountid=11979%0Ahttps://onesearch.lancaster-university.uk/openurl/44LAN/44LAN_services_page?url_ver=Z39.88-

Buccieri, D., Javalgi, R. G., & Jancenelle, V. E. (2021). Dynamic capabilities and performance of emerging market international new ventures: Does international entrepreneurial culture matter? *International Small Business Journal*, *39*(5), 474–499. DOI: 10.1177/0266242620969682

Chin, W. W. (1998). The partial least squares approach to structural equation modeling. *Modern Methods for Business Research*, *295*(2), 295–336.

Davidson, M. J., Fielden, S. L., & Omar, A. (2010). Black, Asian and Minority Ethnic female business owners: Discrimination and social support. *International Journal of Entrepreneurial Behaviour & Research*, *16*(1), 59–81. DOI: 10.1108/13552551011020072

Denis, D. J., & McKeon, S. B. (2021). Persistent negative cash flows, staged financing, and the stockpiling of cash balances. *Journal of Financial Economics*, *142*(1), 293–313. DOI: 10.1016/j.jfineco.2021.04.038

Dibrova, A. (2015). Business Angel Investments: Risks and Opportunities. *Procedia: Social and Behavioral Sciences*, *207*, 280–289. DOI: 10.1016/j.sbspro.2015.10.097

Fowosire, R. A., Elijah, O., & Fowosire, R. (2017). Technopreneurship: A View of Technology, Innovations and Entrepreneurship. *Type: Double Blind Peer Reviewed International Research Journal Publisher: Global Journals Inc, 17*(7).

Hair, J. F., Risher, J. J., Sarstedt, M., & Ringle, C. M. (2019). When to use and how to report the results of PLS-SEM. *European Business Review*, *31*(1), 2–24. DOI: 10.1108/EBR-11-2018-0203

Hassan, Z., Lashari, M. K., & Basit, A. (2021). Cultivating entrepreneurial culture among students in Malaysia. *Entrepreneurial Business and Economics Review*, *9*(1), 119–135. DOI: 10.15678/EBER.2021.090108

Henseler, J., Ringle, C. M., & Sarstedt, M. (2015). A new criterion for assessing discriminant validity in variance-based structural equation modeling. *Journal of the Academy of Marketing Science*, *43*(1), 115–135. DOI: 10.1007/s11747-014-0403-8

Huggins, R., Morgan, B., & Williams, N. (2015). Regional entrepreneurship and the evolution of public policy and governance evidence from three regions. *Journal of Small Business and Enterprise Development*, *22*(3), 473–511. DOI: 10.1108/JSBED-12-2012-0135

Ingram Bogusz, C., Teigland, R., & Vaast, E. (2019). Designed entrepreneurial legitimacy: The case of a Swedish crowdfunding platform. *European Journal of Information Systems*, *28*(3), 318–335. DOI: 10.1080/0960085X.2018.1534039

Joreskog, K. G. (1971). Simultaneous Factor Analysis in Several Populations. *Psychometrika*, *36*(4), 409–426. DOI: 10.1007/BF02291366

Katjiteo, A. (2024). Entrepreneurship and Innovation: The Catalyst for Economic Growth. In *Entrepreneurship Innovation and Education for Performance Improvement* (pp. 249–284). IGI Global.

Khadhraoui, M., Plaisent, M., Lakhal, L., & Bernard, P. (2016). The Impact of Entrepreneurial Culture Dimensions on Entrepreneurial Intention: A Cross Cultural Study. *Universal Journal of Management*, *4*(12), 685–693. DOI: 10.13189/ujm.2016.041205

Klapper, L., Schwert, W., Berger, A., Boot, A., Cetorelli, N., Claessens, S., Desai, M., Djankov, S., Dyck, A., Estrin, S., Fisman, R., Gennaioli, N., Gompers, P., Guiso, L., Haber, S., Hauswald, R., Johnson, S., Kaplan, S., Lamoreaux, N., … Woodruff, C. (2004). *No Title.*

Koe, W. L. (2020). Data on technopreneurial intention among male and female university students: A comparison. *Data in Brief*, *33*, 106423. DOI: 10.1016/j.dib.2020.106423 PMID: 33102642

Lamin, A., & Dunlap, D. (2011). Complex technological capabilities in emerging economy firms: The role of organizational relationships. *Journal of International Management*, *17*(3), 211–228. DOI: 10.1016/j.intman.2011.05.004

Lee, J. D., Lee, K., Meissner, D., Radosevic, S., & Vonortas, N. S. (2021). Local capacity, innovative entrepreneurial places and global connections: An overview. *The Journal of Technology Transfer*, *46*(3), 563–573. DOI: 10.1007/s10961-020-09812-7 PMID: 32836769

Lockett, A., Hayton, J., Ucbasaran, D., Mole, K., & Hodgkinson, G. P. (2015). Entrepreneurial Leadership, Capabilities and Firm Growth: A Review of Existing Evidence. *International Small Business Journal*, *33*(1), 89–105. DOI: 10.1177/0266242614558315

Lukas, E., Mölls, S., & Welling, A. (2016). Venture capital, staged financing and optimal funding policies under uncertainty. *European Journal of Operational Research*, *250*(1), 305–313. DOI: 10.1016/j.ejor.2015.10.051

Mefteh, H., & Benhassen, L. (2015). Impact of information technology and communication on economic growth. International Journal of Economics. *Financial Management*, *4*(2), 90–98.

Modgil, S., Dwivedi, Y. K., Rana, N. P., Gupta, S., & Kamble, S. (2022). Has Covid-19 accelerated opportunities for digital entrepreneurship? An Indian perspective. *Technological Forecasting and Social Change*, *175*, 121415. DOI: 10.1016/j.techfore.2021.121415 PMID: 36536802

Musa, H., Azmi, F. R., Mohamad, N., Shahbodin, F., & Fam, S. (2017). Creative industry learning and development towards craft product: Critical success factors of technopreneurship. *Proceedings of Mechanical Engineering Research Day*, (May), 246–247.

Nambisan, S., Lyytinen, K., & Yoo, Y. (2020). Digital innovation: towards a transdisciplinary perspective. *Handbook of Digital Innovation*, 2–12. DOI: 10.4337/9781788119986.00008

Nguyen, L. (2016). Entrepreneurial culture: Some initial assessments in Vietnam. *Ekonomski Horizonti*, *18*(3), 233–246. DOI: 10.5937/ekonhor1603233N

Nikraftar, T., Hosseini, E., & Mohammadi, E. (2022). The factors influencing technological entrepreneurship in nanotechnology businesses. *Revista de Gestao*, *29*(1), 76–99. DOI: 10.1108/REGE-02-2021-0029

Nwankwo, S., Akunuri, J., & Madichie, N. O. (2010). Supporting black businesses: Narratives of support providers in London. *International Journal of Entrepreneurial Behaviour & Research*, *16*(6), 561–580. DOI: 10.1108/13552551011083541

Ovharhe, H. O. (2024). Business Intelligence and Innovation Moderating Roles on Entrepreneurship and Management Using Champiopreneurship Approach. In *Applying Business Intelligence and Innovation to Entrepreneurship* (pp. 171–223). IGI Global. DOI: 10.4018/979-8-3693-1846-1.ch009

Panda, S. N., & Gopalaswamy, A. K. (2020). An analysis of timing decision in venture capital staged financing: Evidence from India. *Management Research Review*, *43*(12), 1517–1531. DOI: 10.1108/MRR-09-2019-0424

Petti, C., & Zhang, S. (2011). Factors influencing technological entrepreneurship capabilities. *Journal of Technology Management in China*, *6*(1), 7–25. DOI: 10.1108/17468771111105631

Rafiana, N. N. (2024). Technopreneurship strategy to grow entrepreneurship career options for students in higher education. *ADI Journal on Recent Innovation*, *5*(2), 110–126.

Ratinho, T., Amezcua, A., Honig, B., & Zeng, Z. (2020). Supporting entrepreneurs: A systematic review of literature and an agenda for research. *Technological Forecasting and Social Change*, *154*(February), 119956. DOI: 10.1016/j.techfore.2020.119956

Rostam-Afschar, D. (2014). Entry regulation and entrepreneurship: a natural experiment in German craftsmanship. In *Empirical Economics* (Vol. 47, Issue 3). DOI: 10.1007/s00181-013-0773-7

Salhieh, S. M., & Al-Abdallat, Y. (2022). Technopreneurial intentions: The effect of innate innovativeness and academic self-efficacy. *Sustainability (Basel)*, *14*(1), 1–14. DOI: 10.3390/su14010238

Simuka, J., & Masunda, M. M. (2023). Entrepreneurship Education and Women Entrepreneurship Opportunities in Zimbabwe. *Journal of African Education*, *4*(3), 87–107. DOI: 10.31920/2633-2930/2023/v4n3a4

Singhry, H. B. (2015). The Effect of Technology Entrepreneurial Capabilities on Technopreneurial Intention of Nascent Graduates. *European Journal of Business and Management*, *7*(34), 8–20. www.iiste.org

Soekarno, S., & Setiawati, M. (2020). Women and Digital Financial Inclusion in Indonesia As Emerging Market. *International Review of Management and Marketing*, *10*(5), 46–49. DOI: 10.32479/irmm.10212

Soomro, B. A., & Shah, N. (2020). Technopreneurship intention among nonbusiness students: A quantitative assessment. *World Journal of Entrepreneurship, Management and Sustainable Development*, *17*(3), 502–514. DOI: 10.1108/WJEMSD-10-2020-0129

Usman, F. O., Kess-Momoh, A. J., Ibeh, C. V., Elufioye, A. E., Ilojianya, V. I., & Oyeyemi, O. P., (2024). Entrepreneurial innovations and trends: A global review: Examining emerging trends, challenges, and opportunities in the field of entrepreneurship, with a focus on how technology and globalization are shaping new business ventures. *International Journal of Science and Research Archive*, *11*(1), 552–569. DOI: 10.30574/ijsra.2024.11.1.0079

Vu, H. M. (2020). A review of dynamic capabilities, innovation capabilities, entrepreneurial capabilities and their consequences. *The Journal of Asian Finance, Economics and Business*, *7*(8), 485–494. DOI: 10.13106/jafeb.2020.vol7.no8.485

Wilson, N., & Martin, L. (2015). Entrepreneurial opportunities for all?: Entrepreneurial capability and the capabilities approach. *International Journal of Entrepreneurship and Innovation*, *16*(3), 159–169. DOI: 10.5367/ijei.2015.0189

Yeganegi, S., Laplume, A. O., & Dass, P. (2021). The role of information availability: A longitudinal analysis of technology entrepreneurship. *Technological Forecasting and Social Change*, *170*, 120910. Advance online publication. DOI: 10.1016/j.techfore.2021.120910

Zahra, S. A. (2022). International entrepreneurship by family firms post covid. *Journal of Family Business Strategy*, *xxxx*(2), 100482. DOI: 10.1016/j.jfbs.2021.100482

Chapter 6
Impact of Crowdfunding on Women-Led Business Sustainability by Mediation of Alternative Financing in the Horn of Africa

Shashi Kant
https://orcid.org/0000-0003-4722-5736
Bule Hora University, Ethiopia

Tafese Niguse
https://orcid.org/0009-0008-6536-6392
Bule Hora University, Ethiopia

Metasebia Adula
https://orcid.org/0000-0001-5732-2850
Bule Hora University, Ethiopia

ABSTRACT

This investigation looks at the influence of crowdsourcing on the viability of female owned firms in the East Africa, with a special emphasis on the

DOI: 10.4018/979-8-3693-9193-8.ch006

mediating function of alternative means of finance. A quantitative research technique was used to collect information from 385 female venture innovators using structured questionnaires. AMOS software was used to conduct the investigation, which assimilated Kaiser-Meyer-Olkin (KMO) measurements, Exploratory Factor investigation (EFA), and Structural Equation Modeling (SEM). The findings show that crowdsourcing augments access to alternative means of finance, which helps to the long-term viability of female owned firms. The investigation reveals a large direct influence of crowdsourcing on venture viability while emphasizing the considerable intermediary effect of alternative means of finance. Specifically, the findings show that effective crowdsourcing campaigns not only give immediate cash resources but also promote other financing options, hence increasing long-term viability.

INTRODUCTION

In recent years, the global venture innovations landscape has acknowledged the essential role that female owned enterprises play in generating fiscal development and traditional transformation. This recognition is especially important in the East Africa, where female venture innovators confront specific difficulties that limit their access to classical finance options. Crowdsourcing has evolved as an innovative alternative means of finance tool that may help female owned enterprises by providing them with the capitals they need while also encouraging community involvement and assistance. Crowdsourcing's relevance extends beyond regional bounds, as it has been used throughout the globe to democratize access to money and boost entrepreneurial activity, particularly in underrepresented areas (Smagulova & Goncalves, 2023).

Crowdsourcing, which originated in the major realm of communal finance, has gained popularity as a result of the proliferation of digital sources that allow venture innovators and potential investors to contact directly. Empirical research has shown that crowdsourcing may augment venture viability by not just providing financial resources but also confirming venture concepts and forming assistance networks.

According to studies, female venture innovators that use crowdsourcing benefit from higher exposure and legitimacy, which may lead to more sustainable venture approaches. While the potential benefits are clear, infrastructural, cultural, and legislative constraints continue to impede the effective implementation of crowdsourcing in the East Africa (Kromidha et al., 2023). Real globe challenges abound for female owned ventures in the region, including limited financial literacy, lack of access to technology, and societal customs that may discourage female venture innovations. These barriers can limit the effectiveness of crowdsourcing as a viable financing option. Also, empirical studies on the intersection of crowdsourcing, female owned ventures, and alternative means of finance in the East Africa are scarce, revealing a critical research vacuum. This vacuum underscores the need for targeted research that examines how crowdsourcing can be effectively leveraged to enhance the viability of female owned enterprises in this context (Calic et al., 2023).

This chapter seeks to fill these vacuums by investigating the influence of crowdsourcing on the viability of female owned firms, with a special emphasis on the arbitration function of alternative means of finance. This research, which combines empirical information and case studies, will give real globe insights for future scholars and policymakers. It will showcase excellent approaches and approaches for creating a more nurturing ecosystem for female venture innovators. The vital issue underlying this research is: *"How does crowdsourcing affect the viability of female owned firms in the East Africa, and how does alternative means of finance mediate this association?"* By answering this question, the research hopes to shed light on approaches to augment the fiscal resilience of female venture innovators in the region, as well as contribute to the major conversation on sustainable development and sex equity in venture innovations.

BACKGROUND OF INVESTIGATION

The East Africa is characterized by a diverse tapestry of ethos and markets, but it faces vital barriers to the development and viability of female-led companies. Female venture innovators have the capacity to drive fiscal development, but they frequently face institutional restrictions that limit their access to external finance, markets, and resources. Classical external finance systems, such as banks and microfinance firms, routinely neglect female owned ventures, which are generally viewed as riskier. This external finance vacuum is especially visible in the East Africa, where traditional customs and sex stigma compound the difficulties faced by female venture innovators (Nigam& Shatila, 2024). Crowdsourcing has arisen as a viable alternative means of finance approach that might help overcome some of these limitations. By utilizing digital sources, female venture innovators may access a major audience of potential assistance's and investors, allowing them to get finance without the onerous standards of classical monetary institutions. However, implementing crowdsourcing in the East Africa presents real globe challenges. For example, restricted internet access and computer literacy stop many female from effectively utilizing crowdsourcing portals. Female venture innovators in impoverished nations, such as Ethiopia, may find it difficult to interact with online capital raising possibilities, reducing their potential to raise capitals (Calic et al., 2023).

A female's cooperative in Somalia that specializes in handmade crafts serves as a realistic case investigation to illustrate these challenges. While the cooperative attempted to begin a crowdsourcing campaign to assistance the manufacturing of their handcrafted items, they faced substantial challenges. Many members lacked the digital skills required to utilize crowdsourcing portals, and restricted access to dependable internet connections made it difficult to market their campaign effectively. Despite the community's tremendous assistance for their products, the cooperative was unable to get finance owing to logistical hurdles (Smagulova & Goncalves, 2023). Another example is in Kenya, where a group of female venture innovators started a crowdsourcing campaign to assist a sustainable agricultural enterprise. Despite receiving some cash, the campaign emphasized the significance of developing a strong narrative to attract backers. The venture innovators struggled to express their vision and effect, which is critical in crowdsourcing scenarios. This event emphasizes the need of developing narrative and marketing abilities, which are required for effectively engaging potential donors and assuring campaign success (Kromidha et al., 2023). Also, the legislative climate for crowdsourcing in the East Africa is questionable. Many nations lack clear legal frameworks for crowdsourcing operations, raising concerns among potential investors about the authenticity and safety of their contributions. This legislative uncertainty might impede involvement in crowdsourcing activities, particularly among risk-averse investors who prefer classical investment options.

STATEMENT OF PROBLEM

The issue addressed in this paper is the underutilization of crowdsourcing as a feasible financing tool for female-led firms in the East Africa, despite its potential to augment company viability and fiscal empowerment. Ideally, crowdsourcing, with its capacity to democratize access to money, would serve as a strong alternative means of finance option for female venture innovators who face obstacles to established financing channels. However, the reality presents a dissimilar picture in which institutional constraints continue impeding the effective execution of crowdsourcing projects in this setting (Nigam& Shatila, 2024). While crowdsourcing has proven effective in a variety of global contexts, the effect for female owned companies in the East Africa remains unclear. According to research, female venture innovators frequently face particular challenges, such as cultural stigma and restricted access to technology that stops them from participating in crowdsourcing. Also, previous research has yielded mixed results about the effectiveness of crowdsourcing in promoting sustainable venture approaches among female owned firms. Some studies highlight success stories, while others focus on high failure rates, creating a vacuum in knowing the exact elements that lead to these disparate results (Aracil-Jordá et al., 2023).

Theoretical vacuums also exist, as existing crowdsourcing models are mostly focused on Western contexts, ignoring the East Africa's distinctive socio-fiscal and cultural factors. This oversight limits the application of established ideas to the local situation, resulting in a knowledge vacuum that impedes the creation of specialized solutions for female venture innovators. Also, there is a substantial contextual vacuum because the convergence of crowdsourcing, alternative means of finance, and female's venture innovations in the East Africa has not been adequately investigated in the literature. Real globe hurdles complicate the situation for female-led enterprises looking to use crowdsourcing. Crowdsourcing initiatives might fail due to a lack of digital literacy, restricted internet connection, and poor marketing abilities. Also, the legislative climate around crowdsourcing is confusing in many countries across the region, generating confusion for both venture innovators and potential investors (Aracil-Jordá et al., 2023).

This investigation seeks to fill these vacuums by looking into the influence of crowdsourcing on the viability of female owned firms in the East Africa, especially via the angle of alternative means of finance. By combining empirical information, case studies, and theoretical frameworks, this investigation will give a more nuanced understanding of the challenges and potential connected with crowdsourcing in this ecosystem. It will provide policymakers with concrete insights into creating nurturing settings that encourage female's venture innovations and increase access to alternative external finance. Finally, this investigation aims to pave the way for future researchers to investigate the intricate interaction among crowdsourcing and female owned firms, so contributing to a more complete knowledge of sustainable venture innovations in the East Africa (Smagulova & Goncalves, 2023)

RELATED THEORIES

Several theoretical frameworks are used to examine the influence of crowdsourcing on the viability of female owned ventures in the East Africa, providing unique insights into the dynamics of venture innovations, finance, and sex.

Traditional Money view, states that traditional networks and interactions may be useful resources for individuals and firms. In the context of crowdsourcing, this idea focuses on how female venture innovators may use their traditional networks to gain money and assistance. Traditional money may help build trust and teamwork, both of which are necessary for effective crowdsourcing projects. Female owned enterprises that actively engage their networks may find it simpler to recruit investors who share their vision and beliefs (Harrison et al., 2020).

Resource-Based View (RBV), which emphasizes the role of resources—both real and intangible—in creating competitive advantage. According to this hypothesis, the capacity of female owned firms to acquire and effectively use resources, particularly financial money gained through crowdsourcing, is critical to their long-term success. The RBV stresses how distinctive characteristics, such as creative venture models or strong community links, may boost a company's resilience and long-term viability. Using this viewpoint, the research may investigate how female venture innovators in the East Africa might use crowdsourcing not just for immediate financing but also to develop a sustainable resource base (Zhao et al., 2023).

The Innovation Diffusion Theory is also useful in understanding how new ideas and technology, such as crowdsourcing, spread across communities. This hypothesis might assist explain crowdsourcing adoption rates among female venture innovators in the East Africa, taking into account aspects like as awareness, perceived advantages, and traditional network effect. Understanding how innovation spreads can provide light on the challenges that female experience while adopting crowdsourcing and how to overcome them (Kromidha et al., 2023).

Gender and Development Theory serves as the primary theoretical lens. This theory highlights the role of sex dynamics in development processes, stressing how sex disparities can affect access to resources and opportunities. Using this viewpoint, the investigation may critically examine how systemic sex inequalities in the East Africa influence female are access to crowdsourcing and other finance options. It enables a more nuanced view of the junction of sex and venture innovations, examining how cultural, traditional, and fiscal issues influence the experiences of female venture innovators in this region (Calic et al., 2023).

DEFINITION AND ORIGIN OF TERMS

Crowdsourcing is the approach of generating capitals via the combined efforts of a large number of people, usually via online sources. The phrase emerged in the early 2000s by combining the words "crowd," which refers to a big number of people, and "external finance," which refers to financial assistance. Crowdsourcing has progressed from classical capital raising approaches, such as charity events, to a digital framework that uses traditional media and internet sources to connect ventures with a globe wide audience. Its emergence can be ascribed to technological augments and the rising democratization of finance, which allows people and small enterprises to access capitals without the need for established financial institutions (Serwaah, et al., 2024).

Female owned firms are defined as those owned and/or managed by female. This word refers to a wide range of company kinds, from tiny local ventures to vital companies. The notion acquired popularity in the late twentieth century, as the globe wide discourse about sex equality and female's empowerment expanded. It emphasizes the specific obstacles and possibilities that female venture innovators confront, especially in patriarchal settings where resources and chances are limited. Recognizing female owned firms is critical for promoting inclusive fiscal development and closing sex vacuums in venture innovations (Kato, 2023).

Sustainbility is defined as the ability to fulfill current demands without jeopardizing future generations' ability to meet their own needs. The word first appeared in the 1980s, namely in the Brundtland Chapter of the Globe Commission on Ecosystem and Development, which stressed the interdependence of fiscal, traditional, and ecosystem challenges. In the corporate globe, viability has come to mean not simply ecosystem care but also traditional responsibility and fiscal viability. Female owned firms frequently assimilate ethical standards, community involvement, and resource management into their operations to ensure viability (Aracil-Jordá et al., 2023).

Alternative means of finance refers to neoclassical means of getting cash, such as crowdsourcing, peer-to-peer lending, microfinance, and effect investment. This concept gained currency in the early twenty-first century as venture innovators sought new ways to acquire money outside of classical banking institutions. Alternative means of finance has proven especially important for female venture innovators, who frequently encounter challenges to classical external finance owing to systematic sex stigma and a lack of collateral. This notion highlights the rising acknowledgment of a variety of financing sources that might help underrepresented groups in the startup ecosystem (Zhao et al., 2023).

EMPIRICAL LITERATURE REVIEW

Crowdfunding and Female Owned Venture Viability

Crowdfunding sources may be used to validate company concepts, which is especially remarkable for female venture innovators who are frequently questioned about their talents in a male-dominated corporate ecosystem. This validation is critical because it may augment consumer confidence and assistance, so contributing to the long-term viability of female-led firms (Serwaah, et al., 2024). Female are frequently motivated by community assistance and the desire to make a traditional effect, as well as financial benefit. This is consistent with the idea that female owned firms usually prioritize traditional venture innovations and community-oriented aims, which may help them, thrive by cultivating strong consumer loyalty and involvement. Female venture innovators may build a feeling of shared purpose by using their networks, which not only helps them raise cash but also enhances their company foundations (Durga et al., 2024). Also, research shows that effective crowdsourcing campaigns can boost access to following capital raising rounds. Firms who meet their crowdsourcing targets are more likely to obtain venture money and angel investment in the future. This is especially important for female owned enterprises, which frequently face difficulties to acquiring classical finance. By effectively navigating the crowdsourcing market, female venture innovators may establish a track record that increases their reputation and attractiveness to potential investors, assuring better viability for their ventures (Nigam& Shatila, 2024).

However, empirical evidence reveals the hurdles that female venture innovators experience while crowdsourcing. Female owned campaigns may obtain less financing than their male counterparts, although demonstrating identical qualities. This vacuum might be ascribed to sex stigma that still exists in the investing globe, influencing the perceived validity of female owned ventures. Such biases might reduce crowdsourcing's overall influence on venture viability, as insufficient money can restrict development and operational capacities (Srinivas, 2019). Also, studies highlight the significance of digital literacy and marketing abilities in the success of crowdsourcing initiatives. Berglund, (2023) discovered that venture innovators with greater advertising tactics and traditional media involvement were more likely to succeed in their crowdsourcing campaigns. For female venture innovators in the East Africa, where access to technology and training may be restricted, improving digital skills might be critical for reaping the benefits of crowdsourcing (Zhao et al., 2023; Harrison et al., 2020).

> H1: crowdsourcing has remarkable effect on female owned venture viability

Crowdsourcing and Alternative Means of Finance

One of the most remarkable effects of crowdsourcing on alternative means of finance is its capacity to democratize access to cash. Historically, venture innovators, particularly female, have faced difficulties to obtaining money from classical sources such as banks and venture creators. Crowdsourcing sources provide an alternate avenue, allowing ventures to avoid classical gatekeepers. Yu et al, (2024).found that crowdsourcing can act as a bridge for venture innovators who do not fulfill the severe conditions of classical finance. This accessibility is especially important in countries like the East Africa, where financial institutions frequently have sex biases and lack specific solutions for female venture innovators (Kato, 2023). Also, crowdsourcing can increase project visibility and legitimacy. Effective crowdsourcing efforts frequently generate more media coverage and public interest, which can attract further investment from alternative financial sources. Firms who effectively finish a crowdsourcing campaign are more likely to have better chances for follow-on external finance, such as angel investments and venture money. This ripple effect demonstrates how crowdsourcing may serve as a catalyst for extra financial assistance, helping venture innovators to grow operations and sustain their firms in the long run (Panigarhi et al., 2023).

Crowdsourcing also promotes community involvement and assistance, which may be used to strengthen alternative means of finance techniques. Many crowdsourcing projects stress traditional effect, attracting donors who are motivated by community augmentment rather than solely financial gains. This community-oriented strategy may build a devoted customer base that not only contributes to the initial investment but also helps the firm develop over time through repeat purchases and advocacy. Guye et al. (2023) found that enterprises with substantial community assistance are more likely to prosper in the long run, demonstrating the link among crowdsourcing and sustainable venture approaches (Berglund, 2023). However, the link among crowdsourcing and alternative means of finance is not without complications. Despite the potential benefits, many crowdsourcing initiatives fail to meet their capital raising targets. According to studies, female owned campaigns may be especially sensitive to these phenomena as a result of cultural stigma and preconceptions about female venture innovators. Liu et al. (2018) discovered that female owned campaigns frequently obtain less financing than men-led campaigns, while presenting equivalent venture concepts and strategy. This vacuum may hinder crowdsourcing's overall efficacy as a trustworthy alternative means of finance source, thereby reducing the viability of female owned firms (Srinivas, 2019).

Also, not all venture innovators possess the necessary abilities to start a effective crowdsourcing campaign, such as digital marketing, storytelling, and community involvement. Gerber and Hui (2013) found that the efficacy of crowdsourcing is frequently dependent on an entrepreneur's ability to market their campaign effectively. Many female venture innovators, particularly those in the East Africa, struggle to fully utilize crowdsourcing due to a lack of access to digital literacy training and marketing resources.

H2: Crowdsourcing has remarkable effect on Alternative means of finance

Alternative Finance and Female Owned Venture Viability

Empirical information on the influence of alternative means of finance on the viability of female owned firms show a favorable association among access to a variety of external finance sources and increased company viability. According to studies, female venture innovators that use alternative means of finance mechanisms such as microfinance and crowdsourcing have higher development and operational stability than those who only use classical financing. For example, Babar, et al., (2023) discovered that female owned enterprises that obtained microloans saw stronger revenue development and employment creation, emphasizing the importance of accessible finance in assisting company viability. The flexibility provided by microfinance enables female to personalize their financial solutions to their unique requirements, allowing them to spend in critical areas such as inventory, marketing, and skills development (Srinivas, 2019). Also, Dereso et al. (2023) found that crowdsourcing not only offers financial resources but also increases the visibility and legitimacy of female-led companies. Effective crowdsourcing efforts frequently result in greater customer involvement and loyalty, which are critical for long-term viability. The investigation found that female venture innovators that effectively used crowdsourcing sources had a considerable increase in brand recognition and consumer trust, which translated into sustained sales development. This exposure is especially critical in competitive marketplaces, where building a strong brand presence may be a deciding factor in success (Inoubli et al., 2022).

Additionally, empirical research emphasizes the importance of community assistance in alternative means of finance approaches. For example, jabo et al. (2016) discovered that female owned firms that engaged their local communities through crowdsourcing campaigns received more assistance and advocacy, which augmentd their viability. The investigation demonstrated how community engagement not only facilitated external finance but also established a network of devoted consumers who contributed to the company's long-term success. This research emphasizes the role of traditional money and community linkages in increasing the operational resilience of female owned ventures (Berglund, 2023; Harrison et al., 2020).

H3: Crowdsourcing has remarkable effect on Alternative means of finance

Alternative Finance, Crowdsourcing and Female Led Venture Viability

Empirical information on the influence of crowdsourcing on the viability of female owned firms in the East Africa show a strong link mediated by different financing sources. Abate et al. (2021) found that female venture innovators that use crowdsourcing not only get essential financing, but also augment their overall venture viability. The investigation discovered that effective crowdsourcing campaigns frequently result in greater access to alternative means of finance choices such as microloans and peer-to-peer lending, therefore establishing a nurturing financial ecosystem that promotes viability (Adula et al., 2023). Further research reveals that crowdsourcing serves as a validation tool for female owned firms, assisting them in overcoming traditional stigma that frequently limit access to classical finance. Female venture innovators who used crowdsourcing sources were able to demonstrate their company viability to potential investors, increasing their chances of acquiring further external finance from alternative sources. This affirmation is especially important in the East Africa, where female venture innovators regularly encounter doubts about their talents. According to the findings, crowdsourcing not only gives immediate cash help, but it also boosts the legitimacy of female owned ventures, allowing them to access more resources (Kant & Adula, 2024).

Also, empirical research demonstrates the importance of community interaction in crowdsourcing success. Inoubli et al., (2022) discovered that female owned enterprises that effectively organized their traditional networks through crowdsourcing campaigns received greater rates of investment and community assistance. This community assistance not only provided immediate money, but also developed a loyal client base, which is critical for long-term viability. The investigation found that the ties formed during the crowdsourcing process frequently lead to continuous assistance, resulting in a strong ecosystem for female venture innovators (Snellm & Solal, 2023). While the findings are positive, there are still obstacles ahead. Many female venture innovators in the East Africa lack the digital literacy and marketing abilities required operating effective crowdsourcing campaigns. This vacuum may hinder their capacity to exploit crowdsourcing effectively, reducing its potential influence on viability. Also, the investigation found that legislative constraints and restricted access to technology impede the effective implementation of crowdsourcing efforts, implying that systemic reforms are required to fully realize the benefits of crowdsourcing for female venture innovators in the region (Inoubli et al., 2022).

H4: Arbitration effect alternative means of finance in association among crowdsourcing and female led venture viability

CONCEPTUAL FRAMEWORK

Figure 1. Conceptual framework (Authors)

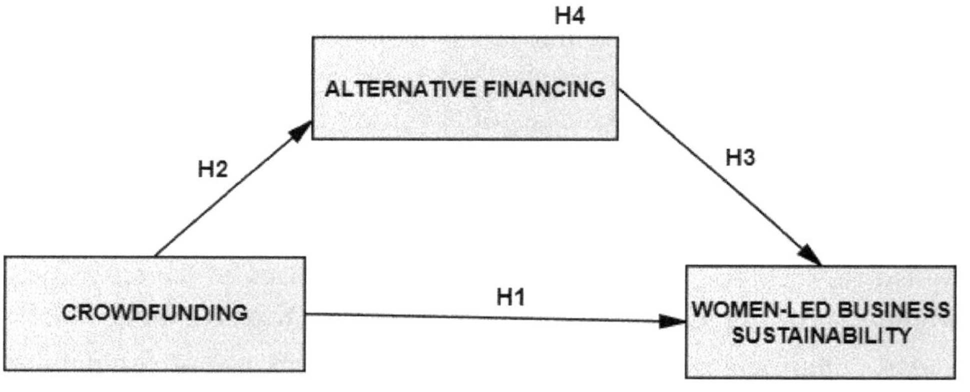

RESEARCH APPROACH

This investigation used a quantitative research technique to evaluate the influence of crowdsourcing on the viability of female owned firms in the East Africa, with a particular emphasis on the arbitration function of alternative means of finance. A sample size of 385 participants was selected via stratified random sampling, guaranteeing a broad representation of female venture innovators from various sectors and areas in the East Africa. The information gathering approach assimilated the use of standardized questionnaires aimed to capture vital factors such as crowdsourcing attitudes, alternative means of finance choices, and company viability metrics. To determine the suitability of the information for factor analysis, the Kaiser-Meyer-Olkin (KMO) measure was calculated, producing a worth's indicating that the sample was acceptable for the investigation. Following that, Exploratory Factor Analysis (EFA) was performed using principal component analysis with varimax rotation to discover the information's underlying structure and corroborate the constructions' dimensions. This stage was critical in refining the measuring scales and ensuring that items were properly put into their relevant factors.

The predicted associations among the components were then tested using Structural Equation Modeling (SEM) with AMOS software. SEM enabled the investigation of direct and indirect effects, offering insights into how crowdsourcing affects venture viability via alternative means of finance. Model fit metrics such as the Comparative Fit Index (CFI), Root Mean Square Error of Approximation (RMSEA), and Chi-square statistics were used to evaluate overall model fit and assure the robustness of the results.

Scale Development

The measuring scales were developed following a comprehensive examination of related literature. Existing scales for crowdsourcing, alternative means of finance, and company viability were analyzed to discover relevant components and dimensions. Items for crowdsourcing were derived from research conducted by (Babar & Abbas, 2023). with an emphasis on financial assistance, community involvement, and venture concept validation. Items for alternative external finance were drawn from the literature on microfinance and peer-to-peer lending, with a focus on accessibility, flexibility, and influence on company development, as noted by (Srinivas, 2019). The viability scale was based on the work Snellman & Solal (2023). and assimilates characteristics of fiscal viability, traditional effect, and ecosystem responsibility.

The first item pool was reviewed by experts to guarantee content authenticity, followed by pilot testing with a smaller sample of female venture innovators to determine clarity and relevance. Feedback from the pilot research influenced further item modifications, resulting in a final set of scales that effectively reflected the components of interest. This thorough scale building procedure was critical for guaranteeing the reproducibility and validity of the measurements utilized in the main investigation, hence adding to the robustness of the empirical results.

DATA ANALYSIS

Table 1. KMO and Bartlett's test

Kaiser-Meyer-Olkin Measure of Sampling Adequacy.		**.850**
Bartlett's Test of Sphericity	Approx. Chi-Square	1321.742
	Df	87
	Sig.	.001

Source: Authors

Table 1 shows the findings of the Kaiser-Meyer-Olkin (KMO) measure of sample adequacy and Bartlett's Test of Sphericity, which are both important in determining the information set's appropriateness for factor analysis. The KMO worth's measured was 0.850, indicating excellent sampling adequacy. KMO worth's typically range from 0 to 1, with worth's around 1 indicating that the information is suitable for factor analysis. A KMO number of 0.7 is regarded acceptable, and worth's above 0.8 are considered good. Thus, the KMO worth's of 0.850 verifies that the sample size and associations among variables are sufficient for further investigation. Bartlett's Test of Sphericity adds to the KMO measure by testing the null hypothesis that the association matrix is an identity matrix, implying that the variables are unrelated and inappropriate for component analysis. The results yield an estimated Chi-Square worth's of 1321.742, with 87 degrees of freedom (df) and a significance level (Sig.) of 0.001. The remarkable result of Bartlett's Test demonstrates that the information set is appropriate for factor analysis, indicating the presence of underlying components that may be retrieved. Overall, the KMO and Bartlett's Test results give a solid source for moving forward with Exploratory Factor Analysis (EFA). The positive KMO worth's and the remarkable result of Bartlett's Test show that the information is not only enough but also acceptable for determining the underlying structure of the constructs assessed in this investigation. This investigation emphasizes the reliability of the information acquired and increases trust in the subsequent conclusions from the factor analysis

Table 2. Total variance explained

Component	Initial Eigen worth's			Extraction Sums of Squared Loadings			Rotation Sums of Squared Loadings		
	Total	% of Variance	Cumulative %	Total	% of Variance	Cumulative %	Total	% of Variance	Cumulative %
1	4.48	31.225	31.225	4.48	31.225	31.225	3.00	20.448	20.448
2	1.41	9.787	41.019	1.41	9.787	41.019	2.16	14.488	34.939
3	1.32	9.087	50.109	1.32	9.087	50.109	1.97	14.168	50.109
4	.951	6.778	56.887						
5	.868	6.218	64.115						
6	.769	5.521	69.634						

Extraction Approach: Principal Component Analysis.
Source: Authors

Table 2 summarizes the overall variance explained by the components collected using Principal Component Analysis (PCA). The initial eigen worth's reflect how much variation each component accounts for before extraction. The first component has an eigen worth's of 4.48 and explains 31.225% of the overall variance. This high proportion indicates that the first component captures a vital piece of the information's underlying structure, making it an important aspect in comprehending the structures under consideration. With an eigen worth's of 1.41, the second component explains 9.787% of the variance, making the cumulative percentage 41.019%. This suggests that the two elements collectively account for a remarkable amount of the overall variation, underscoring their significance within the factor structure. Interestingly, the third component has a remarkable contribution as well, contributing 9.087% to the total variance, which reaches 50.109%, with an eigen worth's of 1.32. This cumulative percentage assistances the idea that many variables are involved in the constructs being studied, since it indicates that three components in total account for half of the variation in the information set.

In conclusion, Table 2's results show that, with a combined contribution of more than 50% to the variance in the information, the first three PCA-extracted components are essential for comprehending information variation. This analysis provides deeper insights into the links among the components under investigation and highlights the efficacy of the factor extraction approach. It also offers a strong foundation for further structural equation modeling.

Confirmatory Principle Component Examination

Confirmatory principle component examination is a sort of statistics that is used to validate the principle component arrangement of a group of directed proxies. Studies can assess hypotheses using CFA based on the underlying frame job and correlatives among observable proxies. The investigation used CFA under table 3 to assess the hypothesis that there is a association among the proxies that are being guided and the latent ideas that assistance them.

Table 3. Co-variances

Covariance			Approximation	S.E.	C.R.	P	Hy.
Alternative means of finance	**<-->**	**Crowdsourcing**	**.245**	**.0241**	**8.235**	***	**H2**
Alternative means of finance	<-->	Female owned venture viability	.313	.042	7.603	***	**H3**
Crowdsourcing	<-->	Female led-venture viability	.256	.26	7.828	***	**H1**

Source: Authors

The co-variances among the three main investigations construct crowdsourcing, female owned venture viability, and alternative means of finance—are shown in Table 3. Knowledge the underlying dynamics in the context of female owned companies in the East Africa requires a knowledge of the co-variances, which offer insights into the direction and intensity of the interactions among these variables. With a standard error (S.E.) of 0.0241, the association among alternative means of finance and crowdsourcing is calculated to be 0.245. The statistical significance of the critical ratio (C.R.) of 8.235 (***) indicates that there is a substantial positive association among the two notions. This research highlights the complimentary nature of different financing approaches by showing that the chance of participating in crowdsourcing augments with access to alternative means of finance. All things considered, Table 3's covariance's show substantial, positive associations among the three concepts, highlighting how crowdsourcing, alternative means of finance, and corporate viability are intertwined. These results provide credence to the investigation's assumptions (H1, H2, and H3), suggesting that alternate financing sources and crowdsourcing are essential for promoting the viability of female-owned enterprises. These kinds of observations are helpful in formulating plans to augment external finance for female venture innovators, which will eventually help them succeed and the region's economy as a whole.

Table 4. Validity concern

	CR	AVE	MSV	MaxR(H)	CF	AF	WLBS
CF	0.727	0.637	0.213	0.847	**0.649**		
AF	0.7600	0.659	0.134	0.765	0.173	**0.668**	
WLBS	0.788	0.600	0.269	0.792	0.379	0.188	**0.679**

Note: CF= Crowdsourcing; AF=Alternative finding; WLBS= Female owned venture viability

Source: Authors

Table 4 lists many validity measures for the three research constructs: female owned venture viability (WLBS), alternative means of finance (AF), and crowdsourcing (CF). In order to evaluate the validity and dependability of the measurement models, these metrics—which assimilate Composite Reliability (CR), Average Variance Extracted (AVE), Maximum Shared Variance (MSV), and Maximum Reliability (MaxR(H))—are crucial. Strong internal consistency is shown by the Composite Reliability (CR) worth's for the constructs: Female owned Venture Viability is at 0.788, Alternative means of finance is at 0.760, and Crowdsourcing is at 0.727. A CR score of more than 0.7 is generally regarded as satisfactory, indicating that all structures show sufficient dependability. Because of its high degree of dependability, each construct's items are guaranteed to dependably represent the underlying theoretical ideas that they are meant to assess. The AVE worth's for each concept are lower than these worth's, which a prerequisite for proving discriminant validity is. This result adds to the measurement model's resilience by showing that the constructions are sufficiently different from one another. Lastly, the constructs' dependability is further assistance by the Maximum Reliability (MaxR(H)) worth'ss, which for Crowdsourcing, Alternative means of finance, and Female owned Venture Viability are 0.847, 0.765, and 0.792, respectively

Mediating Role Examination

Figure 2. Structural equation model

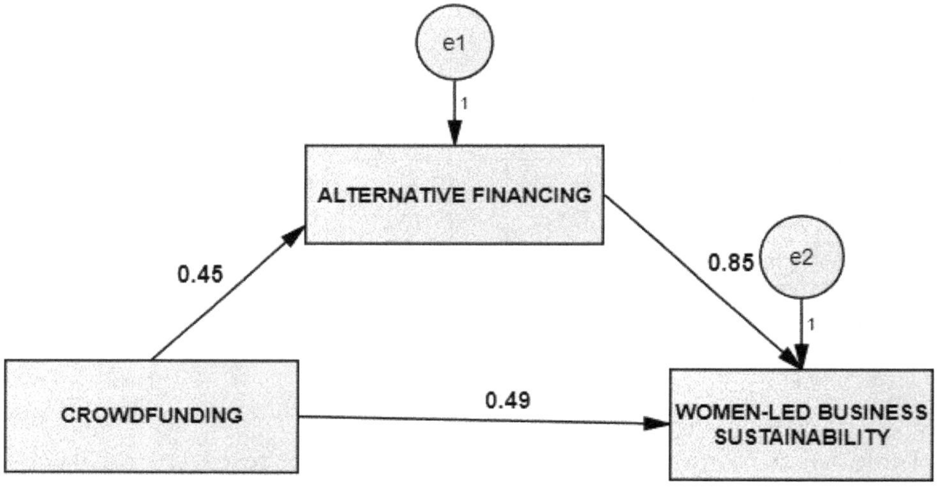

Model Fit Indices

Table 5. Model fitness

Sig.	Chi-Sq	RMR	Fitness Goodness	Fitness Confirmatory	TLI	RMSEA
0.004	1.948	.034	0.926	0.908	0.907	.024

Source: Authors

The model fit indices, shown in Table 5, are crucial for assessing how well the suggested structural equation model fits the observed information. The model is statistically remarkable, indicating that the constructs under investigation have a meaningful association, according to the significance worth's of 0.004. A low p-worth's suggests that the observed information are unlikely to have happened by accident, which assistances the validity of the model. Fit of the model is augmented by the comparatively low Chi-Square worth's of 1.948. A lower Chi-Square worth's in association to the degrees of freedom in structural equation modeling denotes a better fit since it implies that the model does not appreciably differ from the actual information. In this instance, the significance shows that the model accurately captures the information. This statistic is frequently evaluated in combination with the p-worth.

A satisfactory fit is shown by the Root Mean Square Residual (RMR) worth's of 0.034, which is remarkable less than the generally recognized criterion of 0.08. Lower RMR worth's indicate a tighter match. RMR calculates the average difference among the observed and anticipated associations. This suggests that there is good agreement among the model's predictions and the actual information. A excellent fit is indicated by the Fitness Goodness index, which is assessed at 0.926, above the suggested threshold of 0.90. This index evaluates the extent to which the variation in the information is explained by the overall model. The model's suitability in capturing the links among the components is further assistance by the Fitness Confirmatory index (CFI) of 0.908, which also satisfies the acceptable criterion. One other measure of model fit is the Tucker-Lewis Index (TLI), which has a worth's of 0.907. The closer the TLI gets to 1, the better the model fits the information. Worth's greater than 0.90 are often seen as suggestive of a good model fit. Lastly, the excellent Root Mean Square Error of Approximation (RMSEA) score of 0.024 indicates that the model has a close fit to the population covariance matrix because it is much below the 0.06 criterion.

Table 6. Regression examination

Relative			Approx.	S.E.	C.R.	P	Ass.
Alternative means of finance	**<---**	**Crowdsourcing**	**.858**	**.137**	**7.577**	***	**H2**
Female owned venture viability	<---	Alternative means of finance	.334	.137	2.859	***	H3
Female owned venture viability	<---	Crowdsourcing	.950	.185	7.950	***	H1

Source: Authors

The findings of the regression analysis are displayed in Table 6, which also illustrates the connections among the three constructs: alternative means of finance, female owned venture viability, and crowdsourcing. The degree and relevance of each construct's effect on the others are reflected in each pathway, offering insights into the dynamics at work in the context of female owned firms. With a standard error (S.E.) of 0.137, the regression coefficient for the connection among alternative means of finance and crowdsourcing is 0.858. The stated critical ratio (C.R.) is 7.577, indicating a very remarkable result (***). This robustly positive coefficient suggests that greater involvement in crowdsourcing remarkable augments access to alternative external finance sources. This result validates Hypothesis 2 (H2) and shows that crowdsourcing is an important means by which female venture innovators may obtain extra finance.

With a coefficient of 0.334 and a S.E. of 0.137, the second regression route connects female owned venture viability to alternative means of finance. Also statistically remarkable is the C.R. worth's of 2.859, which assistances Hypothesis 3 (H3). This finding implies that, although crowdsourcing has a greater effect, alternative means of finance options have a favorable effect on the viability of female-owned enterprises. This emphasizes how crucial alternative means of finance is as a tool for ensuring the long-term viability of ventures run by female. With a regression worth's of

0.950 and a S.E. of 0.185, crowdsourcing's direct effect on female owned venture viability is clearly remarkable. This association also has a statistically remarkable C.R. of 7.950. This result validates Hypothesis 1 (H1), showing that the viability of female owned firms is remarkable enhanced by effective crowdsourcing initiatives. The high coefficient indicates that crowdsourcing augments these ventures' overall operational stability and development potential in addition to offering instant cash help.

Table 7. Mediating role effect

	Influence	worth	Path Influence
Crowdsourcing→ Female owned venture viability	Direct Influence	.49	Direct influence stated
Crowdsourcing → Alternative means of finance → Female owned venture viability	Indirect Influence	.45*.85=.32	Indirect Influence
	Whole influence	.87	Partial arbitration

Source: Authors

Table 7 presents the function that alternative means of finance plays as a mediator in the link that exists among female owned venture viability and crowdsourcing. This table offers insights into the dynamics of these constructs by clearly breaking out both direct and indirect effects.

The direct influence of crowdsourcing on the viability of female owned ventures is 0.49, showing a substantial positive association. This direct effect implies that the viability of female owned firms is remarkable and immediately effected by effective crowdsourcing initiatives. The phrase "Direct influence stated" highlights the fact that this connection functions without the involvement of any intervening variables, underscoring the usefulness of crowdsourcing as a capital raising tactic for continuing company operations. On the other hand, the chart also illustrates how alternate financing sources, such as crowdsourcing, indirectly affect the viability of female-owned ventures. This path's indirect influence is computed as follows: 0.45 represents the effect of crowdsourcing on alternative means of finance, multiplied by 0.85 represents the effect of alternative means of finance on the viability of female owned ventures.

The phrase "Indirect Influence" denotes that although crowdsourcing has a direct effect on viability, it also has an indirect effect by making alternative means of finance more accessible. This pathway highlights the intricate links among the many parties and implies that, in addition to offering quick money, crowdsourcing may also open up new financial avenues that assistance long-term viability. A summary of the combined direct and indirect effects yields a total influence of 0.87. This impressive sum suggests that crowdsourcing, both directly and indirectly, is essential to the overall viability of female owned firms. The label "Partial arbitration" indicates that although alternative means of finance strengthens the connection among viability and crowdsourcing, crowdsourcing is still a highly reliable independent predictor of viability results.

DISCUSSION

The results of this investigation highlight the important role that crowdsourcing, especially when applied to the East Africa, plays in improving the viability of female owned companies. Empirical information shows that in addition to offering quick access to money, crowdsourcing also makes it easier for female to find other sources of finance, fostering an ecosystem that is beneficial to their venture. This dual approach is vital since crowdsourcing is a critical tool for overcoming the obstacles that many female venture innovators encounter when pursuing classical finance sources. The usefulness of crowdsourcing as a financial strategy is demonstrated by the strong direct influence it has on the viability of female owned ventures. Effective crowdsourcing campaigns allow female venture owners to obtain cash as well as recognition and exposure for their ventures. This result is consistent with previous research that highlights the role that traditional money and community assistance play in crowdsourcing campaigns' success. Long-term company success depends on female venture innovators building trust and loyalty among potential investors through their networks.

The investigation also shows how alternative means of finance functions as a mediator in this connection. Crowdsourcing may help female ventures access additional financial resources, as evidenced by its noteworthy indirect effect on viability through alternative means of finance. This association is especially crucial in areas like the East Africa, where conventional finance institutions might have stigma against companies run by female. Securing alternative means of finance not only increases the operational capabilities of female owned firms, but it also adds to their overall resilience.

CONCLUSION

This investigation demonstrates the remarkable direct and indirect effects of crowdsourcing on the viability of female owned companies around the East Africa. The empirical results show that crowdsourcing not only offers crucial financial resources but also makes alternative means of finance more accessible, improving the financial ecosystem for female venture innovators. Crowdsourcing proved to be a vital motivator for development and operational stability in female owned firms by raising awareness and validating company concepts.

Moreover, the intermediary function of substitute external finance emphasizes the interdependence of monetary assets accessible to female venture innovators. Effective crowdsourcing campaigns can provide alternative means of finance, which augments the resilience and viability of these firms overall and removes some of the structural obstacles that female frequently encounter in classical financing systems. This fruitful collaboration highlights how crucial it is to create strong crowdsourcing programs that are especially designed to assist female ventures. The chapter does, however, also recognize the ongoing difficulties, such as those pertaining to digital literacy, technological accessibility, and cultural stigma that can impede the effective use of crowdsourcing. It is essential to put in place focused training initiatives and assistance networks that enable female venture innovators to effectively negotiate the challenges of alternative means of finance and crowdsourcing in order to optimize the advantages of these external finance sources.

MANAGERIAL IMPLICATIONS

The investigation's conclusions have important management ramifications for assisting female-owned enterprises in the East Africa. First and foremost, the findings emphasize how crucial it is for female venture innovators to assimilate crowdsourcing as a vital part of their financial plan. It is recommended that managers and company leaders proactively endorse crowdsourcing sources as feasible means of obtaining capitals, especially in settings where conventional finance choices are restricted or discriminatory against female. Firms may help female venture innovators to achieve financial independence and accelerate company development by providing access to crowdsourcing.

The chapter also emphasizes how important it is to give female venture innovators access to tools and training targeted at enhancing their digital literacy and marketing abilities. Effective crowdsourcing frequently involves both a strong company concept and the capacity to persuade viable investors of the idea. Supervisors must to think about putting in place mentorship and training programs that provide female the tools they need to start profitable crowdsourcing projects, increasing their chances of getting financing.

REAL WORLD IMPLICATIONS

The investigation's conclusions have a number of useful ramifications for improving the performance of female-owned enterprises in the East Africa by making efficient use of alternative means of finance sources including crowdsourcing. First and foremost, practitioners and firms must to give top priority to creating easily navigable crowdsourcing sources designed especially for female venture innovators. It is important to design interfaces that are easy to use and furnish users with materials that facilitate the crowdsourcing process, so guaranteeing the effective involvement of female from varied backgrounds. Also, it is recommended to incorporate hands-on seminars and training sessions that center on crowdsourcing tactics and digital marketing. These courses may provide female venture innovators the know-how to tell engaging campaign stories, interact with potential assistance's, and effectively use traditional media to reach a wider audience. Such programs can greatly increase the chance of effective capital raising efforts by fostering expertise and confidence.

THEORETICAL IMPLICATIONS

The results of this research, especially when considering the East Africa, add to the theoretical knowledge of the connections among alternative means of finance, crowdsourcing, and the viability of female-owned ventures. This investigation adds to the body of knowledge on entrepreneurial finance by demonstrating the direct connection among crowdsourcing and venture viability. Crowdsourcing is now recognized not only as a source of money but also as a useful instrument that may augment the viability of a company. With this viewpoint, the emphasis is shifted from conventional finance approaches to more creative, inclusive systems that have the potential to strengthen the hand of underprivileged venture innovators.

Also, the investigation's identification of the mediating function of alternative external finance gives the theoretical framework pertaining to the financial avenues open to female venture innovators a more nuanced angle. It emphasizes how crucial it is to see finance possibilities as linked rather than as discrete. This connectivity shows that a effective crowdsourcing campaign may open up new financial avenues, shedding light on a route that other research would have missed. These revelations have the potential to influence research priorities in the future by encouraging researchers to investigate the dynamics of how various external finance sources combine to encourage entrepreneurial ventures.

RECOMMENDATIONS

Several recommendations may be made to augment the efficacy of alternative means of finance and crowdsourcing for female owned firms in the East Africa, based on the investigation's findings. First and foremost, it is imperative to provide training programs that are specifically tailored to the requirements of female venture innovators. These courses ought to assimilate thorough instruction in digital marketing, financial literacy, and crowdsourcing tactics so that female may effectively negotiate the intricacies of the crowdsourcing procedure. Real globe activities that let attendees draft and augment their crowdsourcing pitches should be incorporated into workshops to make sure attendees are ready to interact with viable assistance's. Stakeholders should also place a high priority on creating networks of assistance that link female venture innovators with effective crowdsourcing campaigners, financial institutions, and mentors. Establishing networking and cooperation spaces may strengthen ties within the community and provide female access to important information and tools. Frequent offline and online networking events can promote information exchange among attendees and aid in the development of these ties. In addition, legislators and neighborhood associations ought to collaborate to raise the profile of crowdsourcing as a feasible source of money for female venture innovators. Campaigns that showcase effective case studies have the power to encourage and inspire people to learn more about crowdsourcing. Simplifying the laws governing crowdsourcing can also make it simpler for female venture innovators to utilize these sources, improving their usability.

FUTURE DIRECTIONS

The investigation's conclusions provide a number of directions for future investigation into the workings of alternative means of finance and crowdsourcing as they relate to female-owned enterprises. Undertaking longitudinal research to monitor the long-term effects of crowdsourcing on the viability of ventures is one encouraging avenue. By shedding light on how early crowdsourcing success translates into long-term profitability and development, such investigation may help to a better understanding of the elements that lead to long-term success.

Further research may examine how technology might assistance female venture innovators' efforts at crowdsourcing. Examining how traditional media, mobile applications, and digital source innovations might make it easier to access crowdsourcing resources could provide insightful information. The influence of cultural and socio-fiscal variables on the efficacy of crowdsourcing in various geographic locations is a crucial field for further research. Research comparing the effects of various cultural settings on crowdsourcing campaign performance might shed light on the possibilities and challenges that female venture innovators encounter throughout the globe. This kind of investigation would aid in the creation of customized plans that deal with certain local challenges.

REFERENCES

Adula, M., Birbirsa, Z. A., & Kant, S. (2023). The effect of interpersonal, problem solving and technical training skills on performance of Ethiopia textile industry: Continuance, normative and affective commitment as mediators. *Cogent Business & Management*, *10*(3), 2286672. Advance online publication. DOI: 10.1080/23311975.2023.2286672

Ajiva, O. A., Ejike, O. G., & Abhulimen, A. O. Empowering female venture innovators in the creative sector: Overcoming barriers and strategies for long-term success.

Aracil-Jordá, J., Clemente-Almendros, J. A., Jiménez-Zarco, A. I., & González-González, I. (2023). Improving the traditional performance of female owned microenterprises: The role of traditional media marketing actions. *Technological Forecasting and Traditional Change*, *191*, 122484. DOI: 10.1016/j.techfore.2023.122484

Asefa, K., & Debela, K. L. "Effect of Transformational Leadership on Organizational Performance: The Mediating Role of Employee Commitment and Expert Systems (AI) Inclusion in Ethiopia," *2023 International Conference on Communication, Security and Artificial Intelligence (ICCSAI)*, Greater Noida, India, 2023, pp. 305-310, DOI: 10.1109/ICCSAI59793.2023.10421269

Babar, Z. N., & Abbas, J. (2023). Empowering Female Venture innovators: The influence of Family Assistance and Country of Origin Effects on Financial Inclusion. *Journal of Excellence in Venture Administration*, *1*(2), 39–63.

Babar, Z. N., Al Sulaiti, K., Aldereai, O., Abbas, J., & Al Sulaiti, I. (2023). Empowering Female Venture innovators: The influence of Family Assistance and Country of Origin Effects on Financial Inclusion. *Journal of Excellence in Venture Administration*, *1*(2), 39–63.

Berglund, E. (2023). Changing Tides and Navigating Uncertainty: An ethnographic investigation of NGO resilience in coastal South India.

Birhane, M., Amentie, C., Borji, B., & Kant, S. Are Ethiopian Coffee Farmers Proficient to Predict Capital Structure with Mediation of AI Based Knowledge Systems and Asset Liquidity? In *AI in Agriculture for Sustainable and Economic Management* (pp. 199-215). CRC Press. DOI: 10.1201/9781003451648-15

Calic, G., Lévesque, M., & Shevchenko, A. (2023). On why female-owned ventures take more time to secure microloans. Small Venture Fiscals, 1-22.

Dereso, C. W., Kant, S., Muthuraman, M., & Tufa, G. (2023). Effect of Point of Service on Health Department Student's Creativity in Comprehensive Universities of Ethiopia: Moderating Role of Public-Private Partnership and Mediating Role of Work Place Learning. In: Jain, S., Groppe, S., Mihindukulasooriya, N. (eds) Proceedings of the International Health Informatics Conference. Lecture Notes in Electrical Engineering, vol 990. Springer, Singapore. https://doi.org/DOI: 10.1007/978-981-19-9090-8_13

Durga, P., Godavarthi, D., Kant, S., & Basa, S. S. (2024). Aspect-based drug review classification through a hybrid model with ant colony optimization using deep learning. *Discov Computing*, *27*(1), 19. DOI: 10.1007/s10791-024-09441-w

Dutta, A., & Banerjee, S. (2018). Does microfinance impede sustainable entrepreneurial initiatives among female borrowers? Evidence from rural Bangladesh. *Journal of Rural Studies*, *60*, 70–81. DOI: 10.1016/j.jrurstud.2018.03.007

Guyo, D. M., Kero, C. A., & Kant, S. (2025). Is Marketing Intermediaries' Mediation Required for Livestock and Products Marketing to Improve the Economic Status of Pastoralist Communities in Ethiopia? In *AI in Agriculture for Sustainable and Economic Management* (pp. 216-234). CRC Press.

Guyo, D. M., Kant, S., & Kero, C. A. (2023, November). Mediation of Marketing Intermediaries and AI Adoption Between Livestock Products Marketing and Economic Status of Pastoralist in Ethiopia. In *2023 International Conference on Communication, Security and Artificial Intelligence (ICCSAI)* (pp. 311-316). IEEE.

Harrison, R. T., Botelho, T., & Mason, C. M. (2020). Female on the edge of a breakthrough? A stereotype threat theory of female's angel investing. *International Small Venture Journal*, *38*(8), 768–797.

Inoubli, A., Onkware Sarangé, C., & Adebola, M. (2022). The Agriventure Ecosystem in East and Southern Africa: Exploring the Role and Synergies of Vital Stakeholders in the Space.

Jabo, B., & Kant, S. "Impact of Technical CRM on Ethiopia Bank Human-Computer Interface and Competitive Advantage as Mediators of Performance," *2024 IEEE International Conference on Computing, Power and Communication Technologies (IC2PCT)*, Greater Noida, India, 2024, pp. 679-682, https://doi.org/DOI: 10.1109/IC2PCT60090.2024.10486237

Kant, S., & Adula, M. (2024). AI Learning and Work Attitude Mediation Between Reward and Organizational Support in Ethiopia. In Gomathi Sankar, J., & David, A. (Eds.), *Generative AI for Transformational Management* (pp. 109–136). IGI Global., DOI: 10.4018/979-8-3693-5578-7.ch005

Kant, S., & Adula, M. (2024). Mediated by AI-Based Generative Re-Enforcement Learning and Work Attitude: Are Intrinsic Rewards Transforming Employee Perceived Organizational Support? In Gomathi Sankar, J., & David, A. (Eds.), *Generative AI for Transformational Management* (pp. 83–108). IGI Global., DOI: 10.4018/979-8-3693-5578-7.ch004

Kant, S., & Adula, M. (2024). Human-Machine Interaction in the Metaverse in the Context of Ethiopia. In *Impact and Potential of Machine Learning in the Metaverse* (pp. 196–212). IGI Global., DOI: 10.4018/979-8-3693-5762-0.ch008

Kato, A. I. (2023). Unlocking the Potential of Microfinance Solutions on Urban Woman Venture innovations Development in East Africa: A Bibliometric Analysis Angle. *Viability*, *15*(20), 14862.

Kromidha, E., Yadav, N., & Ilavarasan, P. V. (2023). Digital microfinance crowdsourcing for disconnected female venture innovators in India. International Journal of Venture innovations and Small Venture, 50(4), 459-481.

Nigam, N., & Shatila, K. (2024). Entrepreneurial intention among female venture innovators and the mediating effect of dynamic capabilities: Empirical evidence from Lebanon. *International Journal of Entrepreneurial Behaviour & Research, 30*(4), 916–937. DOI: 10.1108/IJEBR-07-2023-0690

Nyoach, T. D., Lemi, K., Debela, T., & Kant, S. (2024). Does Organizational Commitment Mediate the Relationship between Employee Relationship Management and Bank Performance? The Case of Banks in Ethiopia. *International Journal of Organizational Leadership, 13*(2), 355–376. DOI: 10.33844/ijol.2024.60419

Panigrahi, A., Pati, A., Sahu, B., Das, M. N., Nayak, D. S. K., Sahoo, G., & Kant, S. (2023). En-MinWhale: An ensemble approach based on MRMR and Whale optimization for Cancer diagnosis. *IEEE Access : Practical Innovations, Open Solutions, 11*, 113526–113542. DOI: 10.1109/ACCESS.2023.3318261

Serwaah, P., Shneor, R., Nyarko, S. A., & Nielsen, K. R. (2024). Explaining sex differences in crowdsourcing contribution intentions. *Technology in Society, 76*, 102425. DOI: 10.1016/j.techsoc.2023.102425

Smagulova, G., & Goncalves, M. (2023). Drivers for female venture innovations in Central Asia: A case analysis of Kazakhstani enterprises. *Journal of Transnational Management, 28*(3-4), 249–303. DOI: 10.1080/15475778.2023.2285621

Snellman, K., & Solal, I. (2023). Does investor sex matter for the success of female venture innovators? Sex homophily and the stigma of incompetence in entrepreneurial finance. *Firm Science, 34*(2), 680–699.

Srinivas, S. B. (2019). *Sex and The Crowd: Differential Effectiveness of Justifications Used by Venture innovators in Their Crowdsourcing Pitches*. The University of Texas at Austin.

Yu, W., Fei, J., Peng, G., & Bort, J. (2024). When a crisis hits: An examination of the effect of the global financial crisis and the COVID-19 pandemic on financing for female venture innovators. *Journal of Venture Venturing, 39*(2), 106379. DOI: 10.1016/j.jbusvent.2024.106379

Zhao, K., Wang, H., & Yin, X. (2023). How female venture innovators influence reward-based crowdsourcing performance: The mediating role of traditional and fiscal worth's orientation. International Venture innovations and Management Journal, 19(4), 1771-1802.

Alternative Financing: Alternative financing refers to funding sources outside of traditional bank loans and capital markets. This can include crowdsourcing, peer-to-peer lending, venture capital, angel investing, and other innovative financing methods that often cater to startups or businesses that may struggle to secure conventional funding.

Arbitration: Arbitration is a form of alternative dispute resolution where a neutral third party, known as an arbitrator, is appointed to resolve disputes outside of the court system. The arbitrator's decision is usually binding and can provide a quicker, less formal, and often less expensive resolution than traditional litigation.

Crowd-funding: Crowd-funding is a method of raising capital from a large number of individuals, typically via the internet, to fund a project or business venture. It allows entrepreneurs to solicit small amounts of money from a wide audience, often in exchange for rewards, equity, or other incentives.

Sustainability: Sustainability refers to the ability to maintain or improve certain processes or systems without compromising the ability of future generations to meet their own needs. In a business context, it often involves adopting practices that are environmentally friendly, traditionally responsible, and economically viable over the long term.

Women Owned Business: A women- owned business is an enterprise that is owned, managed, or significantly influenced by women. These businesses are often characterized by their focus on sex equality and may prioritize traditional responsibility, community engagement, and innovative practices.

KEY TERMS AND DEFINITIONS

Chapter 7

The Interplay of Climate Change and Inflation in Sindh

Ghazala Shaukat
University of Sindh, Pakistan

Farhat Jokhiyo
University of Sindh, Pakistan

Saima Shaikh
University of Sindh, Pakistan

ABSTRACT

Sindh, located in southeastern Pakistan, faces significant socio-economic challenges that have been exacerbated by climate change and rising inflation. The 2022 floods, the most devastating in Pakistan's recent history, exposed the province's vulnerability to climate-induced disasters and deepened existing economic and social inequalities. This chapter examines how climate change, particularly floods, has contributed to inflationary pressures in Sindh and analyzes how inflation has, in turn, worsened the province's ability to respond to natural disasters. By focusing on the floods of 2022, we explore the direct and indirect impacts on various sectors, such as health, education, employment, food security, and infrastructure.

DOI: 10.4018/979-8-3693-9193-8.ch007

1. INTRODUCTION

Sindh, located in southeastern Pakistan, faces significant socio-economic challenges that have been exacerbated by climate change and rising inflation. The 2022 floods, the most devastating in Pakistan's recent history, exposed the province's vulnerability to climate-induced disasters and deepened existing economic and social inequalities. This chapter examines how climate change, particularly floods, has contributed to inflationary pressures in Sindh and analyzes how inflation has, in turn, worsened the province's ability to respond to natural disasters. By focusing on the floods of 2022, we explore the direct and indirect impacts on various sectors, such as health, education, employment, food security, and infrastructure.

2. CLIMATE CHANGE AND FLOODS IN SINDH

2.1. Climate Change and Flooding Patterns

Sindh, due to its geographic location, is highly vulnerable to climate change, particularly floods. Rising global temperatures have contributed to unpredictable monsoon patterns, intense rainfall, and glacial melt from the Himalayas and Hindu Kush mountains. The 2022 floods were a direct consequence of these changing weather patterns. According to the *Pakistan Meteorological Department*, Sindh received nearly 500% more rainfall than average during the monsoon season, contributing to catastrophic flooding that submerged vast areas of agricultural land and displaced millions of people (Dawn, 2022).

The floods were worsened by climate change, which has intensified weather events globally. Sindh has experienced a steady rise in average temperatures, leading to accelerated glacial melt, while warmer oceans contribute to increased moisture in the atmosphere, resulting in heavier rains (Patz & Thomson, 2018). These factors combined to create the extreme floods of 2022.

2.2. Poor Infrastructure and Planning

The severe flooding was not just the result of natural causes. Years of poor infrastructure development and inadequate water management policies left Sindh vulnerable to extreme weather events. The province's drainage systems were unable to handle the excess rainfall, while flood protection measures, such as embankments, were insufficient and poorly maintained. Sindh's government had not prioritized upgrading infrastructure to manage such natural disasters, despite previous warnings from experts and international agencies (Express Tribune, 2022).

Prolonged underinvestment in infrastructure can be attributed to the diversion of funds to national security and counterterrorism efforts. Military spending has dominated Pakistan's national budget, leaving fewer resources for critical development projects such as flood defenses (Shah, Khan, & Qureshi, 2019). This failure to invest in climate resilience has made Sindh highly susceptible to floods, exacerbating the socio-economic consequences of climate change.

3. INFLATION: CAUSES AND CONSEQUENCES OF THE FLOODS

3.1. Impact of Floods on Inflation

The 2022 floods severely disrupted Sindh's economy, particularly the agricultural sector, which accounts for a large portion of the province's output. The destruction of crops—including wheat, rice, and cotton—on approximately 1.9 million acres of land resulted in immediate food shortages and price hikes (FAO, 2022). Inflation in essential goods surged to unprecedented levels, with the Consumer Price Index (CPI) reflecting a sharp increase in the prices of vegetables, wheat, and pulses (Pakistan Bureau of Statistics, 2023).

According to the *Pakistan Bureau of Statistics*, food inflation surged by 32.6% after the floods, with the prices of essential commodities like wheat and rice rising by over 35%. The livestock sector, already strained by rising input costs due to inflation, was hit hard by the loss of thousands of animals, further contributing to higher prices for meat and dairy products (Memon & Sharjeel, 2015).

3.2. Supply Chain Disruptions

The damage to roads, bridges, and transportation networks exacerbated inflation by creating supply chain bottlenecks. According to the *National Disaster Management Authority* (NDMA), over 13,000 kilometers of roads and 22 bridges were damaged or destroyed during the floods, limiting access to markets and increasing transportation costs (NDMA, 2022). This disruption in supply chains, especially for food and agricultural products, led to further inflationary pressures as the cost of moving goods rose dramatically.

The inability to restore transport networks quickly meant that prices remained high for months following the floods, making essential goods unaffordable for many families in Sindh (Shoukat, 2020).

4. SOCIO-ECONOMIC IMPACTS OF FLOODS, CLIMATE CHANGE, AND INFLATION

4.1. Education

The destruction of educational infrastructure was another critical impact of the floods. According to *UNICEF*, approximately 20,000 schools were damaged or destroyed, affecting over 2 million children in Sindh (UNICEF, 2022). In rural areas, many schools were turned into shelters for displaced families, further disrupting education. This added to the existing challenges in the province's education system, which has long suffered from poor infrastructure and limited access, particularly for girls.

Girls were disproportionately affected by the disruption in education, as the loss of schools and the economic pressures caused by inflation forced many families to prioritize boys' education over girls'. The long-term impact of this is likely to exacerbate gender inequalities in education and employment in Sindh (Memon & Khaskheli, 2021).

4.2. Health

Health services in Sindh were overwhelmed by the floods, with many healthcare facilities either destroyed or made inaccessible. The stagnant water left behind by the floods became breeding grounds for waterborne diseases, such as cholera, dengue, and malaria, affecting millions of people. The *World Health Organization* (WHO) reported that over 3 million people were impacted by waterborne diseases in the aftermath of the floods (WHO, 2022).

The destruction of healthcare infrastructure, coupled with the rise in inflation, made it difficult for many families to access medical care and essential medicines. Pregnant women and children were particularly vulnerable, with maternal mortality rates rising due to the lack of access to health services (Shah, Khan, & Qureshi, 2019). The limited availability of clean drinking water and proper sanitation facilities further exacerbated the spread of disease, putting immense pressure on Sindh's already fragile healthcare system (Patz & Thomson, 2018).

4.3. Jobs and Livelihoods

The agricultural sector, which employs a significant portion of Sindh's population, was devastated by the floods. Approximately 900,000 jobs were lost in the agricultural sector alone, with farmers and laborers left without work due to the destruction of crops and farmland (PDMA, 2022). In addition, many informal sector workers lost their sources of income as small businesses were destroyed by the floods, and displacement prevented them from accessing markets.

The loss of jobs contributed to a sharp rise in poverty levels across the province, with many families unable to afford basic necessities due to inflation. The long-term economic impact of the floods on employment is likely to be profound, as the agricultural sector struggles to recover and rebuild (Arif et al., 2019).

4.4. Food Scarcity

Food security in Sindh deteriorated rapidly following the floods, as the destruction of agricultural land caused massive reductions in local food production. The *Food and Agriculture Organization* (FAO) estimated that Sindh experienced a 30% reduction in food production after the floods, leading to widespread food scarcity (FAO, 2022). This food shortage not only drove inflation but also led to malnutrition, particularly among children.

The limited availability of food, coupled with rising prices, left many rural households unable to meet their nutritional needs. According to the *National Nutrition Survey* (2018), malnutrition rates spiked in the aftermath of the floods, with children under five experiencing stunted growth due to inadequate food intake (National Nutrition Survey, 2018).

4.5. Shelter and Displacement

The floods displaced millions of people in Sindh, with over 1.7 million homes damaged or destroyed (NDMA, 2022). Displaced families were forced to live in overcrowded temporary camps that lacked basic services, including clean water, sanitation, and electricity. This displacement created long-term instability for many families, as rebuilding efforts were slow and inadequate.

Many families lacked the financial resources to rebuild their homes, leaving them vulnerable to future disasters. The loss of shelter not only exposed displaced populations to further health risks but also contributed to long-term poverty and insecurity (Memon & Khaskheli, 2021).

4.6. Migration

The widespread destruction caused by the floods led to large-scale migration from rural areas to urban centers, particularly Karachi and Hyderabad. Displaced families moved to cities in search of shelter and employment, putting immense pressure on urban infrastructure and resources. The rapid influx of people into cities exacerbated existing challenges related to housing, sanitation, and access to healthcare.

Urban migration also led to social tensions as displaced populations competed with host communities for limited resources. The provincial government has struggled to manage the long-term effects of this migration, which has contributed to overcrowding, increased poverty, and heightened inequality in urban areas (Shoukat, 2020).

5. POLICY RECOMMENDATIONS

To address the challenges posed by the interplay of climate change, inflation, and the impacts of the 2022 floods, a comprehensive policy approach is needed. Key recommendations include:

1. **Strengthening Flood Management Infrastructure**: Investing in the modernization of flood management infrastructure is critical to reducing Sindh's vulnerability to future flooding events. This includes improving embankments, dams, drainage systems, and flood protection measures. A more robust water management system would help mitigate the effects of extreme rainfall, allowing water to be diverted and stored during heavy rains. Integrated floodplain management should also be promoted, with particular focus on areas along the Indus River, which is prone to seasonal flooding. Involving local communities in disaster preparedness training and implementing early warning systems could also significantly reduce loss of life and property during such events (FAO, 2018).
2. **Promoting Climate-Resilient Agriculture**: Agriculture is the backbone of Sindh's economy, and promoting climate-resilient farming practices is essential to protect this sector from future climate-related disasters. This can include supporting farmers in adopting drought-resistant seeds, improving irrigation techniques, and encouraging organic farming. Moreover, the government should establish support programs to help farmers transition to more sustainable and climate-adaptive practices, including access to financial aid, micro-credit schemes, and insurance policies to help recover from crop losses (Arif

et al., 2019). Implementing modern agricultural technology, such as water-efficient drip irrigation systems, will also help mitigate the impact of droughts and floods on food security.

3. **Strengthening Disaster Preparedness and Response**: One of the key lessons from the 2022 floods is the need for a more effective disaster preparedness and response framework. This includes strengthening early warning systems, improving coordination between national and provincial disaster management authorities, and ensuring that relief supplies are pre-positioned in high-risk areas. Investment in data-driven flood modeling systems can also help predict and manage flood risks more effectively. Moreover, establishing contingency plans for post-disaster recovery, including efficient evacuation strategies, relief distribution, and rebuilding efforts, is crucial (NDMA, 2022).
4. **Expanding Social Safety Nets**: Social protection measures are vital for building resilience against inflation and climate-induced disasters, particularly for vulnerable populations such as women, children, and displaced families. Expanding existing social safety net programs, such as cash transfers and food aid, would provide immediate relief to those most affected by inflation and loss of livelihoods during floods. Government schemes should focus on ensuring that low-income households have access to affordable essential goods, housing, and healthcare, particularly during times of crisis. Enhancing support for displaced populations, both in rural and urban areas, should be a key component of disaster response planning (Shah, Khan, & Qureshi, 2019).
5. **Promoting Sustainable Urbanization**: The mass migration of displaced populations from rural areas to urban centers during and after the floods has highlighted the urgent need for sustainable urbanization strategies. The provincial government must invest in affordable housing, strengthen urban infrastructure, and improve basic services in cities such as Karachi and Hyderabad. Upgrading water, sanitation, and health services in urban areas will help mitigate the pressure on existing resources caused by rapid urbanization. Additionally, sustainable urban planning should focus on creating resilient cities that can better withstand the effects of future climate-related disasters (Memon & Khaskheli, 2021).

6. **Improving Health Infrastructure**: The destruction of health facilities and the outbreak of waterborne diseases during the floods demonstrated the critical need for a resilient healthcare system. Strengthening health infrastructure, particularly in rural areas, by rebuilding flood-proof health centers and ensuring access to clean water and sanitation will be essential to safeguard public health in future disasters. Investing in mobile health units and establishing rapid-response medical teams can also help provide immediate relief in disaster-stricken areas. Furthermore, special focus must be given to maternal and child health services, as women and children are disproportionately affected during such crises (WHO, 2022).
7. **Food Security Interventions** Addressing the food scarcity caused by the floods requires a multifaceted approach that includes both short-term relief and long-term sustainability. In the immediate aftermath of disasters, the government must ensure that food aid is rapidly distributed to affected regions. Beyond emergency relief, long-term food security can be promoted through policies that support sustainable agricultural practices, such as crop diversification and investments in post-harvest infrastructure to reduce food waste. Furthermore, community food banks and local-level programs that encourage home gardening and urban farming can help build resilience against food shortages (FAO, 2022).
8. **Livelihood Diversification and Employment Support** The loss of jobs in agriculture and small businesses during the floods highlights the need for livelihood diversification. The government should support programs that provide vocational training and financial aid to help individuals transition into new employment sectors, such as agroforestry, sustainable fisheries, and small-scale manufacturing. Encouraging public-private partnerships and creating new job opportunities in the renewable energy sector can also play a crucial role in reducing dependency on climate-vulnerable sectors. Developing local industries that are less susceptible to environmental disasters will help create more resilient employment opportunities (Memon & Sharjeel, 2015).
9. **Expanding Disaster Insurance and Financial Support**: Providing disaster insurance for farmers, small businesses, and households in flood-prone areas is essential to protect against the financial losses

caused by extreme weather events. Expanding access to affordable disaster insurance can offer a safety net, allowing those affected by the floods to recover more quickly. Additionally, providing low-interest loans or grants for rebuilding homes, infrastructure, and businesses will support long-term recovery and reconstruction efforts. Financial support mechanisms that encourage investment in climate-resilient infrastructure will be crucial to reducing vulnerability in future disasters (Sanchez-Triana et al., 2015; Tunio, et al., 2023).

6. GAPS AND OPPORTUNITIES IN CURRENT POLICIES

While Sindh's climate change policy 2022 provide a framework for addressing the impacts of climate-induced disasters, significant gaps remain that hinder the province's ability to effectively address inflation and socio-economic vulnerabilities:

6.1. Lack of Focus on Inflation and Climate Change Nexus

The Sindh Climate Change Policy lacks a specific focus on the relationship between climate change and inflation. Although the policy addresses disaster management and climate resilience, it does not provide concrete strategies to address the inflationary pressures caused by climate-induced disasters, such as crop failures and supply chain disruptions (Government of Sindh, 2022).

6.2. Insufficient Gender-Inclusive Strategies

While the policy acknowledges the vulnerability of women and marginalized communities, there is a lack of gender-specific interventions that empower women in the recovery and resilience-building process. Women play a critical role in agriculture and community recovery, yet they are often excluded from decision-making processes (Shoukat, 2020; Tunio, et al., 2021).

6.3. Gaps in Urban Migration and Housing Policies

The policy does not adequately address the long-term impacts of climate-induced migration from rural to urban areas. The rapid influx of displaced populations into urban centers during the floods has highlighted the need for sustainable urbanization strategies that provide affordable housing and strengthen infrastructure (Memon & Khaskheli, 2021; Tunio, et al., 2021).

6.4. Weak Monitoring and Evaluation Mechanisms

There is a lack of robust monitoring and evaluation systems to track the progress of disaster management and climate adaptation initiatives. Without effective mechanisms to measure the outcomes of these policies, Sindh risks repeating the same mistakes in future disasters (Sanchez-Triana et al., 2015; Tunio, 2020).

CONCLUSION

The 2022 floods in Sindh underscore the critical interplay between climate change, inflation, and socio-economic vulnerabilities. The devastating impacts of the floods were compounded by decades of poor infrastructure planning, insufficient investment in climate resilience, and a lack of adequate disaster preparedness. Inflation, already a significant challenge in Sindh, worsened in the aftermath of the floods, driving up the cost of essential goods and making it difficult for the most vulnerable communities to recover.

Addressing these challenges requires a comprehensive and multi-sectoral approach that integrates climate resilience into every aspect of policy and planning. By investing in flood management infrastructure, promoting sustainable agriculture, strengthening social safety nets, and improving disaster preparedness, Sindh can build a more resilient future for its people. At the same time, addressing the structural issues that have contributed to Sindh's vulnerability—such as underinvestment in urban planning, health infrastructure, and education—will be essential for long-term stability and development.

REFERENCES

Ali, M., Memon, N., Panhwar, Q., & Bhutto, A. (2019). Impact of climate change on air quality and health in Sindh, Pakistan. *Journal of Environmental Management*, *232*, 469–478.

Arif, G., Riaz, A., Faisal, M., Khattak, M., & Sathar, Z. (2019). *Impact of climate change on agriculture in Pakistan*. Pakistan Agricultural Research Council.

Dawn. (2022). "Flood Devastation: Sindh's Record Rainfall and Its Consequences." *Dawn News*. Retrieved from https://www.dawn.com/news/floods

Express Tribune. (2022). "Climate Change and Infrastructure: A Deadly Combination for Sindh." *The Express Tribune*. Retrieved from https://www.tribune.com.pk/news/climate-change

Food and Agriculture Organization (FAO). (2022). "Impact of Floods on Agriculture in Sindh." *FAO Report*. Retrieved from https://www.fao.org/sindh-flood-report

Government of Sindh. (2022). *Sindh Climate Change Policy 2022*. Environment, Climate Change & Coastal Development Department.

Memon, N., & Khaskheli, M. (2021). *The socioeconomic impacts of climate change on vulnerable populations in Sindh*. Sustainable Development Policy Institute.

Memon, N., & Sharjeel, S. (2015). The aftermath of the 2010 floods in Sindh: Impacts on food security and nutrition. *Nutrition and Health (Berkhamsted, Hertfordshire)*, *22*(3), 165–174.

National Disaster Management Authority (NDMA). (2022). *Flood Damages and Relief Efforts in Sindh*. Retrieved from https://www.ndma.gov.pk/reports

National Nutrition Survey. (2018). Government of Pakistan.

Pakistan Bureau of Statistics. (2023). *Consumer Price Index*. Government of Pakistan.

Patz, J. A., & Thomson, M. C. (2018). Climate change and health: A global perspective. *The Lancet. Planetary Health*, *2*(10), e466–e467.

Sanchez-Triana, E., Enriquez, J., Larsen, M. J., Webster, D., & Afzal, M. (2015). *Environmental health risks in Pakistan: An economic analysis*. World Bank.

Shah, S., Khan, H., & Qureshi, M. (2019). Economic implications of climate change on agriculture in Sindh. *Journal of Agricultural Economics*, *7*(2), 85–100.

Shoukat, G. (2020). Women and Climate Change: A Gender Perspective on Adaptation Strategies in Sindh. *Pakistan Journal of Environmental Studies*, *15*(1), 25–39.

Tunio, M. N. (2020). Academic entrepreneurship in developing countries: contextualizing recent debate. In *Research handbook on entrepreneurship in emerging economies* (pp. 130–146). Edward Elgar Publishing. DOI: 10.4337/9781788973717.00014

Tunio, M. N., Chaudhry, I. S., Shaikh, S., Jariko, M. A., & Brahmi, M. (2021). Determinants of the sustainable entrepreneurial engagement of youth in developing country—An empirical evidence from Pakistan. *Sustainability (Basel)*, *13*(14), 7764. DOI: 10.3390/su13147764

Tunio, M. N., Jariko, M. A., Børsen, T., Shaikh, S., Mushtaque, T., & Brahmi, M. (2021). How entrepreneurship sustains barriers in the entrepreneurial process—A lesson from a developing nation. *Sustainability (Basel)*, *13*(20), 11419. DOI: 10.3390/su132011419

Tunio, M. N., Shaikh, E., Katper, N. K., & Brahmi, M. (2023). Nascent entrepreneurs and challenges in the digital market in developing countries. *International Journal of Public Sector Performance Management*, *12*(1-2), 140–153. DOI: 10.1504/IJPSPM.2023.132244

UNICEF. (2022). "Impact of Floods on Children's Education in Sindh." *UNICEF Report*. Retrieved from https://www.unicef.org/sindh-flood-impact

World Health Organization (WHO). (2022). "Health Crises Following the 2022 Floods in Pakistan." *WHO Emergency Response Report.* Retrieved from https://www.who.int/pakistan-response

Compilation of References

Abbas, A. A. (2018). The Bright Future of Technopreneurship. *International Journal of Scientific and Engineering Research*, *9*(December), 563–566.

Abhilasha, A., Sreenivasulu, A., & Manimozhi, T. KUMAR, P. S., Selvakumar, P., & Singh, P. (2022, April). The Model of Smart Sensing Device For Sensitive Nanoclusters Modification in Sensing Properties. In 2022 2nd International Conference on Advance Computing and Innovative Technologies in Engineering (ICACITE) (pp. 1043-1047). IEEE.

Abubakre, M., & Mkansi, M. (2022). How do technologists do "ICT for development"? A contextualised perspective on ICT4D in South Africa. *European Journal of Information Systems*, *31*(1), 7–24. DOI: 10.1080/0960085X.2021.1978343

Aburas, W., & Alshammari, T. M. (2020). Pharmacists' roles in emergency and disasters: COVID-19 as an example. *Saudi Pharmaceutical Journal : SPJ : the Official Publication of the Saudi Pharmaceutical Society*, *28*(12), 1797–1816. DOI: 10.1016/j.jsps.2020.11.006 PMID: 33257901

Adam, I. O., & Dzang Alhassan, M. (2021). The mediating role of ICT regulation on the effects of ICT access and ICT use on e-participation: Evidence from structural equation modelling and necessary condition analysis. *African Journal of Science, Technology, Innovation and Development*, *0*(0), 1–12. DOI: 10.1080/20421338.2021.1937815

Adedeji, A. S. (2021). Islamic financing and entrepreneurship development: Providing an alternative model for new venture growth. *Finance, Management and Entrepreneurship*, 91.

Adhikari, B., Ozaki, A., Marahatta, S. B., Rijal, K. R., & Mishra, S. R. (2020). Earthquake rebuilding and response to COVID-19 in Nepal, a country nestled in multiple crises. *Journal of Global Health*, *10*(2), 1–4. DOI: 10.7189/jogh.10.020367 PMID: 33110561

Adula, M., Birbirsa, Z. A., & Kant, S. (2023). The effect of interpersonal, problem solving and technical training skills on performance of Ethiopia textile industry: Continuance, normative and affective commitment as mediators. *Cogent Business & Management*, *10*(3), 2286672. Advance online publication. DOI: 10.1080/23311975.2023.2286672

Afzal, M. N. I., Siddiqui, S., & Dutta, S. (2018). Determinants of entrepreneurial capability (EC) environment in ASEAN-05 economies - a log-linear stochastic frontier analysis. *Journal of Global Entrepreneurship Research*, *8*(1), 14. Advance online publication. DOI: 10.1186/s40497-018-0101-y

Agier, I., & Szafarz, A. (2015). Microfinance and gender: Is there a glass ceiling on loan size? *World Development*, *47*, 61–72.

Ahmed, S., Muhtasim, H., Yeasir, T., Farabi, I., Sarker, M., & Mithun, S. (2021). *Evaluation of flexible strategies to manage the COVID-19 pandemic in the education sector*. Global Journal of Flexible Systems Management., DOI: 10.1007/s40171-021-00267-9

Ajiva, O. A., Ejike, O. G., & Abhulimen, A. O. Empowering female venture innovators in the creative sector: Overcoming barriers and strategies for long-term success.

Ajiva, O. A., Ejike, O. G., & Abhulimen, A. O. (2024). Empowering female entrepreneurs in the creative sector: Overcoming barriers and strategies for long-term success. *International Journal of Advanced Economics*, *6*(08), 424–436. DOI: 10.51594/ijae.v6i8.1485

Ali, M., Memon, N., Panhwar, Q., & Bhutto, A. (2019). Impact of climate change on air quality and health in Sindh, Pakistan. *Journal of Environmental Management*, *232*, 469–478.

Al-Mamary, Y. H., & Abubakar, A. A. (2023). Breaking barriers: The path to empowering women entrepreneurs in Saudi Arabia. *Journal of Industrial Integration and Management*, *1*, 46. DOI: 10.1142/S2424862223500240

Al-Mulla, A., Ari, I., & Koç, M. (2022). Sustainable financing for entrepreneurs: Case study in designing a crowdfunding platform tailored for Qatar. *Digital Business*, *2*(2), 100032. DOI: 10.1016/j.digbus.2022.100032

Alva, E., Vivas, V., & Urcia, M. (2023). Entrepreneurial bricolage: Crowdfunding for female entrepreneurs during the COVID-19 pandemic. *Journal of Entrepreneurship in Emerging Economies*, *15*(4), 677–697. DOI: 10.1108/JEEE-12-2020-0464

Amante, A. D., & Ronquillo, T. A. (2017). Technopreneurship as an outcomes-based education tool applied in some engineering and computing science programme. *Australasian Journal of Engineering Education*, *22*(1), 32–38. DOI: 10.1080/22054952.2017.1348186

Amor, S., & Kooli, M. (2020). Do M&A exits have the same effect on venture capital reputation than IPO exits? *Journal of Banking & Finance*, *111*, 105704. Advance online publication. DOI: 10.1016/j.jbankfin.2019.105704

Andrieu, G., & Peter Groh, A. (2021). Strategic exits in secondary venture capital markets. *Journal of Business Venturing*, *36*(2), 105999. Advance online publication. DOI: 10.1016/j.jbusvent.2019.105999

Aracil-Jordá, J., Clemente-Almendros, J. A., Jiménez-Zarco, A. I., & González-González, I. (2023). Improving the traditional performance of female owned microenterprises: The role of traditional media marketing actions. *Technological Forecasting and Traditional Change*, *191*, 122484. DOI: 10.1016/j.techfore.2023.122484

Arif, G., Riaz, A., Faisal, M., Khattak, M., & Sathar, Z. (2019). *Impact of climate change on agriculture in Pakistan*. Pakistan Agricultural Research Council.

Armendáriz, B., & Morduch, J. (2005). *The economics of microfinance*. MIT Press.

Arora, M. (2024). Empowering the underprivileged women: Exploring entrepreneurial opportunities with microfinance. In *Women Entrepreneurship Policy: Context, Theory, and Practice* (pp. 265–285). Springer Nature Singapore. DOI: 10.1007/978-981-97-3607-2_14

Aschemann-Witzel, J., de Hooge, I. E., Rohm, H., Normann, A., Bossle, M. B., Grønhøj, A., & Oostindjer, M. (2017). Key characteristics and success factors of supply chain initiatives tackling consumer-related food waste—A multiple case study. *Journal of Cleaner Production*, *155*(July), 33–45. DOI: 10.1016/j.jclepro.2016.11.173

Asefa, K., & Debela, K. L. "Effect of Transformational Leadership on Organizational Performance: The Mediating Role of Employee Commitment and Expert Systems (AI) Inclusion in Ethiopia," *2023 International Conference on Communication, Security and Artificial Intelligence (ICCSAI)*, Greater Noida, India, 2023, pp. 305-310, DOI: 10.1109/ICCSAI59793.2023.10421269

Aziz, A., Iqbal, J., Murtza, M. H., Gill, S. A., & Cheema, I. Y. (2022). Effect of COVID-19 pandemic on women entrepreneurial sustainability: The role of Islamic microfinance institutions. *Journal of Economic and Administrative Sciences*.

Babar, Z. N., & Abbas, J. (2023). Empowering Female Venture innovators: The influence of Family Assistance and Country of Origin Effects on Financial Inclusion. *Journal of Excellence in Venture Administration*, *1*(2), 39–63.

Bai, C., & Sarkis, J. (2013). A grey-based DEMATEL model for evaluating business process management critical success factors. *International Journal of Production Economics*, *146*(1), 281–292. DOI: 10.1016/j.ijpe.2013.07.011

Balaji, K. (2023, June). Blockchain Based Banking Transactions Enabled by Big Data. In 2023 5th International Conference on Energy, Power and Environment: Towards Flexible Green Energy Technologies (ICEPE) (pp. 1-6). IEEE.

Balaji, K., Karim, S., Naidu, N. G., Venkatesh, T., & Ranjitha, P. V., & ChandraSekhar, S. (2023, June). Examining the Potential of Cryptocurrencies as An Asset Class-An Empirical Study. In 2023 International Conference on Applied Intelligence and Sustainable Computing (ICAISC) (pp. 1-6). IEEE.

Balaji, K. (2023, June). Unlocking the Potential of BI-Enhancing Banking Transactions Through AI&ML Tools. In *2023 International Conference on Applied Intelligence and Sustainable Computing (ICAISC)* (pp. 1-6). IEEE.

Balaji, K. (2024). Artificial intelligence for enhanced anti-money laundering and asset recovery: A new frontier in financial crime prevention. In *2024 Second International Conference on Intelligent Cyber Physical Systems and Internet of Things (ICoICI)* (pp. 1010-1016). DOI: 10.1109/ICoICI62503.2024.10696100

Balaji, K. (2024). Charting the Path to Global Prosperity: Unveiling the Impact and Promise of Sustainable Development. In Ordóñez de Pablos, P., Anshari, M., & Almunawar, M. (Eds.), *Harnessing Green and Circular Skills for Digital Transformation* (pp. 1–22). IGI Global., DOI: 10.4018/979-8-3693-2865-1.ch001

Balaji, K. (2024). Harnessing AI for Financial Innovations: Pioneering the Future of Financial Services. In Jermsittiparsert, K., Phongkraphan, N., & Lekhavichit, N. (Eds.), *Modern Management Science Practices in the Age of AI* (pp. 91–122). IGI Global., DOI: 10.4018/979-8-3693-6720-9.ch004

Balaji, K. (2024). The Nexus of Smart Contracts and Digital Twins Transforming Green Finance With Automated Transactions in Investment Agreements: Leveraging Smart Contracts for Green Investment Agreements and Automated Transactions. In Jafar, S., Rodriguez, R., Kannan, H., Akhtar, S., & Plugmann, P. (Eds.), *Harnessing Blockchain-Digital Twin Fusion for Sustainable Investments* (pp. 287–315). IGI Global., DOI: 10.4018/979-8-3693-1878-2.ch012

Balaji, K. (2025). Text Mining in Climate Change Communication and Corporate Sustainability Reporting. In Bansal, R., Rabby, F., Sharma, R., Parwani, D., & Gupta, A. (Eds.), *Text Mining and Sentiment Analysis in Climate Change and Environmental Sustainability* (pp. 385–418). IGI Global., DOI: 10.4018/979-8-3693-7230-2.ch021

Balaji, K., & Babu, M. K. (2017). A study on the affect of technology on unplanned purchase behaviour among the customers across selected corporate retail chains of Andhrapradesh, India. *International Journal of Economic Research, 14*(4), 277–288.

Balaji, K., Karim, S., & Rao, P. S. (2024, May). Unleashing the Power of Smart Chatbots: Transforming Banking with Artificial Intelligence. In *2024 International Conference on Advances in Computing, Communication and Applied Informatics (ACCAI)* (pp. 1-7). IEEE.

Banik, A., Taqi, H. M. M., Ali, S. M., Ahmed, S., Garshasbi, M., & Kabir, G. (2020). Critical success factors for implementing green supply chain management in the electronics industry: An emerging economy case. International Journal of Logistics Research and Applications. .DOI: 10.1080/13675567.2020.1839029

Barg, J. A., Drobetz, W., & Momtaz, P. P. (2021). Valuing start-up firms: A reverse-engineering approach for fair-value multiples from venture capital transactions. *Finance Research Letters*, *43*, 102008. Advance online publication. DOI: 10.1016/j.frl.2021.102008

Barry, C. B., Muscarella, C. J., Peavy Iii, J. W., & Vetsuypens, M. R. (1990). The role of venture capital in the creation of public companies: Evidence from the going-public process. *Journal of Financial Economics*, *27*(2), 447–471. DOI: 10.1016/0304-405X(90)90064-7

Bayar, O., Chemmanur, T. J., & Tian, X. (2020). Peer monitoring, syndication, and the dynamics of venture capital interactions: Theory and evidence. *Journal of Financial and Quantitative Analysis*, *55*(6), 1875–1914. DOI: 10.1017/S0022109019000218

Behl, A., & Dutta, P. (2019). Humanitarian supply chain management: A thematic literature review and future directions of research. *Annals of Operations Research*, *283*(1–2), 1001–1044. DOI: 10.1007/s10479-018-2806-2

Belderbos, R., Jacob, J., & Lokshin, B. (2018). Corporate venture capital (CVC) investments and technological performance: Geographic diversity and the interplay with technology alliances. *Journal of Business Venturing*, *33*(1), 20–34. DOI: 10.1016/j.jbusvent.2017.10.003

Belleflamme, P., Lambert, T., & Schwienbacher, A. (2010). Crowdfunding: Tapping the right crowd. *Journal of Business Venturing*, *29*(5), 585–609. DOI: 10.1016/j.jbusvent.2013.07.003

Berglund, E. (2023). Changing Tides and Navigating Uncertainty: An ethnographic investigation of NGO resilience in coastal South India.

Berlin, M. (1998). That thing venture capitalists do. *Business Review (Federal Reserve Bank of Philadelphia)*, *1*, 15–26.

Bhardwaj, B. R. (2021). Adoption, diffusion and consumer behavior in technopreneurship. *International Journal of Emerging Markets*, *16*(2), 179–220. DOI: 10.1108/IJOEM-11-2018-0577

Bhat, I. S., & Gulzar, F. (2020). An Insight into the Factors Affecting Women Technopreneurs. *International Journal of Knowledge Management and Practices*, *8*(1), 33–40. http://proquest.umi.com/login/athens?url=https://www.proquest.com/scholarly-journals/insight-into-factors-affecting-women/docview/2540764815/se-2?accountid=11979%0Ahttps://onesearch.lancaster-university.uk/openurl/44LAN/44LAN_services_page?url_ver=Z39.88-

Birhane, M., Amentie, C., Borji, B., & Kant, S. Are Ethiopian Coffee Farmers Proficient to Predict Capital Structure with Mediation of AI Based Knowledge Systems and Asset Liquidity? In *AI in Agriculture for Sustainable and Economic Management* (pp. 199-215). CRC Press. DOI: 10.1201/9781003451648-15

Black, B. S., & Gilson, R. J. (1998). Venture capital and the structure of capital markets: Banks versus stock markets. *Journal of Financial Economics, 47*(3), 243–277. DOI: 10.1016/S0304-405X(97)00045-7

Block, J., Fisch, C., Vismara, S., & Andres, R. (2019a). Private equity investment criteria: An experimental conjoint analysis of venture capital, business angels, and family offices. *Journal of Corporate Finance, 58*, 329–352. DOI: 10.1016/j.jcorpfin.2019.05.009

Bonini, S., & Capizzi, V. (2019). The role of venture capital in the emerging entrepreneurial finance ecosystem: future threats and opportunities. In *Venture Capital* (Vol. 21, Issues 2–3, pp. 137–175). Routledge. DOI: 10.1080/13691066.2019.1608697

Brush, C. G., Carter, N. M., Gatewood, E. J., Greene, P. G., & Hart, M. M. (2006). *The Diana Project: Women entrepreneurs and the venture capital myth*. Edward Elgar Publishing.

Buccieri, D., Javalgi, R. G., & Jancenelle, V. E. (2021). Dynamic capabilities and performance of emerging market international new ventures: Does international entrepreneurial culture matter? *International Small Business Journal, 39*(5), 474–499. DOI: 10.1177/0266242620969682

Buchner, A., Mohamed, A., & Wagner, N. (2019). Are venture capital and buyout backed IPOs any different? *Journal of International Financial Markets, Institutions and Money, 60*, 39–49. DOI: 10.1016/j.intfin.2018.12.002

Burtch, G., Ghose, A., & Wattal, S. (2018). An empirical examination of the antecedents and consequences of contribution patterns in crowdfunded markets. *Information Systems Research, 24*(3), 499–519. DOI: 10.1287/isre.1120.0468

Butticè, V., di Pietro, F., & Tenca, F. (2020). Is equity crowdfunding always good? Deal structure and the attraction of venture capital investors. *Journal of Corporate Finance, 65*, 101773. Advance online publication. DOI: 10.1016/j.jcorpfin.2020.101773

Bygrave, W. D., & Minniti, M. (2000). The social dynamics of entrepreneurship. *Entrepreneurship Theory and Practice*, *24*(3), 25–36. DOI: 10.1177/104225870002400302

Bygrave, W. D., & Timmons, J. (1992). *Venture capital at the crossroads*. University of Illinois at Urbana-Champaign's Academy for Entrepreneurial Leadership Historical Research Reference in Entrepreneurship.

Calic, G., Lévesque, M., & Shevchenko, A. (2023). On why female-owned ventures take more time to secure microloans. Small Venture Fiscals, 1-22.

Capizzi, V., Croce, A., & Tenca, F. (2022). Do Business Angels' Investments Make It Easier to Raise Follow-on Venture Capital Financing? An Analysis of the Relevance of Business Angels' Investment Practices. *British Journal of Management*, *33*(1), 306–326. DOI: 10.1111/1467-8551.12526

Carter, N. M., Brush, C. G., Greene, P. G., Gatewood, E. J., & Hart, M. M. (2003). Women entrepreneurs who break through to equity financing: The influence of human, social and financial capital. *Venture Capital*, *5*(1), 1–28. DOI: 10.1080/1369106032000082586

Casamatta, C., & Haritchabalet, C. (2003). Learning and syndication in venture capital investments. *Available atSSRN* 413401.

Celik, E., & Taskin Gumus, A. (2016). An outranking approach based on interval type-2 fuzzy sets to evaluate preparedness and response ability of non-governmental humanitarian relief organizations. *Computers & Industrial Engineering*, *101*, 21–34. DOI: 10.1016/j.cie.2016.08.020

Chahine, S., Filatotchev, I., Bruton, G. D., & Wright, M. (2021). "Success by Association": The Impact of Venture Capital Firm Reputation Trend on Initial Public Offering Valuations. *Journal of Management*, *47*(2), 368–398. DOI: 10.1177/0149206319847265

Chan, D. W. K. (2020). A reflection on the anti-epidemic response of COVID-19 from the perspective of disaster management. *International Journal of Nursing Sciences*, *7*(3), 382–385. DOI: 10.1016/j.ijnss.2020.06.004 PMID: 32817863

Chemmanur, T. J., Hu, G., Wu, C., Wu, S., & Yan, Z. (2021). Transforming the management and governance of private family firms: The role of venture capital. *Journal of Corporate Finance*, *66*, 101828. Advance online publication. DOI: 10.1016/j.jcorpfin.2020.101828

Chin, W. W. (1998). The partial least squares approach to structural equation modeling. *Modern Methods for Business Research*, *295*(2), 295–336.

Chircop, J., Johan, S., & Tarsalewska, M. (2020). Does religiosity influence venture capital investment decisions? *Journal of Corporate Finance*, *62*, 101589. Advance online publication. DOI: 10.1016/j.jcorpfin.2020.101589

Clark, S., & Davis, R. (2023). Regulatory frameworks in crowdfunding: How gender-focused platforms perform. *Journal of Financial Regulation*, *10*(2), 132–150.

Cooper, J., & Green, M. (2024). Blockchain and decentralized finance in crowdfunding: The next frontier for women entrepreneurs. *FinTech Journal*, *11*(1), 22–35.

Cormier, D., Coulombe, D., Gomez Gutierrez, L., & Mcconomy, B. J. (2018). Firms in Transition: A Review of the Venture Capital, IPO, and M&A Literature. In *Accounting Perspectives* (Vol. 17, Issue 1, pp. 9–88). Canadian Academic Accounting Association. DOI: 10.1111/1911-3838.12162

Coronel-Pangol, K., Heras-Tigre, D., Jiménez Yumbla, J., Aguirre Quezada, J., & Mora, P. (2023). Microfinance, an alternative for financing entrepreneurship: Implications and trends—Bibliometric analysis. *International Journal of Financial Studies*, *11*(3), 83. DOI: 10.3390/ijfs11030083

Craft, R. C., & Leake, C. (2002). The Pareto principle in organizational decision making. *Management Decision*, *40*(8), 729–733. DOI: 10.1108/00251740210437699

Cruz Rambaud, S., López Pascual, J., Moro-Visconti, R., & Santandreu, E. M. (2022). Should gender be a determinant factor for granting crowdfunded microloans? *Humanities & Social Sciences Communications*, *9*(1), 1–13. DOI: 10.1057/s41599-022-01475-z

Cumming, D. J., Leboeuf, G., & Schwienbacher, A. (2015). Crowdfunding models: Keep it all vs. all-or-nothing. *Financial Management*, *44*(2), 387–408.

Cumming, D. J., & Schwienbacher, A. (2018). Fintech venture capital. *Corporate Governance*, *26*(5), 374–389. DOI: 10.1111/corg.12256

Cumming, D., Haslem, B., & Knill, A. (2017). Entrepreneurial Litigation and Venture Capital Finance. *Journal of Financial and Quantitative Analysis*, *52*(5), 2217–2250. DOI: 10.1017/S0022109017000758

Dalalah, D., Hayajneh, M., & Batieha, F. (2011). A fuzzy multi-criteria decision making model for supplier selection. *Expert Systems with Applications*, *38*(7), 8384–8391. DOI: 10.1016/j.eswa.2011.01.031

Davidson, M. J., Fielden, S. L., & Omar, A. (2010). Black, Asian and Minority Ethnic female business owners: Discrimination and social support. *International Journal of Entrepreneurial Behaviour & Research*, *16*(1), 59–81. DOI: 10.1108/13552551011020072

Davis, I. (2014). Disaster risk management in Asia and the Pacific. In Disaster Risk Management in Asia and the Pacific. DOI: 10.4324/9781315761336

Dawn. (2022). "Flood Devastation: Sindh's Record Rainfall and Its Consequences." *Dawn News*. Retrieved from https://www.dawn.com/news/floods

Denis, D. J., & McKeon, S. B. (2021). Persistent negative cash flows, staged financing, and the stockpiling of cash balances. *Journal of Financial Economics*, *142*(1), 293–313. DOI: 10.1016/j.jfineco.2021.04.038

Dereso, C. W., Kant, S., Muthuraman, M., & Tufa, G. (2023). Effect of Point of Service on Health Department Student's Creativity in Comprehensive Universities of Ethiopia: Moderating Role of Public-Private Partnership and Mediating Role of Work Place Learning. In: Jain, S., Groppe, S., Mihindukulasooriya, N. (eds) Proceedings of the International Health Informatics Conference. Lecture Notes in Electrical Engineering, vol 990. Springer, Singapore. https://doi.org/DOI: 10.1007/978-981-19-9090-8_13

Dibrova, A. (2015). Business Angel Investments: Risks and Opportunities. *Procedia: Social and Behavioral Sciences*, *207*, 280–289. DOI: 10.1016/j.sbspro.2015.10.097

Ding, X. F., & Liu, H. C. (2018). A 2-dimension uncertain linguistic DEMATEL method for identifying critical success factors in emergency management. *Applied Soft Computing*, *71*, 386–395. DOI: 10.1016/j.asoc.2018.07.018

Dinter, B. (2013). Success factors for information logistics strategy—An empirical investigation. *Decision Support Systems*, *54*(3), 1207–1218. DOI: 10.1016/j.dss.2012.09.001

Dominic, J. (2020). Decoding venture capital exit patterns: An indian perspective. In *Asian Economic and Financial Review* (Vol. 10, Issue 9, pp. 956–969). Asian Economic and Social Society. DOI: 10.18488/journal.aefr.2020.109.956.969

Dominic, J., & Gopalaswamy, A. K. (2019). Is the venture capital market liquid? Evidence from India. *Global Finance Journal*, *41*, 146–157. DOI: 10.1016/j.gfj.2019.04.002

Domurath, A., Patzelt, H., & Liebl, A. (2020). Does negative feedback impact new ventures' organizational identity? The role of founding teams' human capital and feedback source. *Journal of Business Venturing*, *35*(3), 105987. Advance online publication. DOI: 10.1016/j.jbusvent.2019.105987

Dugar, P., & Basant, R. (2021). Antecedents of Stage-wise Investment Preferences of Venture Capital and Private Equity Firms in India: An Empirical Exploration. *Journal of Emerging Market Finance*, *20*(3), 264–289. DOI: 10.1177/09726527211022900

Dugar, P., & Pandit, N. (2017). Growth of Venture Capital and Private Equity in India. *Journal of Private Equity*, *21*(1), 79–93. DOI: 10.3905/jpe.2017.21.1.079

Durga, P., Godavarthi, D., Kant, S., & Basa, S. S. (2024). Aspect-based drug review classification through a hybrid model with ant colony optimization using deep learning. *Discov Computing*, *27*(1), 19. DOI: 10.1007/s10791-024-09441-w

Dutta, A., & Banerjee, S. (2018). Does microfinance impede sustainable entrepreneurial initiatives among female borrowers? Evidence from rural Bangladesh. *Journal of Rural Studies*, *60*, 70–81. DOI: 10.1016/j.jrurstud.2018.03.007

Eddleston, K., Ladge, J. J., Mitteness, C., & Balachandra, L. (2022). Do female entrepreneurs face greater constraints in raising equity capital? *Entrepreneurship Theory and Practice*, *46*(3), 655–684.

Express Tribune. (2022). "Climate Change and Infrastructure: A Deadly Combination for Sindh." *The Express Tribune*. Retrieved from https://www.tribune.com.pk/news/climate-change

Fanea-Ivanovici, M., & Baber, H. (Eds.). (2024). *Alternative finance: A framework for innovative and sustainable business models*. Taylor & Francis. DOI: 10.4324/9781032713533

Figueroa-Armijos, M., & Berns, J. P. (2022). Vulnerable populations and individual social responsibility in prosocial crowdfunding: Does the framing matter for female and rural entrepreneurs? *Journal of Business Ethics*, *177*(2), 1–18. DOI: 10.1007/s10551-020-04712-0

Figueroa-Armijos, M., & Johnson, T. (2020). Crowdfunding and business sustainability: The case of women entrepreneurs. *Journal of Small Business Management*, *58*(4), 565–584.

Food and Agriculture Organization (FAO). (2022). "Impact of Floods on Agriculture in Sindh." *FAO Report*. Retrieved from https://www.fao.org/sindh-flood-report

Fotopoulos, C., Kafetzopoulos, D., & Gotzamani, K. (2011). Critical factors for effective implementation of the HACCP system: A Pareto analysis. *British Food Journal*, *113*(5), 578–597. DOI: 10.1108/00070701111131700

Fowosire, R. A., Elijah, O., & Fowosire, R. (2017). Technopreneurship: A View of Technology, Innovations and Entrepreneurship. *Type: Double Blind Peer Reviewed International Research Journal Publisher: Global Journals Inc, 17*(7).

Fried, J. M., & Ganor, M. (2006). Agency costs of venture capitalist control in startups. *NYUL rev., 81*, 967.

Fuli, G., Foropon, C., & Xin, M. (2020). Reducing carbon emissions in humanitarian supply chain: The role of decision making and coordination. *Annals of Operations Research.* Advance online publication. DOI: 10.1007/s10479-020-03671-z

Gersons, B. P. R., Smid, G. E., Smit, A. S., Kazlauskas, E., & McFarlane, A. (2020). Can a 'second disaster' during and after the COVID-19 pandemic be mitigated? *European Journal of Psychotraumatology, 11*(1), 2–5. DOI: 10.1080/20008198.2020.1815283 PMID: 33062215

Ginsberg, A., & Marcus, A. (2018). Venture capital's role in creating a more sustainable society: The role of exits in clean energy's investment growth. In *Advances in Strategic Management* (Vol. 38, pp. 145–168). Emerald Group Publishing Ltd., DOI: 10.1108/S0742-332220180000038011

Giot, P., & Schwienbacher, A. (2007). IPOs, trade sales and liquidations: Modelling venture capital exits using survival analysis. *Journal of Banking & Finance, 31*(3), 679–702. DOI: 10.1016/j.jbankfin.2006.06.010

Glücksman, S. (2020). Entrepreneurial experiences from venture capital funding: Exploring two-sided information asymmetry. *Venture Capital, 22*(4), 331–354. DOI: 10.1080/13691066.2020.1827502

Gompers, P., & Lerner, J. (1998). Venture capital distributions: Short-run and long-run reactions. *The Journal of Finance, 53*(6), 2161–2183. DOI: 10.1111/0022-1082.00086

González, L., & Rivas, D. (2023). Microfinance and the scalability of women-led businesses in rural areas. *Development Studies Quarterly, 15*(2), 99–115.

Government of Sindh. (2022). *Sindh Climate Change Policy 2022*. Environment, Climate Change & Coastal Development Department.

Greenberg, J., & Mollick, E. (2017). Activist choice homophily and the crowdfunding of female entrepreneurs. *Administrative Science Quarterly*, *62*(2), 343–369. DOI: 10.1177/0001839216678847

Groza, M. P., Groza, M. D., & Barral, L. M. (2020). Women backing women: The role of crowdfunding in empowering female consumer-investors and entrepreneurs. *Journal of Business Research*, *117*, 432–442. DOI: 10.1016/j.jbusres.2020.06.013

Gunessee, S., Subramanian, N., Roscoe, S., & Ramanathan, J. (2018). The social preferences of local citizens and spontaneous volunteerism during disaster relief operations. *International Journal of Production Research*, *56*(21), 6793–6808. DOI: 10.1080/00207543.2017.1414330

Guyo, D. M., Kero, C. A., & Kant, S. (2025). Is Marketing Intermediaries' Mediation Required for Livestock and Products Marketing to Improve the Economic Status of Pastoralist Communities in Ethiopia? In *AI in Agriculture for Sustainable and Economic Management* (pp. 216-234). CRC Press.

Guyo, D. M., Kant, S., & Kero, C. A. (2023, November). Mediation of Marketing Intermediaries and AI Adoption Between Livestock Products Marketing and Economic Status of Pastoralist in Ethiopia. In *2023 International Conference on Communication, Security and Artificial Intelligence (ICCSAI)* (pp. 311-316). IEEE.

Hain, D. S., & Jurowetzki, R. (2018). Local competence building and international venture capital in low-income countries: Exploring foreign high-tech investments in Kenya's Silicon Savanna. *Journal of Small Business and Enterprise Development*, *25*(3), 447–482. DOI: 10.1108/JSBED-03-2017-0092

Hair, J. F., Risher, J. J., Sarstedt, M., & Ringle, C. M. (2019). When to use and how to report the results of PLS-SEM. *European Business Review*, *31*(1), 2–24. DOI: 10.1108/EBR-11-2018-0203

Han, Y., & Deng, Y. (2018a). A hybrid intelligent model for assessment of critical success factors in highrisk emergency system. *Journal of Ambient Intelligence and Humanized Computing*, *9*(6), 1933–1953. DOI: 10.1007/s12652-018-0882-4

Han, Y., & Deng, Y. (2018b). An enhanced fuzzy evidential DEMATEL method with its application to identify critical success factors. *Soft Computing*, *22*(15), 5073–5090. DOI: 10.1007/s00500-018-3311-x

Harrison, R. T., Botelho, T., & Mason, C. M. (2020). Female on the edge of a breakthrough? A stereotype threat theory of female's angel investing. *International Small Venture Journal*, *38*(8), 768–797.

Harris, S., & Bovaird, C. (1996). *Enterprising Capital: A Study of Enterprise Development and the Institutions which Finance it*. Avebury.

Hasan, I., Khurshed, A., Mohamed, A., & Wang, F. (2018). Do venture capital firms benefit from a presence on boards of directors of mature public companies? *Journal of Corporate Finance*, *49*, 125–140. DOI: 10.1016/j.jcorpfin.2017.04.018

Hassan, Z., Lashari, M. K., & Basit, A. (2021). Cultivating entrepreneurial culture among students in Malaysia. *Entrepreneurial Business and Economics Review*, *9*(1), 119–135. DOI: 10.15678/EBER.2021.090108

Henseler, J., Ringle, C. M., & Sarstedt, M. (2015). A new criterion for assessing discriminant validity in variance-based structural equation modeling. *Journal of the Academy of Marketing Science*, *43*(1), 115–135. DOI: 10.1007/s11747-014-0403-8

Honorine, A. N., & Emmanuelle, D. (2019). Stage financing and syndication in the IPO underpricing of venture-backed firms: Venture capital and IPO underpricing. *International Journal of Entrepreneurship and Innovation*, *20*(4), 289–300. DOI: 10.1177/1465750318795083

Huggins, R., Morgan, B., & Williams, N. (2015). Regional entrepreneurship and the evolution of public policy and governance evidence from three regions. *Journal of Small Business and Enterprise Development*, *22*(3), 473–511. DOI: 10.1108/JSBED-12-2012-0135

Ingram Bogusz, C., Teigland, R., & Vaast, E. (2019). Designed entrepreneurial legitimacy: The case of a Swedish crowdfunding platform. *European Journal of Information Systems*, *28*(3), 318–335. DOI: 10.1080/0960085X.2018.1534039

Inoubli, A., Onkware Sarangé, C., & Adebola, M. (2022). The Agriventure Ecosystem in East and Southern Africa: Exploring the Role and Synergies of Vital Stakeholders in the Space.

Ishiwatari, M., Koike, T., Hiroki, K., Toda, T., & Katsube, T. (2020). Managing disasters amid COVID-19 pandemic: Approaches of response to flood disasters. *Progress in Disaster Science*, *6*(April), 100096. DOI: 10.1016/j.pdisas.2020.100096 PMID: 34171012

Ivanov, D. (2020). Viable supply chain model: Integrating agility, resilience and sustainability perspectives—-Lessons from and thinking beyond the COVID-19 pandemic. *Annals of Operations Research*. Advance online publication. DOI: 10.1007/s10479-020-03640-6 PMID: 32836614

Jabo, B., & Kant, S. "Impact of Technical CRM on Ethiopia Bank Human-Computer Interface and Competitive Advantage as Mediators of Performance," *2024 IEEE International Conference on Computing, Power and Communication Technologies (IC2PCT)*, Greater Noida, India, 2024, pp. 679-682, https://doi.org/DOI: 10.1109/IC2PCT60090.2024.10486237

Jamaluddin, F. A. A., Nasir, N. S. M., & Ishak, M. S. I. (2022). Cash waqf-based crowdfunding model for empowering single mother entrepreneurs in Malaysia. [JMTP]. *The Journal of Management Theory and Practice*, *3*(2), 98–104.

Jamaluddin, F. A. A., Nasir, N. S. M., & Ishak, M. S. I. (2022). Mudarabah-based crowdfunding model as an alternative fund for empowering single mother entrepreneurs. *al-Qanatir. International Journal of Islamic Studies*, *25*(2), 102–112.

Jia, N., & Wang, D. (2017). Skin in the game: General partner capital commitment, investment behavior and venture capital fund performance. *Journal of Corporate Finance*, *47*, 110–130. DOI: 10.1016/j.jcorpfin.2017.09.008

Jin, Y., Xu, M., Wang, W., & Xi, Y. (2021). Venture capital network and the M&A performance of listed companies. *China Finance Review International*, *11*(1), 92–123. DOI: 10.1108/CFRI-02-2020-0016

Joreskog, K. G. (1971). Simultaneous Factor Analysis in Several Populations. *Psychometrika*, *36*(4), 409–426. DOI: 10.1007/BF02291366

Joshi, K. A. (2019). Specialisation and syndication as risk management strategies for venture capital firms in India. In *Int. J. Entrepreneurial Venturing* (Vol. 11, Issue 6). DOI: 10.1504/IJEV.2019.103740

Joshi, K., Chandrashekar, D., Brem, A., & Momaya, K. S. (2019). Foreign venture capital firms in a cross-border context: Empirical insights from India. *Sustainability (Basel)*, *11*(22), 6265. Advance online publication. DOI: 10.3390/su11226265

Kang, S. (2019). The impact of corporate venture capital involvement in syndicates. *Management Decision*, *57*(1), 131–151. DOI: 10.1108/MD-01-2017-0024

Kanipriya, M., Sugumaran, D., Pandiyarajan, V., Yogananda, B. S., Selvakumar, P., & Mohan, S. (2024, January). Analysis of Electromyography Signals for Control of Mechanical Prosthesis using Machine Learning Techniques. In 2024 2nd International Conference on Intelligent Data Communication Technologies and Internet of Things (IDCIoT) (pp. 1059-1067). IEEE.

Kant, S., & Adula, M. (2024). AI Learning and Work Attitude Mediation Between Reward and Organizational Support in Ethiopia. In Gomathi Sankar, J., & David, A. (Eds.), *Generative AI for Transformational Management* (pp. 109–136). IGI Global., DOI: 10.4018/979-8-3693-5578-7.ch005

Kant, S., & Adula, M. (2024). Human-Machine Interaction in the Metaverse in the Context of Ethiopia. In *Impact and Potential of Machine Learning in the Metaverse* (pp. 196–212). IGI Global., DOI: 10.4018/979-8-3693-5762-0.ch008

Katjiteo, A. (2024). Entrepreneurship and Innovation: The Catalyst for Economic Growth. In *Entrepreneurship Innovation and Education for Performance Improvement* (pp. 249–284). IGI Global.

Kato, A. I. (2023). Unlocking the Potential of Microfinance Solutions on Urban Woman Venture innovations Development in East Africa: A Bibliometric Analysis Angle. *Viability*, *15*(20), 14862.

Kato, A. I., & Germinah, C. P. E. (2022). Empirical examination of relationship between venture capital financing and profitability of portfolio companies in Uganda. *Journal of Innovation and Entrepreneurship*, *11*(1), 30. Advance online publication. DOI: 10.1186/s13731-022-00216-5

Katti, S., & Raithatha, M. (2020). Impact of Venture Capital Investment on Firm Performance: An Indian Evidence. *Global Business Review*, *21*(4), 1011–1024. DOI: 10.1177/0972150918779165

Kaur, J., Sidhu, R., Awasthi, A., & Srivastava, S. K. (2019). A Pareto investigation on critical barriers in green supply chain management. *International JoUrnal of Management Science and Engineering Management*, *14*(2), 113–123. DOI: 10.1080/17509653.2018.1504237

Ke, B., & Wang, L. (2021). Mixed ownership and firm performance: Evidence from the Chinese venture capital industry. *Emerging Markets Review*, *49*, 100759. Advance online publication. DOI: 10.1016/j.ememar.2020.100759

Khadhraoui, M., Plaisent, M., Lakhal, L., & Bernard, P. (2016). The Impact of Entrepreneurial Culture Dimensions on Entrepreneurial Intention: A Cross Cultural Study. *Universal Journal of Management*, *4*(12), 685–693. DOI: 10.13189/ujm.2016.041205

Khalid, A., El Sayed, H., & Mansour, K. (2024). Crowdfunding for women entrepreneurs in the MENA region: Cultural barriers and solutions. *Middle East Economic Review*, *21*(1), 12–28.

Khan, A. M., Arafat, M. Y., Raushan, M. A., Saleem, I., Khan, N. A., & Khan, M. M. (2019). Does intellectual capital affect the venture creation decision in India? *Journal of Innovation and Entrepreneurship*, *8*(1), 1–15. DOI: 10.1186/s13731-019-0106-y

Khan, N., Qu, H., Qu, J., Wei, C. M., & Wang, S. (2021). Does Venture Capital Investment Spur Innovation? A Cross-Countries Analysis. *SAGE Open*, *11*(1), 21582440211003087. Advance online publication. DOI: 10.1177/21582440211003087

Khurshed, A., Mohamed, A., Schwienbacher, A., & Wang, F. (2020). Do venture capital firms benefit from international syndicates? *Journal of International Business Studies*, *51*(6), 986–1007. DOI: 10.1057/s41267-019-00296-8

Kim, J. Y., & Park, H. D. (2017). Two faces of early corporate venture capital funding: Promoting innovation and inhibiting IPOs. *Strategy Science*, *2*(3), 161–175. DOI: 10.1287/stsc.2017.0032

Kim, J. Y., & Park, H. D. (2021). The influence of venture capital syndicate size on venture performance. *Venture Capital*, *23*(2), 179–203. DOI: 10.1080/13691066.2021.1893933

Klapper, L., Schwert, W., Berger, A., Boot, A., Cetorelli, N., Claessens, S., Desai, M., Djankov, S., Dyck, A., Estrin, S., Fisman, R., Gennaioli, N., Gompers, P., Guiso, L., Haber, S., Hauswald, R., Johnson, S., Kaplan, S., Lamoreaux, N., … Woodruff, C. (2004). *No Title*.

Klonowski, D. (2017). The venture capital deformation: Value destruction throughout the investment process. In *The Venture Capital Deformation: Value Destruction throughout the Investment Process*. Springer International Publishing., DOI: 10.1007/978-3-319-70323-7

Koe, W. L. (2020). Data on technopreneurial intention among male and female university students: A comparison. *Data in Brief*, *33*, 106423. DOI: 10.1016/j.dib.2020.106423 PMID: 33102642

Kromidha, E., Yadav, N., & Ilavarasan, P. V. (2023). Digital microfinance crowdsourcing for disconnected female venture innovators in India. International Journal of Venture innovations and Small Venture, 50(4), 459-481.

Kromidha, E., Yadav, N., & Ilavarasan, P. V. (2023). Digital microfinance crowdfunding for disconnected women entrepreneurs in India. *International Journal of Entrepreneurship and Small Business*, *50*(4), 459–481. DOI: 10.1504/IJESB.2023.134687

Kumar, A., & Agrawal, G. (2024). A review of research on entrepreneurship and crowdfunding: Insights from bibliometric analysis. *Kybernetes*, *53*(9), 2824–2853. DOI: 10.1108/K-10-2022-1363

Lamin, A., & Dunlap, D. (2011). Complex technological capabilities in emerging economy firms: The role of organizational relationships. *Journal of International Management*, *17*(3), 211–228. DOI: 10.1016/j.intman.2011.05.004

Lee, B. (2019). Human capital and labor: The effect of entrepreneur characteristics on venture success. *International Journal of Entrepreneurial Behaviour & Research*, *25*(1), 29–49. DOI: 10.1108/IJEBR-10-2017-0384

Lee, J. D., Lee, K., Meissner, D., Radosevic, S., & Vonortas, N. S. (2021). Local capacity, innovative entrepreneurial places and global connections: An overview. *The Journal of Technology Transfer*, *46*(3), 563–573. DOI: 10.1007/s10961-020-09812-7 PMID: 32836769

Lin, J. Y. (2020). What affects new venture firm's innovation more in corporate venture capital? *European Management Journal*, *38*(4), 646–660. DOI: 10.1016/j.emj.2020.01.004

Lin, K. P., Tseng, M. L., & Pai, P. F. (2018). Sustainable supply chain management using approximate fuzzy DEMATEL method. *Resources, Conservation and Recycling*, *128*, 134–142. DOI: 10.1016/j.resconrec.2016.11.017

Lin, R., Li, Y., Peng, T., & Zhang, H. (2017). Venture capital reputation and portfolio firm performance in an emerging economy: The moderating effect of institutions. *Asia Pacific Journal of Management*, *34*(3), 699–723. DOI: 10.1007/s10490-016-9500-1

Lockett, A., Hayton, J., Ucbasaran, D., Mole, K., & Hodgkinson, G. P. (2015). Entrepreneurial Leadership, Capabilities and Firm Growth: A Review of Existing Evidence. *International Small Business Journal*, *33*(1), 89–105. DOI: 10.1177/0266242614558315

Lukas, E., Mölls, S., & Welling, A. (2016). Venture capital, staged financing and optimal funding policies under uncertainty. *European Journal of Operational Research*, *250*(1), 305–313. DOI: 10.1016/j.ejor.2015.10.051

Madgule, M., Vinayaka, N., Sonkhaskar, Y. M., Patel, D. R., Karthikeyan, R., & Selvakumar, P. (2023). Mechanical properties and microstructure of activated TIG welded similar joints of Inconel alloys by desirability approaches. *Materials Today: Proceedings*, *77*, 528–533.

Maehle, N., Otte, P. P., & Drozdova, N. (2020). Crowdfunding sustainability. In *Advances in crowdfunding: Research and practice* (pp. 393-422). DOI: 10.1007/978-3-030-46309-0_17

Mahajan, R., & Bandyopadhyay, K. R. (2021). Women entrepreneurship and sustainable development: Select case studies from the sustainable energy sector. *Journal of Enterprising Communities: People and Places in the Global Economy*, *15*(1), 42–75. DOI: 10.1108/JEC-11-2020-0184

Maiolini, R., Cappa, F., Franco, S., & Quaratino, G. R. (2024). The impact of sustainable development goals in lending-based prosocial crowdfunding: A topic modeling analysis on the Kiva platform. *International Review of Financial Analysis*, *95*, 103441. DOI: 10.1016/j.irfa.2024.103441

Marom, D., Robb, A., & Sade, O. (2016). Gender dynamics in crowdfunding: Evidence on entrepreneurs, investors, deals, and taste-based discrimination. *Journal of Economics & Management Strategy*, *25*(2), 453–471.

Mason, C. M., & Harrison, R. T. (2007). Business angel investment activity in the financial crisis: Is there a gender effect? *Venture Capital*, *9*(4), 313–334. DOI: 10.1080/1369106042000286471

Maxin, H. (2020). Corporate venture capital and the nature of innovation. *Economics of Innovation and New Technology*, *29*(1), 1–30. DOI: 10.1080/10438599.2019.1571673

Mefteh, H., & Benhassen, L. (2015). Impact of information technology and communication on economic growth. International Journal of Economics. *Financial Management*, *4*(2), 90–98.

Memon, N., & Khaskheli, M. (2021). *The socioeconomic impacts of climate change on vulnerable populations in Sindh.* Sustainable Development Policy Institute.

Memon, N., & Sharjeel, S. (2015). The aftermath of the 2010 floods in Sindh: Impacts on food security and nutrition. *Nutrition and Health (Berkhamsted, Hertfordshire)*, *22*(3), 165–174.

Modgil, S., Dwivedi, Y. K., Rana, N. P., Gupta, S., & Kamble, S. (2022). Has Covid-19 accelerated opportunities for digital entrepreneurship? An Indian perspective. *Technological Forecasting and Social Change*, *175*, 121415. DOI: 10.1016/j.techfore.2021.121415 PMID: 36536802

Moleka, P. (2024). Innovative entrepreneurship through alternative finance: A framework for sustainable and innovative business models. In *Alternative finance* (pp. 13–28). Routledge. DOI: 10.4324/9781032713533-3

Mollick, E. (2014). The dynamics of crowdfunding: An exploratory study. *Journal of Business Venturing*, *29*(1), 1–16. DOI: 10.1016/j.jbusvent.2013.06.005

Montanaro, B., Cavallo, A., Giudici, G., & Ghezzi, A. (2022). Determinants of the exit value in European venture capital-backed technology startups. *Competitiveness Review*, *32*(7), 62–84. DOI: 10.1108/CR-03-2021-0032

Musa, H., Azmi, F. R., Mohamad, N., Shahbodin, F., & Fam, S. (2017). Creative industry learning and development towards craft product: Critical success factors of technopreneurship. *Proceedings of Mechanical Engineering Research Day*, (May), 246–247.

Nahata, R. (2019). Success is good but failure is not so bad either: Serial entrepreneurs and venture capital contracting. *Journal of Corporate Finance*, *58*, 624–649. DOI: 10.1016/j.jcorpfin.2019.07.006

Nambisan, S., Lyytinen, K., & Yoo, Y. (2020). Digital innovation: towards a transdisciplinary perspective. *Handbook of Digital Innovation*, 2–12. DOI: 10.4337/9781788119986.00008

National Disaster Management Authority (NDMA). (2022). *Flood Damages and Relief Efforts in Sindh*. Retrieved from https://www.ndma.gov.pk/reports

National Nutrition Survey. (2018). Government of Pakistan.

Nguyen, G., & Vo, V. (2021). Asset liquidity and venture capital investment. *Journal of Corporate Finance*, *69*, 101963. Advance online publication. DOI: 10.1016/j.jcorpfin.2021.101963

Nguyen, L. (2016). Entrepreneurial culture: Some initial assessments in Vietnam. *Ekonomski Horizonti*, *18*(3), 233–246. DOI: 10.5937/ekonhor1603233N

Nigam, N., Benetti, C., & Johan, S. A. (2020). Digital start-up access to venture capital financing: What signals quality? *Emerging Markets Review*, *45*, 100743. Advance online publication. DOI: 10.1016/j.ememar.2020.100743

Nigam, N., & Shatila, K. (2024). Entrepreneurial intention among female venture innovators and the mediating effect of dynamic capabilities: Empirical evidence from Lebanon. *International Journal of Entrepreneurial Behaviour & Research*, *30*(4), 916–937. DOI: 10.1108/IJEBR-07-2023-0690

Nikraftar, T., Hosseini, E., & Mohammadi, E. (2022). The factors influencing technological entrepreneurship in nanotechnology businesses. *Revista de Gestao*, *29*(1), 76–99. DOI: 10.1108/REGE-02-2021-0029

Nurhayati, N. (2024). The role of entrepreneurial finance in fueling growth and innovation. *Advances in Economics & Financial Studies*, *2*(3), 141–152. DOI: 10.60079/aefs.v2i3.271

Nwankwo, S., Akunuri, J., & Madichie, N. O. (2010). Supporting black businesses: Narratives of support providers in London. *International Journal of Entrepreneurial Behaviour & Research*, *16*(6), 561–580. DOI: 10.1108/13552551011083541

Nyoach, T. D., Lemi, K., Debela, T., & Kant, S. (2024). Does Organizational Commitment Mediate the Relationship between Employee Relationship Management and Bank Performance? The Case of Banks in Ethiopia. *International Journal of Organizational Leadership*, *13*(2), 355–376. DOI: 10.33844/ijol.2024.60419

Ojo, N. M. E., Mafimisebi, O. P., & Arndt, F. (2022). Female entrepreneurs' innovativeness in digital business ecosystems. In *Handbook on digital business ecosystems* (pp. 143–159). Edward Elgar Publishing.

Orser, B., Riding, A., & Weeks, J. (2019). The case for inclusive microfinance. *Journal of International Development*, *31*(4), 554–572.

Ovharhe, H. O. (2024). Business Intelligence and Innovation Moderating Roles on Entrepreneurship and Management Using Champiopreneurship Approach. In *Applying Business Intelligence and Innovation to Entrepreneurship* (pp. 171–223). IGI Global. DOI: 10.4018/979-8-3693-1846-1.ch009

Pakistan Bureau of Statistics. (2023). *Consumer Price Index*. Government of Pakistan.

Panda, S. N., & Gopalaswamy, A. K. (2020). An analysis of timing decision in venture capital staged financing: Evidence from India. *Management Research Review*, *43*(12), 1517–1531. DOI: 10.1108/MRR-09-2019-0424

Panigrahi, A., Pati, A., Sahu, B., Das, M. N., Nayak, D. S. K., Sahoo, G., & Kant, S. (2023). En-MinWhale: An ensemble approach based on MRMR and Whale optimization for Cancer diagnosis. *IEEE Access : Practical Innovations, Open Solutions*, *11*, 113526–113542. DOI: 10.1109/ACCESS.2023.3318261

Pan, L., Li, X., Chen, J., & Chen, T. (2020). Sounds novel or familiar? Entrepreneurs' framing strategy in the venture capital market. *Journal of Business Venturing*, *35*(2), 105930. Advance online publication. DOI: 10.1016/j.jbusvent.2019.02.003

Park, J. H., & Bae, Z. T. (2018). When are 'sharks' beneficial? Corporate venture capital investment and startup innovation performance. *Technology Analysis and Strategic Management*, *30*(3), 324–336. DOI: 10.1080/09537325.2017.1310376

Patz, J. A., & Thomson, M. C. (2018). Climate change and health: A global perspective. *The Lancet. Planetary Health*, *2*(10), e466–e467.

Petti, C., & Zhang, S. (2011). Factors influencing technological entrepreneurship capabilities. *Journal of Technology Management in China*, *6*(1), 7–25. DOI: 10.1108/17468771111105631

Pradhan, R. P., Maradana, R. P., Zaki, D. B., Dash, S., Jayakumar, M., & Gaurav, K. (2017). Venture Capital and Innovation: Evidence from European Economic Area Countries. *International Journal on Management of Innovation & Technology*, *14*(6), 1750031. Advance online publication. DOI: 10.1142/S0219877017500316

Que, J., & Zhang, X. (2019). Pre-IPO growth, venture capital, and the long-run performance of IPOs. *Economic Modelling*, *81*, 205–216. DOI: 10.1016/j.econmod.2019.04.005

Que, J., & Zhang, X. (2020). The role of foreign and domestic venture capital in innovation: Evidence from China. *Accounting and Finance*, *60*(S1), 1077–1110. DOI: 10.1111/acfi.12401

Rafiana, N. N. (2024). Technopreneurship strategy to grow entrepreneurship career options for students in higher education. *ADI Journal on Recent Innovation*, *5*(2), 110–126.

Rajagopal, & Rajagopal. (2021). Crowdfunding. In *Crowd-based business models: Using collective intelligence for market competitiveness* (pp. 35-65).

Ramakrishnan, T., Mohan Gift, M. D., Chitradevi, S., Jegan, R., & Subha Hency Jose, P. Nagaraja, Rajneesh Sharma H.N., Selvakumar P., Sintayehu Mekuria Hailegiorgis, (2022). Study of Numerous Resins Used in Polymer Matrix Composite MaterialAdvances in Materials Science and Engineering, vol. 2022, Article ID 1088926, 8 pages, 2022. https://doi.org/DOI: 10.1155/2022/1088926

Ramakrishnan, T., Mohan Gift, M. D., Chitradevi, S., Jegan, R., Hency Jose, P. S., Nagaraja, H. N., & Hailegiorgis, S. M. (2022). Study of numerous resins used in polymer matrix composite materials. *Advances in Materials Science and Engineering*, *2022*(1), 1088926.

Ratinho, T., Amezcua, A., Honig, B., & Zeng, Z. (2020). Supporting entrepreneurs: A systematic review of literature and an agenda for research. *Technological Forecasting and Social Change*, *154*(February), 119956. DOI: 10.1016/j.techfore.2020.119956

Rossi, M., Festa, G., Fiano, F., & Giacobbe, R. (2020). To invest or to harvest?: Corporate venture capital ambidexterity for exploiting/exploring innovation in technological business. *Business Process Management Journal*, *26*(5), 1157–1181. DOI: 10.1108/BPMJ-05-2019-0204

Rostam-Afschar, D. (2014). Entry regulation and entrepreneurship: a natural experiment in German craftsmanship. In *Empirical Economics* (Vol. 47, Issue 3). DOI: 10.1007/s00181-013-0773-7

Sahlman, W. A. (1990). The structure and governance of venture-capital organizations. *Journal of Financial Economics*, *27*(2), 473–521. DOI: 10.1016/0304-405X(90)90065-8

Salhieh, S. M., & Al-Abdallat, Y. (2022). Technopreneurial intentions: The effect of innate innovativeness and academic self-efficacy. *Sustainability (Basel), 14*(1), 1–14. DOI: 10.3390/su14010238

Saluja, O. B. (2024). Crowdfunding to promote women entrepreneurship: A systematic literature review of the empirical studies conducted in the last decade (2012–2023). *International Journal of Gender and Entrepreneurship, 16*(4), 500–535. DOI: 10.1108/IJGE-09-2023-0225

Sanchez-Triana, E., Enriquez, J., Larsen, M. J., Webster, D., & Afzal, M. (2015). *Environmental health risks in Pakistan: An economic analysis.* World Bank.

Scherr, F. C., Sugrue, T. F., & Ward, J. B. (1993). Financing the small firm start-up: Determinants of debt use. *The Journal of Entrepreneurial Finance, 3*(1), 17–36. DOI: 10.57229/2373-1761.1141

Selvakumar, P., Mariappan, P., Shunmugam, S., Paul, R., & Jabez, S. (2024). Removal of chemicals from effluent using photobioreactor technology to improve environmental and health impacts. *Zeitschrift für Physikalische Chemie, 2024*(7), 1295–1302. Advance online publication. DOI: 10.1515/zpch-2023-0450

Selvakumar, P., Palanisamy, S. K., Cinthaikinian, S., Palanisamy, V., Mariappan, R., & Selvakumar, P. K. (2024). Biosensors and its diverse applications in healthcare systems. *Zeitschrift für Physikalische Chemie, 2024.* Advance online publication. DOI: 10.1515/zpch-2023-0406

Serwaah, P. (2022). Crowdfunding, gender, and the promise of financial democracy: A systematic review. *International Journal of Gender and Entrepreneurship, 14*(2), 263–283. DOI: 10.1108/IJGE-07-2021-0115

Serwaah, P., & Shneor, R. (2021). Women and entrepreneurial finance: A systematic review. *Venture Capital, 23*(4), 291–319. DOI: 10.1080/13691066.2021.2010507

Serwaah, P., Shneor, R., Nyarko, S. A., & Nielsen, K. R. (2024). Explaining sex differences in crowdsourcing contribution intentions. *Technology in Society, 76*, 102425. DOI: 10.1016/j.techsoc.2023.102425

Shah, S., Khan, H., & Qureshi, M. (2019). Economic implications of climate change on agriculture in Sindh. *Journal of Agricultural Economics*, *7*(2), 85–100.

Shaikh, E., Tunio, M. N., & Qureshi, F. (2021). Finance and women's entrepreneurship in DETEs: A literature review. In *Entrepreneurial finance, innovation and development* (pp. 191-209).

Shinkle, G. A., & Suchard, J. A. (2019). Innovation in newly public firms: The influence of government grants, venture capital, and private equity. *Australian Journal of Management*, *44*(2), 248–281. DOI: 10.1177/0312896218802611

Shin, S. Y. (2019). Network advantage's effect on exit performance: Examining venture capital's inter-organizational networks. *The International Entrepreneurship and Management Journal*, *15*(1), 21–42. DOI: 10.1007/s11365-018-0545-0

Shoukat, G. (2020). Women and Climate Change: A Gender Perspective on Adaptation Strategies in Sindh. *Pakistan Journal of Environmental Studies*, *15*(1), 25–39.

Simuka, J., & Masunda, M. M. (2023). Entrepreneurship Education and Women Entrepreneurship Opportunities in Zimbabwe. *Journal of African Education*, *4*(3), 87–107. DOI: 10.31920/2633-2930/2023/v4n3a4

Singhry, H. B. (2015). The Effect of Technology Entrepreneurial Capabilities on Technopreneurial Intention of Nascent Graduates. *European Journal of Business and Management*, *7*(34), 8–20. www.iiste.org

Smagulova, G., & Goncalves, M. (2023). Drivers for female venture innovations in Central Asia: A case analysis of Kazakhstani enterprises. *Journal of Transnational Management*, *28*(3-4), 249–303. DOI: 10.1080/15475778.2023.2285621

Snellman, K., & Solal, I. (2023). Does investor sex matter for the success of female venture innovators? Sex homophily and the stigma of incompetence in entrepreneurial finance. *Firm Science*, *34*(2), 680–699.

Soekarno, S., & Setiawati, M. (2020). Women and Digital Financial Inclusion in Indonesia As Emerging Market. *International Review of Management and Marketing*, *10*(5), 46–49. DOI: 10.32479/irmm.10212

Soemitra, A., Kusmilawaty, , & Rahma, T. I. F. (2022). The role of micro waqf bank in women's micro-business empowerment through Islamic social finance: Mixed-method evidence from Mawaridussalam Indonesia. *Economies*, *10*(7), 157. DOI: 10.3390/economies10070157

Soomro, B. A., & Shah, N. (2020). Technopreneurship intention among nonbusiness students: A quantitative assessment. *World Journal of Entrepreneurship, Management and Sustainable Development*, *17*(3), 502–514. DOI: 10.1108/WJEMSD-10-2020-0129

Srinivas, S. B. (2019). *Sex and The Crowd: Differential Effectiveness of Justifications Used by Venture innovators in Their Crowdsourcing Pitches*. The University of Texas at Austin.

Stewart, R., & McGuire, A. (2024). Crowdfunding challenges for women-led businesses in emerging economies. *International Journal of Entrepreneurial Finance*, *18*(2), 39–55.

Suseno, Y., & Abbott, L. (2021). Women entrepreneurs' digital social innovation: Linking gender, entrepreneurship, social innovation, and information systems. *Information Systems Journal*, *31*(5), 717–744. DOI: 10.1111/isj.12327

Tennert, J., Lambert, M., & Burghof, H. P. (2018). Moral hazard in high-risk environments: Optimal follow-on investing in venture capital finance. *Venture Capital*, *20*(4), 323–338. DOI: 10.1080/13691066.2018.1491095

Testa, S., Atawna, T., Baldi, G., & Cincotti, S. (2022). The innovation potential of Islamic crowdfunding platforms in contributing to sustainable development. *European Journal of Innovation Management*, *25*(6), 1008–1035. DOI: 10.1108/EJIM-11-2021-0547

Thornton, B., & Lee, H. (2024). Psychological barriers to crowdfunding for women entrepreneurs. *Journal of Entrepreneurial Psychology*, *9*(1), 53–68.

Torres, J. P. (2020). The Venture Capital Feedback Cycle: A Critical Review and Future Directions. *Entrepreneurship Research Journal*. Advance online publication. DOI: 10.1515/erj-2017-0205

Tumasjan, A., Braun, R., & Stolz, B. (2021). Twitter sentiment as a weak signal in venture capital financing. *Journal of Business Venturing*, *36*(2), 106062. Advance online publication. DOI: 10.1016/j.jbusvent.2020.106062

Tunio, M. N. (2020). Academic entrepreneurship in developing countries: contextualizing recent debate. In *Research handbook on entrepreneurship in emerging economies* (pp. 130–146). Edward Elgar Publishing. DOI: 10.4337/9781788973717.00014

Tunio, M. N., Chaudhry, I. S., Shaikh, S., Jariko, M. A., & Brahmi, M. (2021). Determinants of the sustainable entrepreneurial engagement of youth in developing country—An empirical evidence from Pakistan. *Sustainability (Basel)*, *13*(14), 7764. DOI: 10.3390/su13147764

Tunio, M. N., Jariko, M. A., Børsen, T., Shaikh, S., Mushtaque, T., & Brahmi, M. (2021). How entrepreneurship sustains barriers in the entrepreneurial process—A lesson from a developing nation. *Sustainability (Basel)*, *13*(20), 11419. DOI: 10.3390/su132011419

Tunio, M. N., Shaikh, E., Katper, N. K., & Brahmi, M. (2023). Nascent entrepreneurs and challenges in the digital market in developing countries. *International Journal of Public Sector Performance Management*, *12*(1-2), 140–153. DOI: 10.1504/IJPSPM.2023.132244

UNICEF. (2022). "Impact of Floods on Children's Education in Sindh." *UNICEF Report*. Retrieved from https://www.unicef.org/sindh-flood-impact

Usman, F. O., Kess-Momoh, A. J., Ibeh, C. V., Elufioye, A. E., Ilojianya, V. I., & Oyeyemi, O. P., (2024). Entrepreneurial innovations and trends: A global review: Examining emerging trends, challenges, and opportunities in the field of entrepreneurship, with a focus on how technology and globalization are shaping new business ventures. *International Journal of Science and Research Archive*, *11*(1), 552–569. DOI: 10.30574/ijsra.2024.11.1.0079

Vijayakumar, G., Rajkumar, M., Rajiv Chandar, N., Selvakumar, P., & Duraisamy, R. (2024). Muniyandi Rajkumar, Rajiv Chandar N, Selvakumar P and Ramesh Duraisamy, (2024). Environmentally friendly TDS removal from waste water by electrochemical ion exchange batch-type recirculation (EIR) technique. *Environmental Science. Water Research & Technology*, *10*(4), 826–835. DOI: 10.1039/D3EW00793F

Vu, H. M. (2020). A review of dynamic capabilities, innovation capabilities, entrepreneurial capabilities and their consequences. *The Journal of Asian Finance, Economics and Business*, *7*(8), 485–494. DOI: 10.13106/jafeb.2020.vol7.no8.485

Wang, L., Zhou, F., An, Y., & Yang, J. (2019). Corporate venture capital: Technological innovation or value creation? A comparative study of CVC- and IVC-invested Chinese listed companies. *Asian Journal of Technology Innovation*, *27*(3), 257–279. DOI: 10.1080/19761597.2019.1669470

Wilson, N., & Martin, L. (2015). Entrepreneurial opportunities for all?: Entrepreneurial capability and the capabilities approach. *International Journal of Entrepreneurship and Innovation*, *16*(3), 159–169. DOI: 10.5367/ijei.2015.0189

World Health Organization (WHO). (2022). "Health Crises Following the 2022 Floods in Pakistan." *WHO Emergency Response Report*. Retrieved from https://www.who.int/pakistan-response

Yadav, D. K., & Barve, A. (2015). Analysis of critical success factors of humanitarian supply chain: An application of Interpretive Structural Modeling. *International Journal of Disaster Risk Reduction*, *12*, 213–225. DOI: 10.1016/j.ijdrr.2015.01.008

Yeganegi, S., Laplume, A. O., & Dass, P. (2021). The role of information availability: A longitudinal analysis of technology entrepreneurship. *Technological Forecasting and Social Change*, *170*, 120910. Advance online publication. DOI: 10.1016/j.techfore.2021.120910

Yu, W., Fei, J., Peng, G., & Bort, J. (2024). When a crisis hits: An examination of the effect of the global financial crisis and the COVID-19 pandemic on financing for female venture innovators. *Journal of Venture Venturing*, *39*(2), 106379. DOI: 10.1016/j.jbusvent.2024.106379

Zahra, S. A. (2022). International entrepreneurship by family firms post covid. *Journal of Family Business Strategy*, *xxxx*(2), 100482. DOI: 10.1016/j.jfbs.2021.100482

Zhai, L. Y., Khoo, L. P., & Zhong, Z. W. (2008). A rough set enhanced fuzzy approach to quality function deployment. *International Journal of Advanced Manufacturing Technology*, *37*(5–6), 613–624. DOI: 10.1007/s00170-007-0989-9

Zhai, L. Y., Khoo, L. P., & Zhong, Z. W. (2009). Design concept evaluation in product development using rough sets and grey relation analysis. *Expert Systems with Applications*, *36*(3), 7072–7079. DOI: 10.1016/j.eswa.2008.08.068

Zhang, L., Guo, Y., & Sun, G. (2019). How patent signals affect venture capital: The evidence of bio-pharmaceutical start-ups in China. *Technological Forecasting and Social Change*, *145*, 93–104. DOI: 10.1016/j.techfore.2019.05.013

Zhao, K., Wang, H., & Yin, X. (2023). How female venture innovators influence reward-based crowdsourcing performance: The mediating role of traditional and fiscal worth's orientation. International Venture innovations and Management Journal, 19(4), 1771-1802.

Zhou, Q., Huang, W., & Zhang, Y. (2011). Identifying critical success factors in emergency management using a fuzzy DEMATEL method. *Safety Science*, *49*(2), 243–252. DOI: 10.1016/j.ssci.2010.08.005

Zhou, X., Shi, Y., Deng, X., & Deng, Y. (2017). D-DEMATEL: A new method to identify critical success factors in emergency management. *Safety Science*, *91*, 93–104. DOI: 10.1016/j.ssci.2016.06.014

Related References

To continue our tradition of advancing information science and technology research, we have compiled a list of recommended IGI Global readings. These references will provide additional information and guidance to further enrich your knowledge and assist you with your own research and future publications.

Abdul Razak, R., & Mansor, N. A. (2021). Instagram Influencers in Social Media-Induced Tourism: Rethinking Tourist Trust Towards Tourism Destination. In M. Dinis, L. Bonixe, S. Lamy, & Z. Breda (Eds.), *Impact of New Media in Tourism* (pp. 135-144). IGI Global. https://doi.org/10.4018/978-1-7998-7095-1.ch009

Abir, T., & Khan, M. Y. (2022). Importance of ICT Advancement and Culture of Adaptation in the Tourism and Hospitality Industry for Developing Countries. In Ramos, C., Quinteiro, S., & Gonçalves, A. (Eds.), *ICT as Innovator Between Tourism and Culture* (pp. 30–41). IGI Global. https://doi.org/10.4018/978-1-7998-8165-0.ch003

Abir, T., & Khan, M. Y. (2022). Importance of ICT Advancement and Culture of Adaptation in the Tourism and Hospitality Industry for Developing Countries. In Ramos, C., Quinteiro, S., & Gonçalves, A. (Eds.), *ICT as Innovator Between Tourism and Culture* (pp. 30–41). IGI Global. https://doi.org/10.4018/978-1-7998-8165-0.ch003

Abtahi, M. S., Behboudi, L., & Hasanabad, H. M. (2017). Factors Affecting Internet Advertising Adoption in Ad Agencies. *International Journal of Innovation in the Digital Economy*, *8*(4), 18–29. DOI: 10.4018/IJIDE.2017100102

Afenyo-Agbe, E., & Mensah, I. (2022). Principles, Benefits, and Barriers to Community-Based Tourism: Implications for Management. In Mensah, I., & Afenyo-Agbe, E. (Eds.), *Prospects and Challenges of Community-Based Tourism and Changing Demographics* (pp. 1–29). IGI Global. DOI: 10.4018/978-1-7998-7335-8.ch001

Agbo, V. M. (2022). Distributive Justice Issues in Community-Based Tourism. In Mensah, I., & Afenyo-Agbe, E. (Eds.), *Prospects and Challenges of Community-Based Tourism and Changing Demographics* (pp. 107–129). IGI Global. https://doi.org/10.4018/978-1-7998-7335-8.ch005

Agrawal, S. (2017). The Impact of Emerging Technologies and Social Media on Different Business(es): Marketing and Management. In Rishi, O., & Sharma, A. (Eds.), *Maximizing Business Performance and Efficiency Through Intelligent Systems* (pp. 37–49). Hershey, PA: IGI Global. DOI: 10.4018/978-1-5225-2234-8.ch002

Ahmad, A., & Johari, S. (2022). Georgetown as a Gastronomy Tourism Destination: Visitor Awareness Towards Revisit Intention of Nasi Kandar Restaurant. In Valeri, M. (Ed.), *New Governance and Management in Touristic Destinations* (pp. 71–83). IGI Global. https://doi.org/10.4018/978-1-6684-3889-3.ch005

Alkhatib, G., & Bayouq, S. T. (2021). A TAM-Based Model of Technological Factors Affecting Use of E-Tourism. *International Journal of Tourism and Hospitality Management in the Digital Age*, *5*(2), 50–67. https://doi.org/10.4018/IJTHMDA.20210701.oa1

Altinay Ozdemir, M. (2021). Virtual Reality (VR) and Augmented Reality (AR) Technologies for Accessibility and Marketing in the Tourism Industry. In C. Eusébio, L. Teixeira, & M. Carneiro (Eds.), *ICT Tools and Applications for Accessible Tourism* (pp. 277-301). IGI Global. https://doi.org/10.4018/978-1-7998-6428-8.ch013

Anantharaman, R. N., Rajeswari, K. S., Angusamy, A., & Kuppusamy, J. (2017). Role of Self-Efficacy and Collective Efficacy as Moderators of Occupational Stress Among Software Development Professionals. *International Journal of Human Capital and Information Technology Professionals*, *8*(2), 45–58. DOI: 10.4018/IJHCITP.2017040103

Aninze, F., El-Gohary, H., & Hussain, J. (2018). The Role of Microfinance to Empower Women: The Case of Developing Countries. *International Journal of Customer Relationship Marketing and Management*, *9*(1), 54–78. DOI: 10.4018/IJCRMM.2018010104

Antosova, G., Sabogal-Salamanca, M., & Krizova, E. (2021). Human Capital in Tourism: A Practical Model of Endogenous and Exogenous Territorial Tourism Planning in Bahía Solano, Colombia. In Costa, V., Moura, A., & Mira, M. (Eds.), *Handbook of Research on Human Capital and People Management in the Tourism Industry* (pp. 282–302). IGI Global. https://doi.org/10.4018/978-1-7998-4318-4.ch014

Arsenijević, O. M., Orčić, D., & Kastratović, E. (2017). Development of an Optimization Tool for Intangibles in SMEs: A Case Study from Serbia with a Pilot Research in the Prestige by Milka Company. In Vemić, M. (Ed.), *Optimal Management Strategies in Small and Medium Enterprises* (pp. 320–347). Hershey, PA: IGI Global. DOI: 10.4018/978-1-5225-1949-2.ch015

Aryanto, V. D., Wismantoro, Y., & Widyatmoko, K. (2018). Implementing Eco-Innovation by Utilizing the Internet to Enhance Firm's Marketing Performance: Study of Green Batik Small and Medium Enterprises in Indonesia. *International Journal of E-Business Research*, *14*(1), 21–36. DOI: 10.4018/IJEBR.2018010102

Asero, V., & Billi, S. (2022). New Perspective of Networking in the DMO Model. In Valeri, M. (Ed.), *New Governance and Management in Touristic Destinations* (pp. 105–118). IGI Global. https://doi.org/10.4018/978-1-6684-3889-3.ch007

Atiku, S. O., & Fields, Z. (2017). Multicultural Orientations for 21st Century Global Leadership. In Baporikar, N. (Ed.), *Management Education for Global Leadership* (pp. 28–51). Hershey, PA: IGI Global. DOI: 10.4018/978-1-5225-1013-0.ch002

Atiku, S. O., & Fields, Z. (2018). Organisational Learning Dimensions and Talent Retention Strategies for the Service Industries. In Baporikar, N. (Ed.), *Global Practices in Knowledge Management for Societal and Organizational Development* (pp. 358–381). Hershey, PA: IGI Global. DOI: 10.4018/978-1-5225-3009-1.ch017

Atsa'am, D. D., & Kuset Bodur, E. (2021). Pattern Mining on How Organizational Tenure Affects the Psychological Capital of Employees Within the Hospitality and Tourism Industry: Linking Employees' Organizational Tenure With PsyCap. *International Journal of Tourism and Hospitality Management in the Digital Age*, *5*(2), 17–28. https://doi.org/10.4018/IJTHMDA.2021070102

Ávila, L., & Teixeira, L. (2018). The Main Concepts Behind the Dematerialization of Business Processes. In M. Khosrow-Pour, D.B.A. (Ed.), *Encyclopedia of Information Science and Technology, Fourth Edition* (pp. 888-898). Hershey, PA: IGI Global. https://doi.org/DOI: 10.4018/978-1-5225-2255-3.ch076

Ayorekire, J., Mugizi, F., Obua, J., & Ampaire, G. (2022). Community-Based Tourism and Local People's Perceptions Towards Conservation: The Case of Queen Elizabeth Conservation Area, Uganda. In Mensah, I., & Afenyo-Agbe, E. (Eds.), *Prospects and Challenges of Community-Based Tourism and Changing Demographics* (pp. 56–82). IGI Global. https://doi.org/10.4018/978-1-7998-7335-8.ch003

Baleiro, R. (2022). Tourist Literature and the Architecture of Travel in Olga Tokarczuk and Patti Smith. In R. Baleiro & R. Pereira (Eds.), *Global Perspectives on Literary Tourism and Film-Induced Tourism* (pp. 202-216). IGI Global. https://doi.org/10.4018/978-1-7998-8262-6.ch011

Barat, S. (2021). Looking at the Future of Medical Tourism in Asia. *International Journal of Tourism and Hospitality Management in the Digital Age*, *5*(1), 19–33. https://doi.org/10.4018/IJTHMDA.2021010102

Barbosa, C. A., Magalhães, M., & Nunes, M. R. (2021). Travel Instagramability: A Way of Choosing a Destination? In M. Dinis, L. Bonixe, S. Lamy, & Z. Breda (Eds.), *Impact of New Media in Tourism* (pp. 173-190). IGI Global. https://doi.org/10.4018/978-1-7998-7095-1.ch011

Bari, M. W., & Khan, Q. (2021). Pakistan as a Destination of Religious Tourism. In E. Alaverdov & M. Bari (Eds.), *Global Development of Religious Tourism* (pp. 1-10). IGI Global. https://doi.org/10.4018/978-1-7998-5792-1.ch001

Bartens, Y., Chunpir, H. I., Schulte, F., & Voß, S. (2017). Business/IT Alignment in Two-Sided Markets: A COBIT 5 Analysis for Media Streaming Business Models. In De Haes, S., & Van Grembergen, W. (Eds.), *Strategic IT Governance and Alignment in Business Settings* (pp. 82–111). Hershey, PA: IGI Global. DOI: 10.4018/978-1-5225-0861-8.ch004

Bashayreh, A. M. (2018). Organizational Culture and Organizational Performance. In Lee, W., & Sabetzadeh, F. (Eds.), *Contemporary Knowledge and Systems Science* (pp. 50–69). Hershey, PA: IGI Global. DOI: 10.4018/978-1-5225-5655-8.ch003

Bechthold, L., Lude, M., & Prügl, R. (2021). Crisis Favors the Prepared Firm: How Organizational Ambidexterity Relates to Perceptions of Organizational Resilience. In Zehrer, A., Glowka, G., Schwaiger, K., & Ranacher-Lackner, V. (Eds.), *Resiliency Models and Addressing Future Risks for Family Firms in the Tourism Industry* (pp. 178–205). IGI Global. https://doi.org/10.4018/978-1-7998-7352-5.ch008

Bedford, D. A. (2018). Sustainable Knowledge Management Strategies: Aligning Business Capabilities and Knowledge Management Goals. In Baporikar, N. (Ed.), *Global Practices in Knowledge Management for Societal and Organizational Development* (pp. 46–73). Hershey, PA: IGI Global. DOI: 10.4018/978-1-5225-3009-1.ch003

Bekjanov, D., & Matyusupov, B. (2021). Influence of Innovative Processes in the Competitiveness of Tourist Destination. In Soares, J. (Ed.), *Innovation and Entrepreneurial Opportunities in Community Tourism* (pp. 243–263). IGI Global. https://doi.org/10.4018/978-1-7998-4855-4.ch014

Bharwani, S., & Musunuri, D. (2018). Reflection as a Process From Theory to Practice. In M. Khosrow-Pour, D.B.A. (Ed.), *Encyclopedia of Information Science and Technology, Fourth Edition* (pp. 1529-1539). Hershey, PA: IGI Global. DOI: 10.4018/978-1-5225-2255-3.ch132

Bhatt, G. D., Wang, Z., & Rodger, J. A. (2017). Information Systems Capabilities and Their Effects on Competitive Advantages: A Study of Chinese Companies. *Information Resources Management Journal, 30*(3), 41–57. DOI: 10.4018/IRMJ.2017070103

Bhushan, M., & Yadav, A. (2017). Concept of Cloud Computing in ESB. In Bhadoria, R., Chaudhari, N., Tomar, G., & Singh, S. (Eds.), *Exploring Enterprise Service Bus in the Service-Oriented Architecture Paradigm* (pp. 116–127). Hershey, PA: IGI Global. DOI: 10.4018/978-1-5225-2157-0.ch008

Bhushan, S. (2017). System Dynamics Base-Model of Humanitarian Supply Chain (HSCM) in Disaster Prone Eco-Communities of India: A Discussion on Simulation and Scenario Results. *International Journal of System Dynamics Applications, 6*(3), 20–37. DOI: 10.4018/IJSDA.2017070102

Binder, D., & Miller, J. W. (2021). A Generations' Perspective on Employer Branding in Tourism. In Costa, V., Moura, A., & Mira, M. (Eds.), *Handbook of Research on Human Capital and People Management in the Tourism Industry* (pp. 152–174). IGI Global. https://doi.org/10.4018/978-1-7998-4318-4.ch008

Birch Freeman, A. A., Mensah, I., & Antwi, K. B. (2022). Smiling vs. Frowning Faces: Community Participation for Sustainable Tourism in Ghanaian Communities. In Mensah, I., & Afenyo-Agbe, E. (Eds.), *Prospects and Challenges of Community-Based Tourism and Changing Demographics* (pp. 83–106). IGI Global. https://doi.org/10.4018/978-1-7998-7335-8.ch004

Biswas, A., & De, A. K. (2017). On Development of a Fuzzy Stochastic Programming Model with Its Application to Business Management. In Trivedi, S., Dey, S., Kumar, A., & Panda, T. (Eds.), *Handbook of Research on Advanced Data Mining Techniques and Applications for Business Intelligence* (pp. 353–378). Hershey, PA: IGI Global. DOI: 10.4018/978-1-5225-2031-3.ch021

Boragnio, A., & Faracce Macia, C. (2021). "Taking Care of Yourself at Home": Use of E-Commerce About Food and Care During the COVID-19 Pandemic in the City of Buenos Aires. In Korstanje, M. (Ed.), *Socio-Economic Effects and Recovery Efforts for the Rental Industry: Post-COVID-19 Strategies* (pp. 45–71). IGI Global. https://doi.org/10.4018/978-1-7998-7287-0.ch003

Borges, V. D. (2021). Happiness: The Basis for Public Policy in Tourism. In Perinotto, A., Mayer, V., & Soares, J. (Eds.), *Rebuilding and Restructuring the Tourism Industry: Infusion of Happiness and Quality of Life* (pp. 1–25). IGI Global. https://doi.org/10.4018/978-1-7998-7239-9.ch001

Bücker, J., & Ernste, K. (2018). Use of Brand Heroes in Strategic Reputation Management: The Case of Bacardi, Adidas, and Daimler. In Erdemir, A. (Ed.), *Reputation Management Techniques in Public Relations* (pp. 126–150). Hershey, PA: IGI Global. DOI: 10.4018/978-1-5225-3619-2.ch007

Buluk Eşitti, B. (2021). COVID-19 and Alternative Tourism: New Destinations and New Tourism Products. In Demir, M., Dalgıç, A., & Ergen, F. (Eds.), *Handbook of Research on the Impacts and Implications of COVID-19 on the Tourism Industry* (pp. 786–805). IGI Global. https://doi.org/10.4018/978-1-7998-8231-2.ch038

Bureš, V. (2018). Industry 4.0 From the Systems Engineering Perspective: Alternative Holistic Framework Development. In Brunet-Thornton, R., & Martinez, F. (Eds.), *Analyzing the Impacts of Industry 4.0 in Modern Business Environments* (pp. 199–223). Hershey, PA: IGI Global. DOI: 10.4018/978-1-5225-3468-6.ch011

Buzady, Z. (2017). Resolving the Magic Cube of Effective Case Teaching: Benchmarking Case Teaching Practices in Emerging Markets – Insights from the Central European University Business School, Hungary. In Latusek, D. (Ed.), *Case Studies as a Teaching Tool in Management Education* (pp. 79–103). Hershey, PA: IGI Global. DOI: 10.4018/978-1-5225-0770-3.ch005

Camillo, A. (2021). *Legal Matters, Risk Management, and Risk Prevention: From Forming a Business to Legal Representation*. IGI Global. DOI: 10.4018/978-1-7998-4342-9.ch004

Căpusneanu, S., & Topor, D. I. (2018). Business Ethics and Cost Management in SMEs: Theories of Business Ethics and Cost Management Ethos. In Oncioiu, I. (Ed.), *Ethics and Decision-Making for Sustainable Business Practices* (pp. 109–127). Hershey, PA: IGI Global. DOI: 10.4018/978-1-5225-3773-1.ch007

Chan, R. L., Mo, P. L., & Moon, K. K. (2018). Strategic and Tactical Measures in Managing Enterprise Risks: A Study of the Textile and Apparel Industry. In Strang, K., Korstanje, M., & Vajjhala, N. (Eds.), *Research, Practices, and Innovations in Global Risk and Contingency Management* (pp. 1–19). Hershey, PA: IGI Global. DOI: 10.4018/978-1-5225-4754-9.ch001

Charlier, S. D., Burke-Smalley, L. A., & Fisher, S. L. (2018). Undergraduate Programs in the U.S: A Contextual and Content-Based Analysis. In Mendy, J. (Ed.), *Teaching Human Resources and Organizational Behavior at the College Level* (pp. 26–57). Hershey, PA: IGI Global. DOI: 10.4018/978-1-5225-2820-3.ch002

Chumillas, J., Güell, M., & Quer, P. (2022). The Use of ICT in Tourist and Educational Literary Routes: The Role of the Guide. In Ramos, C., Quinteiro, S., & Gonçalves, A. (Eds.), *ICT as Innovator Between Tourism and Culture* (pp. 15–29). IGI Global. https://doi.org/10.4018/978-1-7998-8165-0.ch002

Dahlberg, T., Kivijärvi, H., & Saarinen, T. (2017). IT Investment Consistency and Other Factors Influencing the Success of IT Performance. In De Haes, S., & Van Grembergen, W. (Eds.), *Strategic IT Governance and Alignment in Business Settings* (pp. 176–208). Hershey, PA: IGI Global. DOI: 10.4018/978-1-5225-0861-8.ch007

Damnjanović, A. M. (2017). Knowledge Management Optimization through IT and E-Business Utilization: A Qualitative Study on Serbian SMEs. In Vemić, M. (Ed.), *Optimal Management Strategies in Small and Medium Enterprises* (pp. 249–267). Hershey, PA: IGI Global. DOI: 10.4018/978-1-5225-1949-2.ch012

Daneshpour, H. (2017). Integrating Sustainable Development into Project Portfolio Management through Application of Open Innovation. In Vemić, M. (Ed.), *Optimal Management Strategies in Small and Medium Enterprises* (pp. 370–387). Hershey, PA: IGI Global. DOI: 10.4018/978-1-5225-1949-2.ch017

Daniel, A. D., & Reis de Castro, V. (2018). Entrepreneurship Education: How to Measure the Impact on Nascent Entrepreneurs. In Carrizo Moreira, A., Guilherme Leitão Dantas, J., & Manuel Valente, F. (Eds.), *Nascent Entrepreneurship and Successful New Venture Creation* (pp. 85–110). Hershey, PA: IGI Global. DOI: 10.4018/978-1-5225-2936-1.ch004

David, R., Swami, B. N., & Tangirala, S. (2018). Ethics Impact on Knowledge Management in Organizational Development: A Case Study. In Baporikar, N. (Ed.), *Global Practices in Knowledge Management for Societal and Organizational Development* (pp. 19–45). Hershey, PA: IGI Global. DOI: 10.4018/978-1-5225-3009-1.ch002

De Uña-Álvarez, E., & Villarino-Pérez, M. (2022). Fostering Ecocultural Resources, Identity, and Tourism in Inland Territories (Galicia, NW Spain). In G. Fernandes (Ed.), *Challenges and New Opportunities for Tourism in Inland Territories: Ecocultural Resources and Sustainable Initiatives* (pp. 1-16). IGI Global. https://doi.org/10.4018/978-1-7998-7339-6.ch001

Delias, P., & Lakiotaki, K. (2018). Discovering Process Horizontal Boundaries to Facilitate Process Comprehension. *International Journal of Operations Research and Information Systems*, *9*(2), 1–31. DOI: 10.4018/IJORIS.2018040101

Denholm, J., & Lee-Davies, L. (2018). Success Factors for Games in Business and Project Management. In *Enhancing Education and Training Initiatives Through Serious Games* (pp. 34–68). Hershey, PA: IGI Global. DOI: 10.4018/978-1-5225-3689-5.ch002

Deshpande, M. (2017). Best Practices in Management Institutions for Global Leadership: Policy Aspects. In Baporikar, N. (Ed.), *Management Education for Global Leadership* (pp. 1–27). Hershey, PA: IGI Global. DOI: 10.4018/978-1-5225-1013-0.ch001

Deshpande, M. (2018). Policy Perspectives for SMEs Knowledge Management. In Baporikar, N. (Ed.), *Knowledge Integration Strategies for Entrepreneurship and Sustainability* (pp. 23–46). Hershey, PA: IGI Global. DOI: 10.4018/978-1-5225-5115-7.ch002

Dezdar, S. (2017). ERP Implementation Projects in Asian Countries: A Comparative Study on Iran and China. *International Journal of Information Technology Project Management*, *8*(3), 52–68. DOI: 10.4018/IJITPM.2017070104

Domingos, D., Respício, A., & Martinho, R. (2017). Reliability of IoT-Aware BPMN Healthcare Processes. In Reis, C., & Maximiano, M. (Eds.), *Internet of Things and Advanced Application in Healthcare* (pp. 214–248). Hershey, PA: IGI Global. DOI: 10.4018/978-1-5225-1820-4.ch008

Dosumu, O., Hussain, J., & El-Gohary, H. (2017). An Exploratory Study of the Impact of Government Policies on the Development of Small and Medium Enterprises in Developing Countries: The Case of Nigeria. *International Journal of Customer Relationship Marketing and Management*, *8*(4), 51–62. DOI: 10.4018/IJCRMM.2017100104

Durst, S., Bruns, G., & Edvardsson, I. R. (2017). Retaining Knowledge in Smaller Building and Construction Firms. *International Journal of Knowledge and Systems Science*, *8*(3), 1–12. DOI: 10.4018/IJKSS.2017070101

Edvardsson, I. R., & Durst, S. (2017). Outsourcing, Knowledge, and Learning: A Critical Review. *International Journal of Knowledge-Based Organizations*, *7*(2), 13–26. DOI: 10.4018/IJKBO.2017040102

Edwards, J. S. (2018). Integrating Knowledge Management and Business Processes. In M. Khosrow-Pour, D.B.A. (Ed.), *Encyclopedia of Information Science and Technology, Fourth Edition* (pp. 5046-5055). Hershey, PA: IGI Global. DOI: 10.4018/978-1-5225-2255-3.ch437

Eichelberger, S., & Peters, M. (2021). Family Firm Management in Turbulent Times: Opportunities for Responsible Tourism. In Zehrer, A., Glowka, G., Schwaiger, K., & Ranacher-Lackner, V. (Eds.), *Resiliency Models and Addressing Future Risks for Family Firms in the Tourism Industry* (pp. 103–124). IGI Global. https://doi.org/10.4018/978-1-7998-7352-5.ch005

Eide, D., Hjalager, A., & Hansen, M. (2022). Innovative Certifications in Adventure Tourism: Attributes and Diffusion. In R. Augusto Costa, F. Brandão, Z. Breda, & C. Costa (Eds.), *Planning and Managing the Experience Economy in Tourism* (pp. 161-175). IGI Global. https://doi.org/10.4018/978-1-7998-8775-1.ch009

Ejiogu, A. O. (2018). Economics of Farm Management. In *Agricultural Finance and Opportunities for Investment and Expansion* (pp. 56–72). Hershey, PA: IGI Global. DOI: 10.4018/978-1-5225-3059-6.ch003

Ekanem, I., & Abiade, G. E. (2018). Factors Influencing the Use of E-Commerce by Small Enterprises in Nigeria. *International Journal of ICT Research in Africa and the Middle East*, *7*(1), 37–53. DOI: 10.4018/IJICTRAME.2018010103

Ekanem, I., & Alrossais, L. A. (2017). Succession Challenges Facing Family Businesses in Saudi Arabia. In Zgheib, P. (Ed.), *Entrepreneurship and Business Innovation in the Middle East* (pp. 122–146). Hershey, PA: IGI Global. DOI: 10.4018/978-1-5225-2066-5.ch007

El Faquih, L., & Fredj, M. (2017). Ontology-Based Framework for Quality in Configurable Process Models. *Journal of Electronic Commerce in Organizations*, *15*(2), 48–60. DOI: 10.4018/JECO.2017040104

Faisal, M. N., & Talib, F. (2017). Building Ambidextrous Supply Chains in SMEs: How to Tackle the Barriers? *International Journal of Information Systems and Supply Chain Management*, *10*(4), 80–100. DOI: 10.4018/IJISSCM.2017100105

Fernandes, T. M., Gomes, J., & Romão, M. (2017). Investments in E-Government: A Benefit Management Case Study. *International Journal of Electronic Government Research*, *13*(3), 1–17. DOI: 10.4018/IJEGR.2017070101

Figueira, L. M., Honrado, G. R., & Dionísio, M. S. (2021). Human Capital Management in the Tourism Industry in Portugal. In Costa, V., Moura, A., & Mira, M. (Eds.), *Handbook of Research on Human Capital and People Management in the Tourism Industry* (pp. 1–19). IGI Global. DOI: 10.4018/978-1-7998-4318-4.ch001

Gao, S. S., Oreal, S., & Zhang, J. (2018). Contemporary Financial Risk Management Perceptions and Practices of Small-Sized Chinese Businesses. In I. Management Association (Ed.), *Global Business Expansion: Concepts, Methodologies, Tools, and Applications* (pp. 917-931). Hershey, PA: IGI Global. DOI: 10.4018/978-1-5225-5481-3.ch041

Garg, R., & Berning, S. C. (2017). Indigenous Chinese Management Philosophies: Key Concepts and Relevance for Modern Chinese Firms. In Christiansen, B., & Koc, G. (Eds.), *Transcontinental Strategies for Industrial Development and Economic Growth* (pp. 43–57). Hershey, PA: IGI Global. DOI: 10.4018/978-1-5225-2160-0.ch003

Gencer, Y. G. (2017). Supply Chain Management in Retailing Business. In Akkucuk, U. (Ed.), *Ethics and Sustainability in Global Supply Chain Management* (pp. 197–210). Hershey, PA: IGI Global. DOI: 10.4018/978-1-5225-2036-8.ch011

Gera, R., Arora, S., & Malik, S. (2021). Emotional Labor in the Tourism Industry: Strategies, Antecedents, and Outcomes. In Costa, V., Moura, A., & Mira, M. (Eds.), *Handbook of Research on Human Capital and People Management in the Tourism Industry* (pp. 73–91). IGI Global. https://doi.org/10.4018/978-1-7998-4318-4.ch004

Giacosa, E. (2018). The Increasing of the Regional Development Thanks to the Luxury Business Innovation. In Carvalho, L. (Ed.), *Handbook of Research on Entrepreneurial Ecosystems and Social Dynamics in a Globalized World* (pp. 260–273). Hershey, PA: IGI Global. DOI: 10.4018/978-1-5225-3525-6.ch011

Glowka, G., Tusch, M., & Zehrer, A. (2021). The Risk Perception of Family Business Owner-Manager in the Tourism Industry: A Qualitative Comparison of the Intra-Firm Senior and Junior Generation. In Zehrer, A., Glowka, G., Schwaiger, K., & Ranacher-Lackner, V. (Eds.), *Resiliency Models and Addressing Future Risks for Family Firms in the Tourism Industry* (pp. 126–153). IGI Global. https://doi.org/10.4018/978-1-7998-7352-5.ch006

Glykas, M., & George, J. (2017). Quality and Process Management Systems in the UAE Maritime Industry. *International Journal of Productivity Management and Assessment Technologies*, *5*(1), 20–39. DOI: 10.4018/IJPMAT.2017010102

Glykas, M., Valiris, G., Kokkinaki, A., & Koutsoukou, Z. (2018). Banking Business Process Management Implementation. *International Journal of Productivity Management and Assessment Technologies*, *6*(1), 50–69. DOI: 10.4018/IJPMAT.2018010104

Gomes, J., & Romão, M. (2017). The Balanced Scorecard: Keeping Updated and Aligned with Today's Business Trends. *International Journal of Productivity Management and Assessment Technologies*, *5*(2), 1–15. DOI: 10.4018/IJPMAT.2017070101

Gomes, J., & Romão, M. (2017). Aligning Information Systems and Technology with Benefit Management and Balanced Scorecard. In De Haes, S., & Van Grembergen, W. (Eds.), *Strategic IT Governance and Alignment in Business Settings* (pp. 112–131). Hershey, PA: IGI Global. DOI: 10.4018/978-1-5225-0861-8.ch005

Goyal, A. (2021). Communicating and Building Destination Brands With New Media. In M. Dinis, L. Bonixe, S. Lamy, & Z. Breda (Eds.), *Impact of New Media in Tourism* (pp. 1-20). IGI Global. https://doi.org/10.4018/978-1-7998-7095-1.ch001

Grefen, P., & Turetken, O. (2017). Advanced Business Process Management in Networked E-Business Scenarios. *International Journal of E-Business Research*, *13*(4), 70–104. DOI: 10.4018/IJEBR.2017100105

Guasca, M., Van Broeck, A. M., & Vanneste, D. (2021). Tourism and the Social Reintegration of Colombian Ex-Combatants. In J. da Silva, Z. Breda, & F. Carbone (Eds.), *Role and Impact of Tourism in Peacebuilding and Conflict Transformation* (pp. 66-86). IGI Global. https://doi.org/10.4018/978-1-7998-5053-3.ch005

Haider, A., & Saetang, S. (2017). Strategic IT Alignment in Service Sector. In Rozenes, S., & Cohen, Y. (Eds.), *Handbook of Research on Strategic Alliances and Value Co-Creation in the Service Industry* (pp. 231–258). Hershey, PA: IGI Global. DOI: 10.4018/978-1-5225-2084-9.ch012

Hajilari, A. B., Ghadaksaz, M., & Fasghandis, G. S. (2017). Assessing Organizational Readiness for Implementing ERP System Using Fuzzy Expert System Approach. *International Journal of Enterprise Information Systems*, *13*(1), 67–85. DOI: 10.4018/IJEIS.2017010105

Haldorai, A., Ramu, A., & Murugan, S. (2018). Social Aware Cognitive Radio Networks: Effectiveness of Social Networks as a Strategic Tool for Organizational Business Management. In Bansal, H., Shrivastava, G., Nguyen, G., & Stanciu, L. (Eds.), *Social Network Analytics for Contemporary Business Organizations* (pp. 188–202). Hershey, PA: IGI Global. DOI: 10.4018/978-1-5225-5097-6.ch010

Hall, O. P.Jr. (2017). Social Media Driven Management Education. *International Journal of Knowledge-Based Organizations*, *7*(2), 43–59. DOI: 10.4018/IJKBO.2017040104

Hanifah, H., Halim, H. A., Ahmad, N. H., & Vafaei-Zadeh, A. (2017). Innovation Culture as a Mediator Between Specific Human Capital and Innovation Performance Among Bumiputera SMEs in Malaysia. In Ahmad, N., Ramayah, T., Halim, H., & Rahman, S. (Eds.), *Handbook of Research on Small and Medium Enterprises in Developing Countries* (pp. 261–279). Hershey, PA: IGI Global. DOI: 10.4018/978-1-5225-2165-5.ch012

Hartlieb, S., & Silvius, G. (2017). Handling Uncertainty in Project Management and Business Development: Similarities and Differences. In Raydugin, Y. (Ed.), *Handbook of Research on Leveraging Risk and Uncertainties for Effective Project Management* (pp. 337–362). Hershey, PA: IGI Global. DOI: 10.4018/978-1-5225-1790-0.ch016

Hass, K. B. (2017). Living on the Edge: Managing Project Complexity. In Raydugin, Y. (Ed.), *Handbook of Research on Leveraging Risk and Uncertainties for Effective Project Management* (pp. 177–201). Hershey, PA: IGI Global. DOI: 10.4018/978-1-5225-1790-0.ch009

Hawking, P., & Carmine Sellitto, C. (2017). Developing an Effective Strategy for Organizational Business Intelligence. In Tavana, M. (Ed.), *Enterprise Information Systems and the Digitalization of Business Functions* (pp. 222–237). Hershey, PA: IGI Global. DOI: 10.4018/978-1-5225-2382-6.ch010

Hawking, P., & Sellitto, C. (2017). A Fast-Moving Consumer Goods Company and Business Intelligence Strategy Development. *International Journal of Enterprise Information Systems*, *13*(2), 22–33. DOI: 10.4018/IJEIS.2017040102

Hawking, P., & Sellitto, C. (2017). Business Intelligence Strategy: Two Case Studies. *International Journal of Business Intelligence Research*, *8*(2), 17–30. DOI: 10.4018/IJBIR.2017070102

Hee, W. J., Jalleh, G., Lai, H., & Lin, C. (2017). E-Commerce and IT Projects: Evaluation and Management Issues in Australian and Taiwanese Hospitals. *International Journal of Public Health Management and Ethics*, *2*(1), 69–90. DOI: 10.4018/IJPHME.2017010104

Hernandez, A. A. (2018). Exploring the Factors to Green IT Adoption of SMEs in the Philippines. *Journal of Cases on Information Technology*, *20*(2), 49–66. DOI: 10.4018/JCIT.2018040104

Hollman, A., Bickford, S., & Hollman, T. (2017). Cyber InSecurity: A Post-Mortem Attempt to Assess Cyber Problems from IT and Business Management Perspectives. *Journal of Cases on Information Technology*, *19*(3), 42–70. DOI: 10.4018/JCIT.2017070104

Ibrahim, F., & Zainin, N. M. (2021). Exploring the Technological Impacts: The Case of Museums in Brunei Darussalam. *International Journal of Tourism and Hospitality Management in the Digital Age*, *5*(1), 1–18. https://doi.org/10.4018/IJTHMDA.2021010101

Igbinakhase, I. (2017). Responsible and Sustainable Management Practices in Developing and Developed Business Environments. In Fields, Z. (Ed.), *Collective Creativity for Responsible and Sustainable Business Practice* (pp. 180–207). Hershey, PA: IGI Global. DOI: 10.4018/978-1-5225-1823-5.ch010

Iwata, J. J., & Hoskins, R. G. (2017). Managing Indigenous Knowledge in Tanzania: A Business Perspective. In Jain, P., & Mnjama, N. (Eds.), *Managing Knowledge Resources and Records in Modern Organizations* (pp. 198–214). Hershey, PA: IGI Global. DOI: 10.4018/978-1-5225-1965-2.ch012

Jain, P. (2017). Ethical and Legal Issues in Knowledge Management Life-Cycle in Business. In Jain, P., & Mnjama, N. (Eds.), *Managing Knowledge Resources and Records in Modern Organizations* (pp. 82–101). Hershey, PA: IGI Global. DOI: 10.4018/978-1-5225-1965-2.ch006

James, S., & Hauli, E. (2017). Holistic Management Education at Tanzanian Rural Development Planning Institute. In Baporikar, N. (Ed.), *Management Education for Global Leadership* (pp. 112–136). Hershey, PA: IGI Global. DOI: 10.4018/978-1-5225-1013-0.ch006

Janošková, M., Csikósová, A., & Čulková, K. (2018). Measurement of Company Performance as Part of Its Strategic Management. In Leon, R. (Ed.), *Managerial Strategies for Business Sustainability During Turbulent Times* (pp. 309–335). Hershey, PA: IGI Global. DOI: 10.4018/978-1-5225-2716-9.ch017

Jean-Vasile, A., & Alecu, A. (2017). Theoretical and Practical Approaches in Understanding the Influences of Cost-Productivity-Profit Trinomial in Contemporary Enterprises. In Jean Vasile, A., & Nicolò, D. (Eds.), *Sustainable Entrepreneurship and Investments in the Green Economy* (pp. 28–62). Hershey, PA: IGI Global. DOI: 10.4018/978-1-5225-2075-7.ch002

Joia, L. A., & Correia, J. C. (2018). CIO Competencies From the IT Professional Perspective: Insights From Brazil. *Journal of Global Information Management*, *26*(2), 74–103. DOI: 10.4018/JGIM.2018040104

Juma, A., & Mzera, N. (2017). Knowledge Management and Records Management and Competitive Advantage in Business. In Jain, P., & Mnjama, N. (Eds.), *Managing Knowledge Resources and Records in Modern Organizations* (pp. 15–28). Hershey, PA: IGI Global. DOI: 10.4018/978-1-5225-1965-2.ch002

K., I., & A, V. (2018). Monitoring and Auditing in the Cloud. In K. Munir (Ed.), *Cloud Computing Technologies for Green Enterprises* (pp. 318-350). Hershey, PA: IGI Global. https://doi.org/DOI: 10.4018/978-1-5225-3038-1.ch013

Kabra, G., Ghosh, V., & Ramesh, A. (2018). Enterprise Integrated Business Process Management and Business Intelligence Framework for Business Process Sustainability. In Paul, A., Bhattacharyya, D., & Anand, S. (Eds.), *Green Initiatives for Business Sustainability and Value Creation* (pp. 228–238). Hershey, PA: IGI Global. DOI: 10.4018/978-1-5225-2662-9.ch010

Kaoud, M. (2017). Investigation of Customer Knowledge Management: A Case Study Research. *International Journal of Service Science, Management, Engineering, and Technology*, *8*(2), 12–22. DOI: 10.4018/IJSSMET.2017040102

Katuu, S. (2018). A Comparative Assessment of Enterprise Content Management Maturity Models. In Gwangwava, N., & Mutingi, M. (Eds.), *E-Manufacturing and E-Service Strategies in Contemporary Organizations* (pp. 93–118). Hershey, PA: IGI Global. DOI: 10.4018/978-1-5225-3628-4.ch005

Khan, M. Y., & Abir, T. (2022). The Role of Social Media Marketing in the Tourism and Hospitality Industry: A Conceptual Study on Bangladesh. In Ramos, C., Quinteiro, S., & Gonçalves, A. (Eds.), *ICT as Innovator Between Tourism and Culture* (pp. 213–229). IGI Global. https://doi.org/10.4018/978-1-7998-8165-0.ch013

Kinnunen, S., Ylä-Kujala, A., Marttonen-Arola, S., Kärri, T., & Baglee, D. (2018). Internet of Things in Asset Management: Insights from Industrial Professionals and Academia. *International Journal of Service Science, Management, Engineering, and Technology*, *9*(2), 104–119. DOI: 10.4018/IJSSMET.2018040105

Klein, A. Z., Sabino de Freitas, A., Machado, L., Freitas, J. C.Jr, Graziola, P. G.Jr, & Schlemmer, E. (2017). Virtual Worlds Applications for Management Education. In Tomei, L. (Ed.), *Exploring the New Era of Technology-Infused Education* (pp. 279–299). Hershey, PA: IGI Global. DOI: 10.4018/978-1-5225-1709-2.ch017

Kővári, E., Saleh, M., & Steinbachné Hajmásy, G. (2022). The Impact of Corporate Digital Responsibility (CDR) on Internal Stakeholders' Satisfaction in Hungarian Upscale Hotels. In Valeri, M. (Ed.), *New Governance and Management in Touristic Destinations* (pp. 35–51). IGI Global. https://doi.org/10.4018/978-1-6684-3889-3.ch003

Kożuch, B., & Jabłoński, A. (2017). Adopting the Concept of Business Models in Public Management. In Lewandowski, M., & Kożuch, B. (Eds.), *Public Sector Entrepreneurship and the Integration of Innovative Business Models* (pp. 10–46). Hershey, PA: IGI Global. DOI: 10.4018/978-1-5225-2215-7.ch002

Kumar, J., Adhikary, A., & Jha, A. (2017). Small Active Investors' Perceptions and Preferences Towards Tax Saving Mutual Fund Schemes in Eastern India: An Empirical Note. *International Journal of Asian Business and Information Management*, *8*(2), 35–45. DOI: 10.4018/IJABIM.2017040103

Latusi, S., & Fissore, M. (2021). Pilgrimage Routes to Happiness: Comparing the Camino de Santiago and Via Francigena. In Perinotto, A., Mayer, V., & Soares, J. (Eds.), *Rebuilding and Restructuring the Tourism Industry: Infusion of Happiness and Quality of Life* (pp. 157–182). IGI Global. https://doi.org/10.4018/978-1-7998-7239-9.ch008

Lavassani, K. M., & Movahedi, B. (2017). Applications Driven Information Systems: Beyond Networks toward Business Ecosystems. *International Journal of Innovation in the Digital Economy*, *8*(1), 61–75. DOI: 10.4018/IJIDE.2017010104

Lazzareschi, V. H., & Brito, M. S. (2017). Strategic Information Management: Proposal of Business Project Model. In Jamil, G., Soares, A., & Pessoa, C. (Eds.), *Handbook of Research on Information Management for Effective Logistics and Supply Chains* (pp. 59–88). Hershey, PA: IGI Global. DOI: 10.4018/978-1-5225-0973-8.ch004

Lechuga Sancho, M. P., & Martín Navarro, A. (2022). Evolution of the Literature on Social Responsibility in the Tourism Sector: A Systematic Literature Review. In Fernandes, G. (Ed.), *Challenges and New Opportunities for Tourism in Inland Territories: Ecocultural Resources and Sustainable Initiatives* (pp. 169–186). IGI Global. https://doi.org/10.4018/978-1-7998-7339-6.ch010

Lederer, M., Kurz, M., & Lazarov, P. (2017). Usage and Suitability of Methods for Strategic Business Process Initiatives: A Multi Case Study Research. *International Journal of Productivity Management and Assessment Technologies*, *5*(1), 40–51. DOI: 10.4018/IJPMAT.2017010103

Lee, I. (2017). A Social Enterprise Business Model and a Case Study of Pacific Community Ventures (PCV). In Potocan, V., Ünğan, M., & Nedelko, Z. (Eds.), *Handbook of Research on Managerial Solutions in Non-Profit Organizations* (pp. 182–204). Hershey, PA: IGI Global. DOI: 10.4018/978-1-5225-0731-4.ch009

Leon, L. A., Seal, K. C., Przasnyski, Z. H., & Wiedenman, I. (2017). Skills and Competencies Required for Jobs in Business Analytics: A Content Analysis of Job Advertisements Using Text Mining. *International Journal of Business Intelligence Research*, *8*(1), 1–25. DOI: 10.4018/IJBIR.2017010101

Levy, C. L., & Elias, N. I. (2017). SOHO Users' Perceptions of Reliability and Continuity of Cloud-Based Services. In Moore, M. (Ed.), *Cybersecurity Breaches and Issues Surrounding Online Threat Protection* (pp. 248–287). Hershey, PA: IGI Global. DOI: 10.4018/978-1-5225-1941-6.ch011

Levy, M. (2018). Change Management Serving Knowledge Management and Organizational Development: Reflections and Review. In Baporikar, N. (Ed.), *Global Practices in Knowledge Management for Societal and Organizational Development* (pp. 256–270). Hershey, PA: IGI Global. DOI: 10.4018/978-1-5225-3009-1.ch012

Lewandowski, M. (2017). Public Organizations and Business Model Innovation: The Role of Public Service Design. In Lewandowski, M., & Kożuch, B. (Eds.), *Public Sector Entrepreneurship and the Integration of Innovative Business Models* (pp. 47–72). Hershey, PA: IGI Global. DOI: 10.4018/978-1-5225-2215-7.ch003

Lhannaoui, H., Kabbaj, M. I., & Bakkoury, Z. (2017). A Survey of Risk-Aware Business Process Modelling. *International Journal of Risk and Contingency Management*, *6*(3), 14–26. DOI: 10.4018/IJRCM.2017070102

Li, J., Sun, W., Jiang, W., Yang, H., & Zhang, L. (2017). How the Nature of Exogenous Shocks and Crises Impact Company Performance?: The Effects of Industry Characteristics. *International Journal of Risk and Contingency Management*, *6*(4), 40–55. DOI: 10.4018/IJRCM.2017100103

Lopez-Fernandez, M., Perez-Perez, M., Serrano-Bedia, A., & Cobo-Gonzalez, A. (2021). Small and Medium Tourism Enterprise Survival in Times of Crisis: "El Capricho de Gaudí. In Toubes, D., & Araújo-Vila, N. (Eds.), *Risk, Crisis, and Disaster Management in Small and Medium-Sized Tourism Enterprises* (pp. 103–129). IGI Global. DOI: 10.4018/978-1-7998-6996-2.ch005

Mahajan, A., Maidullah, S., & Hossain, M. R. (2022). Experience Toward Smart Tour Guide Apps in Travelling: An Analysis of Users' Reviews on Audio Odigos and Trip My Way. In R. Augusto Costa, F. Brandão, Z. Breda, & C. Costa (Eds.), *Planning and Managing the Experience Economy in Tourism* (pp. 255-273). IGI Global. https://doi.org/10.4018/978-1-7998-8775-1.ch014

Malega, P. (2017). Small and Medium Enterprises in the Slovak Republic: Status and Competitiveness of SMEs in the Global Markets and Possibilities of Optimization. In Vemić, M. (Ed.), *Optimal Management Strategies in Small and Medium Enterprises* (pp. 102–124). Hershey, PA: IGI Global. DOI: 10.4018/978-1-5225-1949-2.ch006

Malewska, K. M. (2017). Intuition in Decision-Making on the Example of a Non-Profit Organization. In Potocan, V., Ünğan, M., & Nedelko, Z. (Eds.), *Handbook of Research on Managerial Solutions in Non-Profit Organizations* (pp. 378–399). Hershey, PA: IGI Global. DOI: 10.4018/978-1-5225-0731-4.ch018

Maroofi, F. (2017). Entrepreneurial Orientation and Organizational Learning Ability Analysis for Innovation and Firm Performance. In Baporikar, N. (Ed.), *Innovation and Shifting Perspectives in Management Education* (pp. 144–165). Hershey, PA: IGI Global. DOI: 10.4018/978-1-5225-1019-2.ch007

Marques, M., Moleiro, D., Brito, T. M., & Marques, T. (2021). Customer Relationship Management as an Important Relationship Marketing Tool: The Case of the Hospitality Industry in Estoril Coast. In M. Dinis, L. Bonixe, S. Lamy, & Z. Breda (Eds.), *Impact of New Media in Tourism* (pp. 39-56). IGI Global. https://doi.org/DOI: 10.4018/978-1-7998-7095-1.ch003

Martins, P. V., & Zacarias, M. (2017). A Web-based Tool for Business Process Improvement. *International Journal of Web Portals*, *9*(2), 68–84. DOI: 10.4018/IJWP.2017070104

Matthies, B., & Coners, A. (2017). Exploring the Conceptual Nature of e-Business Projects. *Journal of Electronic Commerce in Organizations*, *15*(3), 33–63. DOI: 10.4018/JECO.2017070103

Mayer, V. F., Fraga, C. C., & Silva, L. C. (2021). Contributions of Neurosciences to Studies of Well-Being in Tourism. In Perinotto, A., Mayer, V., & Soares, J. (Eds.), *Rebuilding and Restructuring the Tourism Industry: Infusion of Happiness and Quality of Life* (pp. 108–128). IGI Global. https://doi.org/10.4018/978-1-7998-7239-9.ch006

McKee, J. (2018). Architecture as a Tool to Solve Business Planning Problems. In M. Khosrow-Pour, D.B.A. (Ed.), *Encyclopedia of Information Science and Technology, Fourth Edition* (pp. 573-586). Hershey, PA: IGI Global. DOI: 10.4018/978-1-5225-2255-3.ch050

McMurray, A. J., Cross, J., & Caponecchia, C. (2018). The Risk Management Profession in Australia: Business Continuity Plan Practices. In Bajgoric, N. (Ed.), *Always-On Enterprise Information Systems for Modern Organizations* (pp. 112–129). Hershey, PA: IGI Global. DOI: 10.4018/978-1-5225-3704-5.ch006

Meddah, I. H., & Belkadi, K. (2018). Mining Patterns Using Business Process Management. In Hamou, R. (Ed.), *Handbook of Research on Biomimicry in Information Retrieval and Knowledge Management* (pp. 78–89). Hershey, PA: IGI Global. DOI: 10.4018/978-1-5225-3004-6.ch005

Melian, A. G., & Camprubí, R. (2021). The Accessibility of Museum Websites: The Case of Barcelona. In Eusébio, C., Teixeira, L., & Carneiro, M. (Eds.), *ICT Tools and Applications for Accessible Tourism* (pp. 234–255). IGI Global. https://doi.org/10.4018/978-1-7998-6428-8.ch011

Mendes, L. (2017). TQM and Knowledge Management: An Integrated Approach Towards Tacit Knowledge Management. In Jaziri-Bouagina, D., & Jamil, G. (Eds.), *Handbook of Research on Tacit Knowledge Management for Organizational Success* (pp. 236–263). Hershey, PA: IGI Global. DOI: 10.4018/978-1-5225-2394-9.ch009

Menezes, V. D., & Cavagnaro, E. (2021). Communicating Sustainable Initiatives in the Hotel Industry: The Case of the Hotel Jakarta Amsterdam. In F. Brandão, Z. Breda, R. Costa, & C. Costa (Eds.), *Handbook of Research on the Role of Tourism in Achieving Sustainable Development Goals* (pp. 224-234). IGI Global. https://doi.org/10.4018/978-1-7998-5691-7.ch013

Menezes, V. D., & Cavagnaro, E. (2021). Communicating Sustainable Initiatives in the Hotel Industry: The Case of the Hotel Jakarta Amsterdam. In F. Brandão, Z. Breda, R. Costa, & C. Costa (Eds.), *Handbook of Research on the Role of Tourism in Achieving Sustainable Development Goals* (pp. 224-234). IGI Global. https://doi.org/10.4018/978-1-7998-5691-7.ch013

Mitas, O., Bastiaansen, M., & Boode, W. (2022). If You're Happy, I'm Happy: Emotion Contagion at a Tourist Information Center. In R. Augusto Costa, F. Brandão, Z. Breda, & C. Costa (Eds.), *Planning and Managing the Experience Economy in Tourism* (pp. 122-140). IGI Global. https://doi.org/10.4018/978-1-7998-8775-1.ch007

Mnjama, N. M. (2017). Preservation of Recorded Information in Public and Private Sector Organizations. In Jain, P., & Mnjama, N. (Eds.), *Managing Knowledge Resources and Records in Modern Organizations* (pp. 149–167). Hershey, PA: IGI Global. DOI: 10.4018/978-1-5225-1965-2.ch009

Mokoqama, M., & Fields, Z. (2017). Principles of Responsible Management Education (PRME): Call for Responsible Management Education. In Fields, Z. (Ed.), *Collective Creativity for Responsible and Sustainable Business Practice* (pp. 229–241). Hershey, PA: IGI Global. DOI: 10.4018/978-1-5225-1823-5.ch012

Monteiro, A., Lopes, S., & Carbone, F. (2021). Academic Mobility: Bridging Tourism and Peace Education. In J. da Silva, Z. Breda, & F. Carbone (Eds.), *Role and Impact of Tourism in Peacebuilding and Conflict Transformation* (pp. 275-301). IGI Global. https://doi.org/10.4018/978-1-7998-5053-3.ch016

Muniapan, B. (2017). Philosophy and Management: The Relevance of Vedanta in Management. In Ordóñez de Pablos, P. (Ed.), *Managerial Strategies and Solutions for Business Success in Asia* (pp. 124–139). Hershey, PA: IGI Global. DOI: 10.4018/978-1-5225-1886-0.ch007

Murad, S. E., & Dowaji, S. (2017). Using Value-Based Approach for Managing Cloud-Based Services. In Turuk, A., Sahoo, B., & Addya, S. (Eds.), *Resource Management and Efficiency in Cloud Computing Environments* (pp. 33–60). Hershey, PA: IGI Global. DOI: 10.4018/978-1-5225-1721-4.ch002

Mutahar, A. M., Daud, N. M., Thurasamy, R., Isaac, O., & Abdulsalam, R. (2018). The Mediating of Perceived Usefulness and Perceived Ease of Use: The Case of Mobile Banking in Yemen. *International Journal of Technology Diffusion*, *9*(2), 21–40. DOI: 10.4018/IJTD.2018040102

Naidoo, V. (2017). E-Learning and Management Education at African Universities. In Baporikar, N. (Ed.), *Management Education for Global Leadership* (pp. 181–201). Hershey, PA: IGI Global. DOI: 10.4018/978-1-5225-1013-0.ch009

Naidoo, V., & Igbinakhase, I. (2018). Opportunities and Challenges of Knowledge Retention in SMEs. In Baporikar, N. (Ed.), *Knowledge Integration Strategies for Entrepreneurship and Sustainability* (pp. 70–94). Hershey, PA: IGI Global. DOI: 10.4018/978-1-5225-5115-7.ch004

Naumov, N., & Costandachi, G. (2021). Creativity and Entrepreneurship: Gastronomic Tourism in Mexico. In Soares, J. (Ed.), *Innovation and Entrepreneurial Opportunities in Community Tourism* (pp. 90–108). IGI Global. https://doi.org/10.4018/978-1-7998-4855-4.ch006

Nayak, S., & Prabhu, N. (2017). Paradigm Shift in Management Education: Need for a Cross Functional Perspective. In Baporikar, N. (Ed.), *Management Education for Global Leadership* (pp. 241–255). Hershey, PA: IGI Global. DOI: 10.4018/978-1-5225-1013-0.ch012

Nedelko, Z., & Potocan, V. (2017). Management Solutions in Non-Profit Organizations: Case of Slovenia. In Potocan, V., Üngan, M., & Nedelko, Z. (Eds.), *Handbook of Research on Managerial Solutions in Non-Profit Organizations* (pp. 1–22). Hershey, PA: IGI Global. DOI: 10.4018/978-1-5225-0731-4.ch001

Nedelko, Z., & Potocan, V. (2017). Priority of Management Tools Utilization among Managers: International Comparison. In Wang, V. (Ed.), *Encyclopedia of Strategic Leadership and Management* (pp. 1083–1094). Hershey, PA: IGI Global. DOI: 10.4018/978-1-5225-1049-9.ch075

Nedelko, Z., Raudeliūnienė, J., & Črešnar, R. (2018). Knowledge Dynamics in Supply Chain Management. In Baporikar, N. (Ed.), *Knowledge Integration Strategies for Entrepreneurship and Sustainability* (pp. 150–166). Hershey, PA: IGI Global. DOI: 10.4018/978-1-5225-5115-7.ch008

Nguyen, H. T., & Hipsher, S. A. (2018). Innovation and Creativity Used by Private Sector Firms in a Resources-Constrained Environment. In Hipsher, S. (Ed.), *Examining the Private Sector's Role in Wealth Creation and Poverty Reduction* (pp. 219–238). Hershey, PA: IGI Global. DOI: 10.4018/978-1-5225-3117-3.ch010

Obicci, P. A. (2017). Risk Sharing in a Partnership. In *Risk Management Strategies in Public-Private Partnerships* (pp. 115–152). Hershey, PA: IGI Global. DOI: 10.4018/978-1-5225-2503-5.ch004

Obidallah, W. J., & Raahemi, B. (2017). Managing Changes in Service Oriented Virtual Organizations: A Structural and Procedural Framework to Facilitate the Process of Change. *Journal of Electronic Commerce in Organizations*, *15*(1), 59–83. DOI: 10.4018/JECO.2017010104

Ojo, O. (2017). Impact of Innovation on the Entrepreneurial Success in Selected Business Enterprises in South-West Nigeria. *International Journal of Innovation in the Digital Economy*, *8*(2), 29–38. DOI: 10.4018/IJIDE.2017040103

Okdinawati, L., Simatupang, T. M., & Sunitiyoso, Y. (2017). Multi-Agent Reinforcement Learning for Value Co-Creation of Collaborative Transportation Management (CTM). *International Journal of Information Systems and Supply Chain Management*, *10*(3), 84–95. DOI: 10.4018/IJISSCM.2017070105

Olivera, V. A., & Carrillo, I. M. (2021). Organizational Culture: A Key Element for the Development of Mexican Micro and Small Tourist Companies. In Soares, J. (Ed.), *Innovation and Entrepreneurial Opportunities in Community Tourism* (pp. 227–242). IGI Global. DOI: 10.4018/978-1-7998-4855-4.ch013

Ossorio, M. (2022). Corporate Museum Experiences in Enogastronomic Tourism. In R. Augusto Costa, F. Brandão, Z. Breda, & C. Costa (Eds.), *Planning and Managing the Experience Economy in Tourism* (pp. 107-121). IGI Global. https://doi.org/DOI: 10.4018/978-1-7998-8775-1.ch006

Ossorio, M. (2022). Enogastronomic Tourism in Times of Pandemic. In Fernandes, G. (Ed.), *Challenges and New Opportunities for Tourism in Inland Territories: Ecocultural Resources and Sustainable Initiatives* (pp. 241–255). IGI Global. https://doi.org/10.4018/978-1-7998-7339-6.ch014

Özekici, Y. K. (2022). ICT as an Acculturative Agent and Its Role in the Tourism Context: Introduction, Acculturation Theory, Progress of the Acculturation Theory in Extant Literature. In Ramos, C., Quinteiro, S., & Gonçalves, A. (Eds.), *ICT as Innovator Between Tourism and Culture* (pp. 42–66). IGI Global. https://doi.org/10.4018/978-1-7998-8165-0.ch004

Pal, K. (2018). Building High Quality Big Data-Based Applications in Supply Chains. In Kumar, A., & Saurav, S. (Eds.), *Supply Chain Management Strategies and Risk Assessment in Retail Environments* (pp. 1–24). Hershey, PA: IGI Global. DOI: 10.4018/978-1-5225-3056-5.ch001

Palos-Sanchez, P. R., & Correia, M. B. (2018). Perspectives of the Adoption of Cloud Computing in the Tourism Sector. In Rodrigues, J., Ramos, C., Cardoso, P., & Henriques, C. (Eds.), *Handbook of Research on Technological Developments for Cultural Heritage and eTourism Applications* (pp. 377–400). Hershey, PA: IGI Global. DOI: 10.4018/978-1-5225-2927-9.ch018

Papadopoulou, G. (2021). Promoting Gender Equality and Women Empowerment in the Tourism Sector. In F. Brandão, Z. Breda, R. Costa, & C. Costa (Eds.), *Handbook of Research on the Role of Tourism in Achieving Sustainable Development Goals* (pp. 152-174). IGI Global. https://doi.org/DOI: 10.4018/978-1-7998-5691-7.ch009

Papp-Váry, Á. F., & Tóth, T. Z. (2022). Analysis of Budapest as a Film Tourism Destination. In R. Baleiro & R. Pereira (Eds.), *Global Perspectives on Literary Tourism and Film-Induced Tourism* (pp. 257-279). IGI Global. https://doi.org/10.4018/978-1-7998-8262-6.ch014

Patiño, B. E. (2017). New Generation Management by Convergence and Individual Identity: A Systemic and Human-Oriented Approach. In Baporikar, N. (Ed.), *Innovation and Shifting Perspectives in Management Education* (pp. 119–143). Hershey, PA: IGI Global. DOI: 10.4018/978-1-5225-1019-2.ch006

Patro, C. S. (2021). Digital Tourism: Influence of E-Marketing Technology. In M. Dinis, L. Bonixe, S. Lamy, & Z. Breda (Eds.), *Impact of New Media in Tourism* (pp. 234-254). IGI Global. https://doi.org/10.4018/978-1-7998-7095-1.ch014

Pawliczek, A., & Rössler, M. (2017). Knowledge of Management Tools and Systems in SMEs: Knowledge Transfer in Management. In Bencsik, A. (Ed.), *Knowledge Management Initiatives and Strategies in Small and Medium Enterprises* (pp. 180–203). Hershey, PA: IGI Global. DOI: 10.4018/978-1-5225-1642-2.ch009

Pejic-Bach, M., Omazic, M. A., Aleksic, A., & Zoroja, J. (2018). Knowledge-Based Decision Making: A Multi-Case Analysis. In Leon, R. (Ed.), *Managerial Strategies for Business Sustainability During Turbulent Times* (pp. 160–184). Hershey, PA: IGI Global. DOI: 10.4018/978-1-5225-2716-9.ch009

Perano, M., Hysa, X., & Calabrese, M. (2018). Strategic Planning, Cultural Context, and Business Continuity Management: Business Cases in the City of Shkoder. In Presenza, A., & Sheehan, L. (Eds.), *Geopolitics and Strategic Management in the Global Economy* (pp. 57–77). Hershey, PA: IGI Global. DOI: 10.4018/978-1-5225-2673-5.ch004

Pereira, R., Mira da Silva, M., & Lapão, L. V. (2017). IT Governance Maturity Patterns in Portuguese Healthcare. In De Haes, S., & Van Grembergen, W. (Eds.), *Strategic IT Governance and Alignment in Business Settings* (pp. 24–52). Hershey, PA: IGI Global. DOI: 10.4018/978-1-5225-0861-8.ch002

Pérez-Uribe, R. I., Torres, D. A., Jurado, S. P., & Prada, D. M. (2018). Cloud Tools for the Development of Project Management in SMEs. In Perez-Uribe, R., Salcedo-Perez, C., & Ocampo-Guzman, D. (Eds.), *Handbook of Research on Intrapreneurship and Organizational Sustainability in SMEs* (pp. 95–120). Hershey, PA: IGI Global. DOI: 10.4018/978-1-5225-3543-0.ch005

Petrisor, I., & Cozmiuc, D. (2017). Global Supply Chain Management Organization at Siemens in the Advent of Industry 4.0. In Saglietto, L., & Cezanne, C. (Eds.), *Global Intermediation and Logistics Service Providers* (pp. 123–142). Hershey, PA: IGI Global. DOI: 10.4018/978-1-5225-2133-4.ch007

Pierce, J. M., Velliaris, D. M., & Edwards, J. (2017). A Living Case Study: A Journey Not a Destination. In Silton, N. (Ed.), *Exploring the Benefits of Creativity in Education, Media, and the Arts* (pp. 158–178). Hershey, PA: IGI Global. DOI: 10.4018/978-1-5225-0504-4.ch008

Pipia, S., & Pipia, S. (2021). Challenges of Religious Tourism in the Conflict Region: An Example of Jerusalem. In E. Alaverdov & M. Bari (Eds.), *Global Development of Religious Tourism* (pp. 135-148). IGI Global. https://doi.org/10.4018/978-1-7998-5792-1.ch009

Poulaki, P., Kritikos, A., Vasilakis, N., & Valeri, M. (2022). The Contribution of Female Creativity to the Development of Gastronomic Tourism in Greece: The Case of the Island of Naxos in the South Aegean Region. In Valeri, M. (Ed.), *New Governance and Management in Touristic Destinations* (pp. 246–258). IGI Global. https://doi.org/10.4018/978-1-6684-3889-3.ch015

Radosavljevic, M., & Andjelkovic, A. (2017). Multi-Criteria Decision Making Approach for Choosing Business Process for the Improvement: Upgrading of the Six Sigma Methodology. In Stanković, J., Delias, P., Marinković, S., & Rochhia, S. (Eds.), *Tools and Techniques for Economic Decision Analysis* (pp. 225–247). Hershey, PA: IGI Global. DOI: 10.4018/978-1-5225-0959-2.ch011

Radovic, V. M. (2017). Corporate Sustainability and Responsibility and Disaster Risk Reduction: A Serbian Overview. In Camilleri, M. (Ed.), *CSR 2.0 and the New Era of Corporate Citizenship* (pp. 147–164). Hershey, PA: IGI Global. DOI: 10.4018/978-1-5225-1842-6.ch008

Raghunath, K. M., Devi, S. L., & Patro, C. S. (2018). Impact of Risk Assessment Models on Risk Factors: A Holistic Outlook. In Strang, K., Korstanje, M., & Vajjhala, N. (Eds.), *Research, Practices, and Innovations in Global Risk and Contingency Management* (pp. 134–153). Hershey, PA: IGI Global. DOI: 10.4018/978-1-5225-4754-9.ch008

Raman, A., & Goyal, D. P. (2017). Extending IMPLEMENT Framework for Enterprise Information Systems Implementation to Information System Innovation. In Tavana, M. (Ed.), *Enterprise Information Systems and the Digitalization of Business Functions* (pp. 137–177). Hershey, PA: IGI Global. DOI: 10.4018/978-1-5225-2382-6.ch007

Rao, Y., & Zhang, Y. (2017). The Construction and Development of Academic Library Digital Special Subject Databases. In Ruan, L., Zhu, Q., & Ye, Y. (Eds.), *Academic Library Development and Administration in China* (pp. 163–183). Hershey, PA: IGI Global. DOI: 10.4018/978-1-5225-0550-1.ch010

Ravasan, A. Z., Mohammadi, M. M., & Hamidi, H. (2018). An Investigation Into the Critical Success Factors of Implementing Information Technology Service Management Frameworks. In Jakobs, K. (Ed.), *Corporate and Global Standardization Initiatives in Contemporary Society* (pp. 200–218). Hershey, PA: IGI Global. DOI: 10.4018/978-1-5225-5320-5.ch009

Rezaie, S., Mirabedini, S. J., & Abtahi, A. (2018). Designing a Model for Implementation of Business Intelligence in the Banking Industry. *International Journal of Enterprise Information Systems*, *14*(1), 77–103. DOI: 10.4018/IJEIS.2018010105

Richards, V., Matthews, N., Williams, O. J., & Khan, Z. (2021). The Challenges of Accessible Tourism Information Systems for Tourists With Vision Impairment: Sensory Communications Beyond the Screen. In Eusébio, C., Teixeira, L., & Carneiro, M. (Eds.), *ICT Tools and Applications for Accessible Tourism* (pp. 26–54). IGI Global. https://doi.org/10.4018/978-1-7998-6428-8.ch002

Rodrigues de Souza Neto, V., & Marques, O. (2021). Rural Tourism Fostering Welfare Through Sustainable Development: A Conceptual Approach. In Perinotto, A., Mayer, V., & Soares, J. (Eds.), *Rebuilding and Restructuring the Tourism Industry: Infusion of Happiness and Quality of Life* (pp. 38–57). IGI Global. https://doi.org/10.4018/978-1-7998-7239-9.ch003

Romano, L., Grimaldi, R., & Colasuonno, F. S. (2017). Demand Management as a Success Factor in Project Portfolio Management. In Romano, L. (Ed.), *Project Portfolio Management Strategies for Effective Organizational Operations* (pp. 202–219). Hershey, PA: IGI Global. DOI: 10.4018/978-1-5225-2151-8.ch008

Rubio-Escuderos, L., & García-Andreu, H. (2021). Competitiveness Factors of Accessible Tourism E-Travel Agencies. In Eusébio, C., Teixeira, L., & Carneiro, M. (Eds.), *ICT Tools and Applications for Accessible Tourism* (pp. 196–217). IGI Global. https://doi.org/10.4018/978-1-7998-6428-8.ch009

Rucci, A. C., Porto, N., Darcy, S., & Becka, L. (2021). Smart and Accessible Cities?: Not Always – The Case for Accessible Tourism Initiatives in Buenos Aries and Sydney. In Eusébio, C., Teixeira, L., & Carneiro, M. (Eds.), *ICT Tools and Applications for Accessible Tourism* (pp. 115–145). IGI Global. https://doi.org/10.4018/978-1-7998-6428-8.ch006

Ruhi, U. (2018). Towards an Interdisciplinary Socio-Technical Definition of Virtual Communities. In M. Khosrow-Pour, D.B.A. (Ed.), *Encyclopedia of Information Science and Technology, Fourth Edition* (pp. 4278-4295). Hershey, PA: IGI Global. DOI: 10.4018/978-1-5225-2255-3.ch371

Ryan, L., Catena, M., Ros, P., & Stephens, S. (2021). Designing Entrepreneurial Ecosystems to Support Resource Management in the Tourism Industry. In Costa, V., Moura, A., & Mira, M. (Eds.), *Handbook of Research on Human Capital and People Management in the Tourism Industry* (pp. 265–281). IGI Global. https://doi.org/10.4018/978-1-7998-4318-4.ch013

Sabuncu, I. (2021). Understanding Tourist Perceptions and Expectations During Pandemic Through Social Media Big Data. In Demir, M., Dalgıç, A., & Ergen, F. (Eds.), *Handbook of Research on the Impacts and Implications of COVID-19 on the Tourism Industry* (pp. 330–350). IGI Global. https://doi.org/10.4018/978-1-7998-8231-2.ch016

Safari, M. R., & Jiang, Q. (2018). The Theory and Practice of IT Governance Maturity and Strategies Alignment: Evidence From Banking Industry. *Journal of Global Information Management*, *26*(2), 127–146. DOI: 10.4018/JGIM.2018040106

Sahoo, J., Pati, B., & Mohanty, B. (2017). Knowledge Management as an Academic Discipline: An Assessment. In Gunjal, B. (Ed.), *Managing Knowledge and Scholarly Assets in Academic Libraries* (pp. 99–126). Hershey, PA: IGI Global. DOI: 10.4018/978-1-5225-1741-2.ch005

Saini, D. (2017). Relevance of Teaching Values and Ethics in Management Education. In Baporikar, N. (Ed.), *Management Education for Global Leadership* (pp. 90–111). Hershey, PA: IGI Global. DOI: 10.4018/978-1-5225-1013-0.ch005

Sambhanthan, A. (2017). Assessing and Benchmarking Sustainability in Organisations: An Integrated Conceptual Model. *International Journal of Systems and Service-Oriented Engineering*, *7*(4), 22–43. DOI: 10.4018/IJSSOE.2017100102

Sambhanthan, A., & Potdar, V. (2017). A Study of the Parameters Impacting Sustainability in Information Technology Organizations. *International Journal of Knowledge-Based Organizations*, *7*(3), 27–39. DOI: 10.4018/IJKBO.2017070103

Sánchez-Fernández, M. D., & Manríquez, M. R. (2018). The Entrepreneurial Spirit Based on Social Values: The Digital Generation. In Isaias, P., & Carvalho, L. (Eds.), *User Innovation and the Entrepreneurship Phenomenon in the Digital Economy* (pp. 173–193). Hershey, PA: IGI Global. DOI: 10.4018/978-1-5225-2826-5.ch009

Sanchez-Ruiz, L., & Blanco, B. (2017). Process Management for SMEs: Barriers, Enablers, and Benefits. In Vemić, M. (Ed.), *Optimal Management Strategies in Small and Medium Enterprises* (pp. 293–319). Hershey, PA: IGI Global. DOI: 10.4018/978-1-5225-1949-2.ch014

Sanz, L. F., Gómez-Pérez, J., & Castillo-Martinez, A. (2018). Analysis of the European ICT Competence Frameworks. In Ahuja, V., & Rathore, S. (Eds.), *Multidisciplinary Perspectives on Human Capital and Information Technology Professionals* (pp. 225–245). Hershey, PA: IGI Global. DOI: 10.4018/978-1-5225-5297-0.ch012

Sarvepalli, A., & Godin, J. (2017). Business Process Management in the Classroom. *Journal of Cases on Information Technology*, *19*(2), 17–28. DOI: 10.4018/JCIT.2017040102

Saxena, G. G., & Saxena, A. (2021). Host Community Role in Medical Tourism Development. In Singh, M., & Kumaran, S. (Eds.), *Growth of the Medical Tourism Industry and Its Impact on Society: Emerging Research and Opportunities* (pp. 105–127). IGI Global. https://doi.org/10.4018/978-1-7998-3427-4.ch006

Saygili, E. E., Ozturkoglu, Y., & Kocakulah, M. C. (2017). End Users' Perceptions of Critical Success Factors in ERP Applications. *International Journal of Enterprise Information Systems*, *13*(4), 58–75. DOI: 10.4018/IJEIS.2017100104

Saygili, E. E., & Saygili, A. T. (2017). Contemporary Issues in Enterprise Information Systems: A Critical Review of CSFs in ERP Implementations. In Tavana, M. (Ed.), *Enterprise Information Systems and the Digitalization of Business Functions* (pp. 120–136). Hershey, PA: IGI Global. DOI: 10.4018/978-1-5225-2382-6.ch006

Schwaiger, K. M., & Zehrer, A. (2021). The COVID-19 Pandemic and Organizational Resilience in Hospitality Family Firms: A Qualitative Approach. In Zehrer, A., Glowka, G., Schwaiger, K., & Ranacher-Lackner, V. (Eds.), *Resiliency Models and Addressing Future Risks for Family Firms in the Tourism Industry* (pp. 32–49). IGI Global. https://doi.org/10.4018/978-1-7998-7352-5.ch002

Scott, N., & Campos, A. C. (2022). Cognitive Science of Tourism Experiences. In R. Augusto Costa, F. Brandão, Z. Breda, & C. Costa (Eds.), *Planning and Managing the Experience Economy in Tourism* (pp. 1-21). IGI Global. https://doi.org/DOI: 10.4018/978-1-7998-8775-1.ch001

Seidenstricker, S., & Antonino, A. (2018). Business Model Innovation-Oriented Technology Management for Emergent Technologies. In M. Khosrow-Pour, D.B.A. (Ed.), *Encyclopedia of Information Science and Technology, Fourth Edition* (pp. 4560-4569). Hershey, PA: IGI Global. DOI: 10.4018/978-1-5225-2255-3.ch396

Selvi, M. S. (2021). Changes in Tourism Sales and Marketing Post COVID-19. In Demir, M., Dalgıç, A., & Ergen, F. (Eds.), *Handbook of Research on the Impacts and Implications of COVID-19 on the Tourism Industry* (pp. 437–460). IGI Global. DOI: 10.4018/978-1-7998-8231-2.ch021

Senaratne, S., & Gunarathne, A. D. (2017). Excellence Perspective for Management Education from a Global Accountants' Hub in Asia. In Baporikar, N. (Ed.), *Management Education for Global Leadership* (pp. 158–180). Hershey, PA: IGI Global. DOI: 10.4018/978-1-5225-1013-0.ch008

Sensuse, D. I., & Cahyaningsih, E. (2018). Knowledge Management Models: A Summative Review. *International Journal of Information Systems in the Service Sector*, *10*(1), 71–100. DOI: 10.4018/IJISSS.2018010105

Seth, M., Goyal, D., & Kiran, R. (2017). Diminution of Impediments in Implementation of Supply Chain Management Information System for Enhancing its Effectiveness in Indian Automobile Industry. *Journal of Global Information Management*, *25*(3), 1–20. DOI: 10.4018/JGIM.2017070101

Seyal, A. H., & Rahman, M. N. (2017). Investigating Impact of Inter-Organizational Factors in Measuring ERP Systems Success: Bruneian Perspectives. In Tavana, M. (Ed.), *Enterprise Information Systems and the Digitalization of Business Functions* (pp. 178–204). Hershey, PA: IGI Global. DOI: 10.4018/978-1-5225-2382-6.ch008

Shaqrah, A. A. (2018). Analyzing Business Intelligence Systems Based on 7s Model of McKinsey. *International Journal of Business Intelligence Research*, *9*(1), 53–63. DOI: 10.4018/IJBIR.2018010104

Sharma, A. J. (2017). Enhancing Sustainability through Experiential Learning in Management Education. In Baporikar, N. (Ed.), *Management Education for Global Leadership* (pp. 256–274). Hershey, PA: IGI Global. DOI: 10.4018/978-1-5225-1013-0.ch013

Shetty, K. P. (2017). Responsible Global Leadership: Ethical Challenges in Management Education. In Baporikar, N. (Ed.), *Innovation and Shifting Perspectives in Management Education* (pp. 194–223). Hershey, PA: IGI Global. DOI: 10.4018/978-1-5225-1019-2.ch009

Sinthupundaja, J., & Kohda, Y. (2017). Effects of Corporate Social Responsibility and Creating Shared Value on Sustainability. *International Journal of Sustainable Entrepreneurship and Corporate Social Responsibility*, *2*(1), 27–38. DOI: 10.4018/IJSECSR.2017010103

Škarica, I., & Hrgović, A. V. (2018). Implementation of Total Quality Management Principles in Public Health Institutes in the Republic of Croatia. *International Journal of Productivity Management and Assessment Technologies*, *6*(1), 1–16. DOI: 10.4018/IJPMAT.2018010101

Skokic, V. (2021). How Small Hotel Owners Practice Resilience: Longitudinal Study Among Small Family Hotels in Croatia. In Zehrer, A., Glowka, G., Schwaiger, K., & Ranacher-Lackner, V. (Eds.), *Resiliency Models and Addressing Future Risks for Family Firms in the Tourism Industry* (pp. 50–73). IGI Global. DOI: 10.4018/978-1-7998-7352-5.ch003

Smuts, H., Kotzé, P., Van der Merwe, A., & Loock, M. (2017). Framework for Managing Shared Knowledge in an Information Systems Outsourcing Context. *International Journal of Knowledge Management*, *13*(4), 1–30. DOI: 10.4018/IJKM.2017100101

Sousa, M. J., Cruz, R., Dias, I., & Caracol, C. (2017). Information Management Systems in the Supply Chain. In Jamil, G., Soares, A., & Pessoa, C. (Eds.), *Handbook of Research on Information Management for Effective Logistics and Supply Chains* (pp. 469–485). Hershey, PA: IGI Global. DOI: 10.4018/978-1-5225-0973-8.ch025

Spremic, M., Turulja, L., & Bajgoric, N. (2018). Two Approaches in Assessing Business Continuity Management Attitudes in the Organizational Context. In Bajgoric, N. (Ed.), *Always-On Enterprise Information Systems for Modern Organizations* (pp. 159–183). Hershey, PA: IGI Global. DOI: 10.4018/978-1-5225-3704-5.ch008

Steenkamp, A. L. (2018). Some Insights in Computer Science and Information Technology. In *Examining the Changing Role of Supervision in Doctoral Research Projects: Emerging Research and Opportunities* (pp. 113–133). Hershey, PA: IGI Global. DOI: 10.4018/978-1-5225-2610-0.ch005

Stipanović, C., Rudan, E., & Zubović, V. (2022). Reaching the New Tourist Through Creativity: Sustainable Development Challenges in Croatian Coastal Towns. In Valeri, M. (Ed.), *New Governance and Management in Touristic Destinations* (pp. 231–245). IGI Global. https://doi.org/10.4018/978-1-6684-3889-3.ch014

Tabach, A., & Croteau, A. (2017). Configurations of Information Technology Governance Practices and Business Unit Performance. *International Journal of IT/Business Alignment and Governance*, *8*(2), 1–27. DOI: 10.4018/IJITBAG.2017070101

Talaue, G. M., & Iqbal, T. (2017). Assessment of e-Business Mode of Selected Private Universities in the Philippines and Pakistan. *International Journal of Online Marketing*, *7*(4), 63–77. DOI: 10.4018/IJOM.2017100105

Tam, G. C. (2017). Project Manager Sustainability Competence. In *Managerial Strategies and Green Solutions for Project Sustainability* (pp. 178–207). Hershey, PA: IGI Global. DOI: 10.4018/978-1-5225-2371-0.ch008

Tambo, T. (2018). Fashion Retail Innovation: About Context, Antecedents, and Outcome in Technological Change Projects. In I. Management Association (Ed.), *Fashion and Textiles: Breakthroughs in Research and Practice* (pp. 233-260). Hershey, PA: IGI Global. https://doi.org/DOI: 10.4018/978-1-5225-3432-7.ch010

Tantau, A. D., & Frăţilă, L. C. (2018). Information and Management System for Renewable Energy Business. In *Entrepreneurship and Business Development in the Renewable Energy Sector* (pp. 200–244). Hershey, PA: IGI Global. DOI: 10.4018/978-1-5225-3625-3.ch006

Teixeira, N., Pardal, P. N., & Rafael, B. G. (2018). Internationalization, Financial Performance, and Organizational Challenges: A Success Case in Portugal. In Carvalho, L. (Ed.), *Handbook of Research on Entrepreneurial Ecosystems and Social Dynamics in a Globalized World* (pp. 379–423). Hershey, PA: IGI Global. DOI: 10.4018/978-1-5225-3525-6.ch017

Teixeira, P., Teixeira, L., Eusébio, C., Silva, S., & Teixeira, A. (2021). The Impact of ICTs on Accessible Tourism: Evidence Based on a Systematic Literature Review. In Eusébio, C., Teixeira, L., & Carneiro, M. (Eds.), *ICT Tools and Applications for Accessible Tourism* (pp. 1–25). IGI Global. DOI: 10.4018/978-1-7998-6428-8.ch001

Trad, A., & Kalpić, D. (2018). The Business Transformation Framework, Agile Project and Change Management. In M. Khosrow-Pour, D.B.A. (Ed.), *Encyclopedia of Information Science and Technology, Fourth Edition* (pp. 620-635). Hershey, PA: IGI Global. https://doi.org/DOI: 10.4018/978-1-5225-2255-3.ch054

Trad, A., & Kalpić, D. (2018). The Business Transformation and Enterprise Architecture Framework: The Financial Engineering E-Risk Management and E-Law Integration. In Sergi, B., Fidanoski, F., Ziolo, M., & Naumovski, V. (Eds.), *Regaining Global Stability After the Financial Crisis* (pp. 46–65). Hershey, PA: IGI Global. DOI: 10.4018/978-1-5225-4026-7.ch003

Trengereid, V. (2022). Conditions of Network Engagement: The Quest for a Common Good. In R. Augusto Costa, F. Brandão, Z. Breda, & C. Costa (Eds.), *Planning and Managing the Experience Economy in Tourism* (pp. 69-84). IGI Global. https://doi.org/10.4018/978-1-7998-8775-1.ch004

Turulja, L., & Bajgoric, N. (2018). Business Continuity and Information Systems: A Systematic Literature Review. In Bajgoric, N. (Ed.), *Always-On Enterprise Information Systems for Modern Organizations* (pp. 60–87). Hershey, PA: IGI Global. DOI: 10.4018/978-1-5225-3704-5.ch004

Vargas-Hernández, J. G. (2017). Professional Integrity in Business Management Education. In Baporikar, N. (Ed.), *Management Education for Global Leadership* (pp. 70–89). Hershey, PA: IGI Global. DOI: 10.4018/978-1-5225-1013-0.ch004

Varnacı Uzun, F. (2021). The Destination Preferences of Foreign Tourists During the COVID-19 Pandemic and Attitudes Towards: Marmaris, Turkey. In Demir, M., Dalgıç, A., & Ergen, F. (Eds.), *Handbook of Research on the Impacts and Implications of COVID-19 on the Tourism Industry* (pp. 285–306). IGI Global. https://doi.org/10.4018/978-1-7998-8231-2.ch014

Vasista, T. G., & AlAbdullatif, A. M. (2017). Role of Electronic Customer Relationship Management in Demand Chain Management: A Predictive Analytic Approach. *International Journal of Information Systems and Supply Chain Management, 10*(1), 53–67. DOI: 10.4018/IJISSCM.2017010104

Vieru, D., & Bourdeau, S. (2017). Survival in the Digital Era: A Digital Competence-Based Multi-Case Study in the Canadian SME Clothing Industry. *International Journal of Social and Organizational Dynamics in IT, 6*(1), 17–34. DOI: 10.4018/IJSODIT.2017010102

Vijayan, G., & Kamarulzaman, N. H. (2017). An Introduction to Sustainable Supply Chain Management and Business Implications. In Khan, M., Hussain, M., & Ajmal, M. (Eds.), *Green Supply Chain Management for Sustainable Business Practice* (pp. 27–50). Hershey, PA: IGI Global. DOI: 10.4018/978-1-5225-0635-5.ch002

Vlachvei, A., & Notta, O. (2017). Firm Competitiveness: Theories, Evidence, and Measurement. In Vlachvei, A., Notta, O., Karantininis, K., & Tsounis, N. (Eds.), *Factors Affecting Firm Competitiveness and Performance in the Modern Business World* (pp. 1–42). Hershey, PA: IGI Global. DOI: 10.4018/978-1-5225-0843-4.ch001

Wang, C., Schofield, M., Li, X., & Ou, X. (2017). Do Chinese Students in Public and Private Higher Education Institutes Perform at Different Level in One of the Leadership Skills: Critical Thinking?: An Exploratory Comparison. In Wang, V. (Ed.), *Encyclopedia of Strategic Leadership and Management* (pp. 160–181). Hershey, PA: IGI Global. DOI: 10.4018/978-1-5225-1049-9.ch013

Wang, J. (2017). Multi-Agent based Production Management Decision System Modelling for the Textile Enterprise. *Journal of Global Information Management, 25*(4), 1–15. DOI: 10.4018/JGIM.2017100101

Wiedemann, A., & Gewald, H. (2017). Examining Cross-Domain Alignment: The Correlation of Business Strategy, IT Management, and IT Business Value. *International Journal of IT/Business Alignment and Governance, 8*(1), 17–31. DOI: 10.4018/IJITBAG.2017010102

Wolf, R., & Thiel, M. (2018). Advancing Global Business Ethics in China: Reducing Poverty Through Human and Social Welfare. In Hipsher, S. (Ed.), *Examining the Private Sector's Role in Wealth Creation and Poverty Reduction* (pp. 67–84). Hershey, PA: IGI Global. DOI: 10.4018/978-1-5225-3117-3.ch004

Yablonsky, S. (2018). Innovation Platforms: Data and Analytics Platforms. In *Multi-Sided Platforms (MSPs) and Sharing Strategies in the Digital Economy: Emerging Research and Opportunities* (pp. 72–95). Hershey, PA: IGI Global. DOI: 10.4018/978-1-5225-5457-8.ch003

Yaşar, B. (2021). The Impact of COVID-19 on Volatility of Tourism Stocks: Evidence From BIST Tourism Index. In Demir, M., Dalgıç, A., & Ergen, F. (Eds.), *Handbook of Research on the Impacts and Implications of COVID-19 on the Tourism Industry* (pp. 23–44). IGI Global. https://doi.org/10.4018/978-1-7998-8231-2.ch002

Yusoff, A., Ahmad, N. H., & Halim, H. A. (2017). Agropreneurship among Gen Y in Malaysia: The Role of Academic Institutions. In Ahmad, N., Ramayah, T., Halim, H., & Rahman, S. (Eds.), *Handbook of Research on Small and Medium Enterprises in Developing Countries* (pp. 23–47). Hershey, PA: IGI Global. DOI: 10.4018/978-1-5225-2165-5.ch002

Zacher, D., & Pechlaner, H. (2021). Resilience as an Opportunity Approach: Challenges and Perspectives for Private Sector Participation on a Community Level. In Zehrer, A., Glowka, G., Schwaiger, K., & Ranacher-Lackner, V. (Eds.), *Resiliency Models and Addressing Future Risks for Family Firms in the Tourism Industry* (pp. 75–102). IGI Global. https://doi.org/10.4018/978-1-7998-7352-5.ch004

Zanin, F., Comuzzi, E., & Costantini, A. (2018). The Effect of Business Strategy and Stock Market Listing on the Use of Risk Assessment Tools. In *Management Control Systems in Complex Settings: Emerging Research and Opportunities* (pp. 145–168). Hershey, PA: IGI Global. DOI: 10.4018/978-1-5225-3987-2.ch007

Zgheib, P. W. (2017). Corporate Innovation and Intrapreneurship in the Middle East. In Zgheib, P. (Ed.), *Entrepreneurship and Business Innovation in the Middle East* (pp. 37–56). Hershey, PA: IGI Global. DOI: 10.4018/978-1-5225-2066-5.ch003

About the Contributors

Naveeda Akhter Katper is an esteemed academician, researcher, and author specializing in finance, economics, entrepreneurship, and human resource management. Serving as an Assistant Professor at IBA, University of Sindh, she has over 15 years of teaching and research experience. Holding a Ph.D. from the University of Malaya, she has authored 30 research publications and contributed book chapters. She is an HEC-recognized Ph.D. supervisor, award-winning researcher, and poet. Actively engaged in academic and literary circles, she has delivered guest lectures, reviewed for prestigious journals, and contributed to socio-economic discussions, making a significant impact in academia and beyond.

***

Zelda Arku is a PhD candidate at the University of Ghana offering PhD Information Systems. She obtained her Mphil (Management Information Systems) qualification from the University of Ghana, and BSc (Information Technology) degrees from University of Cape Coast, Ghana. Ms Arku's research interest are digital transformation, technopreneurship, creator economy, Artificial intelligence.

K. Balaji is an Assistant Professor in Business and Management, Christ University, Bangalore. He did Ph.D. from KLU Business School, KL University, Vijayawada. He is having 12 years of teaching experience. He has to his credit 23 Research Articles published in reputed National and International Journals. He has participated and presented more than

12 papers in both National and International Seminars/Conferences and also attended more than 50 workshops/FDPS organized by various reputed organizations. He has also participated in more than 50 seminars / webinars organized by various reputed organizations. He has also attended in 6 Short Term Training programs. He has successfully conducted 3 webinars, one 5-day FDP and one International Conference on Reimaging marketing in New Normal. He is a ratified as Assistant Professor by both JNTUH, JNTU Anantapur and Sri Venkateswara University, Tirupati. His specialized areas include, Accounting and Financial management, Marketing Management, Retailing Management, Consumer Behavior studies, Entrepreneurship and Business Laws.

Sheena Lovia Boateng is a Senior Lecturer at the Department of Marketing and Entrepreneurship at the University of Ghana Business School. She is the Communications Coordinator for the College of Humanities, University of Ghana. She is an Associate Editor and member of the Editorial Board for the Springer journal, Humanities & Social Sciences Communications. Her research has been published in the International Journal of Electronic Marketing and Retailing, Information Development, International Journal of Customer Relationship Marketing and Management, International Journal of Bank Marketing, Journal of Financial Services Marketing, Smart Learning Environments, and the Journal of Educational Technology Systems. She has co-edited two Routledge Books on Empowering Women in the Digital Economy and Delivering Distinctive Value in Emerging Economies, and a Springer Book on Digital Innovations, Business and Society in Africa.

Stephen Boateng is a Doctoral Candidate at the University of Mines and Technology (UMaT), specializing in Management Information Systems. His research focuses on Cloud Computing, Cybersecurity, Technopreneurship, Digital Transformation, and ASGM Financing, addressing critical challenges in technology and entrepreneurship. Stephen has authored research papers on emerging trends in MIS and is actively involved in projects that drive innovation and sustainable development in both academic and practical contexts. He has contributed to conferences and workshops that explore the intersection of technology and business, further solidifying his expertise. With a commitment to advancing knowledge, Stephen collaborates with academic and industry partners to develop practical solutions that enhance digital transformation and financial inclusion.

Shiney Chib is presently working as Professor, Dean Academics and Research Head at, Datta Meghe Institute of Management Studies, Nagpur. Is the Former Director (2015-2023- (8 years)), of the same Institute. Appointed as Adjunct Faculty with SEGI University Malaysia. Proven ability in team building and direction, Organized National and International conferences, MDPs, FDPs and organized various intra and inter college events.

Farhat Jokhio is PhD in Sociology and working a permanent faculty at University of Sindh, Jamshoro, Pakistan.

Desmond Kwadjo Kumi is the CEO of DAL Consultancy Company Limited Ghana and a PhD Candidate in Information Systems at the University of Ghana Business School. He holds an undergraduate degree in Computer Science and Mathematics with First Class Honours from the University of Ghana, Legon, and a master's in Management and Information Systems from Cranfield University, United Kingdom. He has co-authored 13 peer-reviewed journal articles with over 490 citations. He has published in Total Quality Management and Business Excellence, Journal of Small Business and Enterprise Development, International Journal of Bank Marketing, International Journal of Managing Projects in Business, International Journal of Health Care Quality Assurance, Journal of International Consumer Marketing, Research in Transportation Business & Management, Journal of Information, Communication and Ethics in Society, Global Knowledge, Memory, and Communication, and Journal of Risk and Financial Management.

Karthigeyan M. is an assistant professor in the Department of Mathematics at Karpaga Vinayaga College of Engineering and Technology, located in Chengalpattu, Tamil Nadu. With a strong academic background, Mr. Karthigeyan has been contributing to the field of mathematics through both teaching and research. His expertise is reflected in his commitment to guiding students in understanding complex mathematical concepts and helping them apply these in engineering contexts. The college is situated in Chengalpattu, Tamil Nadu, with a postal code of 603308.

T. C. Manjunath is a distinguished professor in the Department of Computer Science & Engineering at Rajarajeswari College of Engineering, located in Bangalore, Karnataka. He specializes in IoT Cybersecurity and Blockchain Technology and currently serves as the Dean of Research & Development at the institution. With extensive academic and research experience, Dr. Manjunath has contributed significantly to the advancement of technology in his fields of expertise. His work and leadership in research have made him a prominent figure in the academic community. The college is located on Mysore Road, Ramohalli Cross, Kumbalgodu Post, in Bangalore, with the postal code 560074.

Nupur Mishra is affiliated with the School of Finance and Commerce at Galgotias University.

P. Selvakumar is currently an Associate Professor in the Department of Science and Humanities at Nehru Institute of Technology, Coimbatore, Tamil Nadu, India. Since 2023, he has served as the Department IQAC Coordinator at the institute. Prior to joining Nehru Institute of Technology, he held positions as an Assistant Professor in the Department of Science and Humanities various engineering colleges in Coimbatore, Tamil Nadu, India, spanning from 2011 to 2023. Dr. P. Selvakumar's academic and research interests lie primarily in the field of phytochemistry. He has made significant contributions to his field, with an impressive record that includes 30 journal publications, 12 patents, and 20 conference papers. Additionally, he has organized 5 seminars and conferences, further demonstrating his commitment to academic and scientific exchange. Throughout his career, Dr. P.Selvakumar has been recognized for his dedication and excellence in teaching, having been honored with several awards, including the Best Teacher Awards. He holds a prominent position in the academic community, contributing actively to research.

Falguni Pawar is an MBA department at Datta Meghe Institute of Management Studies, Nagpur. With a keen interest in management and business strategies, she is dedicated to developing her skills in leadership, decision-making, and organizational growth. Falguni is committed to excelling in her academic journey and preparing for a successful career in the field of management.

Neena P. C. has a blend of corporate and academic experience spanning two decades in leading business schools and corporate firms, including a short stint abroad. As an academician, she has made significant contributions at various levels, such as in Accreditation, IQAC, Research, Board of studies, Certification and Executive programs, and other activities. She has presented and published research papers in national and international journals including articles in Scopus & Web of Science. Her diverse experience also includes roles as a Manager of Operations and HR, Program Manager, and Academic Coordinator

Saima is Professor at the Department of Sociology.

Mohd Shamshad is an Associate Professor at the School of Finance and Commerce (SFC), Galgotias University, Uttar Pradesh, India. He is also the coordinator of research and division chair of accounting. He has done his MBA in Finance and Ph.D. in sustainability & banking from Aligarh Muslim University, Uttar Pradesh, India. His research focuses on interdisciplinary areas like corporate governance, banking, finance, sustainability, etc. which have a significant social impact. He has published research papers in journals of national and international repute, including Scopus Indexed 'B' Category Journals in ABDC. He has also been awarded the best paper awards at various international conferences. He has also published eight patents of national and international importance. He teaches courses like Accounting & Finance, Financial Management, Income Tax, and Research Methodology.

Mohit is a research scholar at the Institute of Management Studies and Research, Maharshi Dayanand University, Rohtak, Haryana, India. His research focuses on the dynamic relationship between brand image and purchase intentions, particularly in the context of brand extensions within the FMCG sector. He has co-authored several scholarly works and continues to contribute to the academic community. Mohit can be reached at mohitattri.rs.imsar@mdurohtak.ac.in

Ghazala Shaukat is pursuing a postdoctoral under National Post-Doctoral Fellowship Programme (Phase-I) by Sindh Higher Education Commission, Government of Sindh, Karachi. Project Title is "Empowering Women's Leadership for Political Representation in Sindh: A Multi-Dimentional Analysis" to be carried out at National Institute of Historical & Cultural Research, Quaid-i-Azam University. Dr. Ghazala Shoukat is a distinguished scholar and thought leader in the field of sociology, renowned for her profound insights and scholarly contributions. With a career spanning over two decades, Dr. Shoukat has established herself as a trailblazer in advancing our understanding of complex societal dynamics and fostering dialogue on critical social issues. Armed with a Ph.D. in Sociology from the prestigious University of Sindh, Dr. Shoukat's academic journey has been marked by a relentless pursuit of knowledge and intellectual inquiry. Her scholarly endeavors have traversed diverse domains within sociology, from gender studies and social problems to poverty alleviation and community development. Dr. Shoukat's rigorous research methodologies and interdisciplinary approach have earned her acclaim and recognition among peers and scholars worldwide. Dr. Shoukat's scholarly repertoire boasts an impressive array of publications, including research papers, book chapters, and monographs, that have left an indelible mark on the field of sociology. Her seminal works delve into pressing societal issues, offering nuanced analyses and empirical insights that illuminate the complexities of contemporary social phenomena. Through her writings, Dr. Shoukat challenges conventional wisdom, stimulates critical discourse, and propels the boundaries of sociological inquiry. As an Associate Professor at the University of Sindh, Dr. Shoukat has played a pivotal role in shaping the intellectual landscape of sociology education. Her passion for teaching and mentorship has inspired generations of students, instilling in them a deep appreciation for the intricacies of social theory and research methodology. Dr. Shoukat's leadership extends beyond the classroom, as she spearheads initiatives to foster interdisciplinary collaboration, promote diversity, and cultivate a culture of academic excellence. Driven by a steadfast commitment to social justice and equity, Dr. Shoukat's scholarship transcends the confines of academia to catalyze positive change in society. Her research endeavors have shed light on marginalized voices, advocated for gender equality, and championed the rights of the underserved. Through community engagement, policy advocacy, and scholarly activism, Dr. Shoukat remains at the forefront of efforts to create a more inclusive and egalitarian world. In her UNLOCKING SOCIETY: ADVANCED PERSPECTIVES IN SOCIOLOGY book, Dr. Ghazala Shoukat invites readers on a transformative journey through the intricate tapestry of sociological inquiry. Drawing upon her wealth of knowledge and expertise, she offers a comprehensive exploration of advanced concepts in sociology, unraveling the complexities of human behavior, social institutions, and global dynamics. With clarity, rigor, and a deep sense of empathy, Dr. Shoukat's work promises to inspire scholars, students, and practitioners to engage critically with the pressing challenges of our time and envision pathways towards a more just and sustainable future.

Poonam Singh has been serving as an Assistant Professor at the School of Commerce, Manav Rachna International Institute of Research and Studies since August 2023. With over 5 years of teaching experience in Commerce and Finance, she earned her Ph.D. in 2018 and secured Net/JRF in management in 2010. Driven by a passion for teaching, she actively engages in research, boasting a record of 4 research papers in various Scopus Indexed Journals, 1 in an ABDC journal, and 3 in non-indexed journals. She has also contributed two book chapters, a case study, and a book while publishing two patents. Dr. Singh has participated in numerous national and international conferences, FDPs, and workshops.

Muhammad Usman Tariq has more than 16+ year's experience in industry and academia. He has authored more than 200+ research articles, 110+ case studies, 115+ book chapters and several books other than 4 patents. He is founder and CEO of The Case HQ, a unique repository for courses, narrative and video case studies. He has been working as a consultant and trainer for industries representing six sigma, quality, health and safety, environmental systems, project management, and information security standards. His work has encompassed sectors in aviation, manufacturing, food, hospitality, education, finance, research, software and transportation. He has diverse and significant experience working with accreditation agencies of ABET, ACBSP, AACSB, WASC, CAA, EFQM and NCEAC. Additionally, Dr. Tariq has operational experience in incubators, research labs, government research projects, private sector startups, program creation and management at various industrial and academic levels. He is Certified Higher Education Teacher from Harvard University, USA, Certified Online Educator from HMBSU, Certified Six Sigma Master Black Belt and has been awarded PFHEA, SFSEDA, SMIEEE, and CMBE.

Index

A

Alternative Financing 1, 2, 5, 6, 13, 14, 15, 17, 18, 27, 34, 65, 66, 67, 68, 69, 70, 71, 72, 73, 74, 76, 77, 78, 79, 80, 81, 82, 83, 85, 87, 88, 90, 91, 92, 93, 94, 95, 171, 204
Analyze the Factors 35
Arbitration 173, 184, 193, 194, 204

B

Bibliometric analysis 31, 32, 101, 105, 111, 202

C

Climate 8, 45, 69, 97, 174, 176, 205, 206, 207, 208, 211, 212, 213, 214, 215, 216, 217
Contributed to their Success 35
Crowdfunding 1, 2, 3, 4, 5, 6, 7, 8, 9, 10, 11, 12, 13, 14, 15, 16, 17, 18, 19, 20, 21, 22, 23, 24, 25, 26, 27, 28, 29, 30, 31, 32, 33, 34, 65, 66, 67, 68, 69, 70, 71, 72, 73, 74, 75, 76, 77, 78, 79, 80, 81, 82, 83, 84, 85, 86, 87, 88, 89, 90, 91, 92, 93, 94, 95, 97, 98, 99, 100, 124, 166, 171, 179

D

Developing Economy 133, 136, 142

E

Entrepreneurial growth 162
Exit routes 104, 115
Exit strategy 103, 104, 106, 107, 112, 113, 116, 120

G

Growth 1, 2, 5, 6, 10, 12, 13, 21, 25, 31, 33, 36, 37, 40, 46, 48, 49, 50, 51, 52, 53, 54, 55, 56, 57, 58, 65, 66, 67, 70, 71, 72, 77, 78, 80, 81, 82, 93, 94, 95, 102, 126, 129, 133, 134, 135, 136, 137, 138, 139, 140, 141, 150, 151, 152, 154, 155, 156, 157, 158, 159, 160, 161, 162, 163, 166, 167, 210

I

Impact Investing 1, 4, 5, 8, 10, 12, 13, 29, 34
India 12, 21, 32, 35, 65, 70, 97, 101, 102, 103, 108, 113, 114, 117, 119, 120, 125, 126, 127, 128, 168, 200, 202
Inflation 9, 16, 205, 206, 207, 208, 209, 210, 211, 212, 214, 215
IPOs 103, 110, 112, 113, 114, 124, 126, 128, 129

L

Lessons Learned 35, 55, 56, 58

M

mergers and acquisitions 103, 113, 114
Microfinance 1, 5, 6, 7, 8, 10, 11, 12, 13, 14, 15, 16, 20, 25, 29, 31, 32, 34, 65, 66, 67, 68, 69, 70, 71, 76, 96, 98, 99, 174, 178, 181, 182, 185, 201, 202

P

Peer-To-Peer Lending 1, 7, 8, 9, 10, 15, 16, 19, 20, 34, 65, 66, 69, 70, 71, 75, 76, 77, 100, 178, 183, 185, 204
PLS-SEM 134, 142, 143, 165

S

Sindh 205, 206, 207, 208, 209, 210, 211, 214, 215, 216, 217
Sustainability 1, 4, 8, 10, 12, 13, 14, 19, 30, 31, 33, 40, 43, 45, 50, 56, 57, 62,

65, 67, 69, 70, 71, 72, 84, 85, 87, 89, 93, 94, 95, 97, 98, 127, 162, 168, 171, 204, 213, 217
Sustainable Business Growth 1
Systematic 33, 39, 47, 101, 106, 118, 168, 178

W

Women Entrepreneurs 1, 2, 3, 4, 5, 6, 7, 8, 9, 10, 14, 15, 16, 17, 18, 19, 20, 21, 22, 23, 24, 25, 26, 27, 28, 29, 30, 31, 32, 34, 65, 66, 67, 68, 69, 70, 71, 72, 76, 77, 78, 80, 82, 83, 84, 85, 86, 87, 88, 89, 90, 93, 94, 95, 97, 98, 99
Women-led businesses 27, 65, 66, 67, 68, 69, 70, 71, 72, 81, 94, 95, 98, 99
Women Technopreneurship 133, 138, 139, 140, 141, 146, 152, 154, 155, 161

www.ingramcontent.com/pod-product-compliance
Lightning Source LLC
LaVergne TN
LVHW081333300926
849161LV00008B/1966
* 9 7 9 8 3 6 9 3 9 1 9 3 8 *